PENGUIN  CLASSICS

ETHICS

ADVISORY EDITOR: BETTY RADICE

ARISTOTLE was born at Stageira, in the dominion of the kings of Macedon, in 384 B.C. He studied in Athens under Plato, on whose death he left, and some time later became tutor of the young Alexander the Great. When Alexander succeeded to the throne in 335, Aristotle returned to Athens and established the Lyceum, where his vast erudition attracted a large number of scholars. After Alexander's death he was regarded in some quarters with suspicion, having been Alexander's friend; he was accused of impiety, and in 322 B.C. fled to Chalcis in Euboea, where he died the same year. His writings were of extraordinary range, and many of them have survived. Among the most famous are the *Ethics* and the *Politics*, both Penguin Classics.

J. A. K. THOMSON was Professor Emeritus of Classics at King's College, London, until his death in 1959, and was educated at Aberdeen and Oxford Universities. He was a lecturer at the Universities of Aberdeen, St Andrews, Harvard and Bryn Mawr College, U.S.A. Among his publications are *Greeks and Barbarians* (1921), *Shakespeare and the Classics* (1952) and *Classical Influences on English Prose* (1955).

HUGH TREDENNICK was born in 1899 and educated at King Edward's, Birmingham, and Trinity Hall, Cambridge, where he got a double first in Classics. He was Professor of Classics at Royal Holloway College from 1946 until 1966. He was Dean of the Faculty of Arts at London University from 1956 to 1960, and joint editor of the *Classical Review* from 1961 to 1967. His translation of Xenophon's *Memoirs of Socrates* is a Penguin Classic, and he also edited and translated works by Aristotle. He died in 1982.

JONATHAN BARNES is Professor of Ancient Philosophy and Fellow of Balliol College, Oxford. He was educated at the City of London School and at Balliol. He has held visiting posts at the University of Chicago, at the Institute for Advanced Study in Princeton, at the University of Massachusetts in Amherst and at the University of

Texas. For ten years he was a Fellow of Oriel College, Oxford. His publications include *The Ontological Argument* (1972). *Aristotle's Posterior Analytics* (1975), *The Presocratic Philosophers* (1979), *Aristotle* (1982) and *Early Greek Philosophy* (1987).

THE
ETHICS OF ARISTOTLE

THE NICOMACHEAN ETHICS

*

TRANSLATED BY
J. A. K. THOMSON

REVISED WITH NOTES AND APPENDICES BY
HUGH TREDENNICK

INTRODUCTION AND BIBLIOGRAPHY BY
JONATHAN BARNES

PENGUIN BOOKS

PENGUIN BOOKS

Published by the Penguin Group
Penguin Books Ltd, 27 Wrights Lane, London W8 5TZ, England
Penguin Books USA Inc., 375 Hudson Street, New York, New York 10014, USA
Penguin Books Australia Ltd, Ringwood, Victoria, Australia
Penguin Books Canada Ltd, 10 Alcorn Avenue, Toronto, Ontario, Canada M4V 3B2
Penguin Books (NZ) Ltd, 182–190 Wairau Road, Auckland 10, New Zealand

Penguin Books Ltd, Registered Offices: Harmondsworth, Middlesex, England

This translation by J. A. K. Thomson first published by Allen & Unwin 1953
Published in Penguin Classics 1955
Revised edition 1976
19 20 18

Translation copyright 1953 by J. A. K. Thomson
Revised translation copyright © Hugh Tredennick, 1976
Introduction and Bibliography copyright © Jonathan Barnes, 1976
All rights reserved

Printed in England by Clays Ltd, St Ives plc

CONTENTS

PREFACE

THERE were several reasons why J. A. K. Thomson's translation of the *Ethics* called for a revision. It was written more than twenty years ago, with the object of providing an English version, not of the Greek text, which in many parts of the work is hardly more than a minimal expansion of lecture notes, but of the lectures which Aristotle may be supposed to have actually delivered. The result, although eminently readable, was not achieved without some licence: passages that seemed repetitious or otherwise dispensable were omitted; others that seemed loosely parenthetical were represented as footnotes; and such comments or elucidations of Aristotle's meaning as seemed desirable were conveyed by means of expansion or paraphrase.

This revised version, which is intended both for the general reader and for students of philosophy, attempts to keep close to the Greek without too much sacrifice of readability, and to supply some aids towards the understanding of Aristotle's notions and doctrines. The new Introduction by Jonathan Barnes, who also compiled the informative Bibliography, takes account of the most recent work on Aristotle, and challenges some of the traditional estimates of his ethical theory, whereas the reviser adheres to a more conservative view, although he gladly acknowledges a very great debt to his partner's expert knowledge, critical acumen and generous help. Mrs Betty Radice has supervised the collaborative effort with even more than her usual wisdom and patience. It may be hoped that Thomson would have given his approval to the revision, which was undertaken largely *pietatis causa*.

H.T.

7

INTRODUCTION

THE system which Aristotle expounds and advocates in the *Nicomachean Ethics* stands as one of the most celebrated and influential of moral philosophies. Since its construction in the fourth century B.C. it has had a profound and lasting effect: by later philosophers it has been fervently embraced and critically rejected, but never coldly ignored; and in certain crucial respects it has helped to shape and mould the common moral consciousness. Thus the modern reader who takes up the *Ethics* for the first time will find himself already familiar, at least to some degree, with several of its leading notions. And the comparative simplicity of the work's grand structure may encourage him to sail with a specious celerity through its long and winding channels of argument.

Yet any but the most shallow reading of the *Ethics* soon strikes on shoals and reefs; and the deeper the reading, the more frequently those obstacles appear and the slower the voyage through them becomes. They are diverse in nature and in magnitude: sometimes a whole chapter may seem perversely repetitious, or curiously alien to a treatise on morality, or unintelligibly oblique in purport; sometimes a short stretch of argument will appear unendurably crabbed, or incomprehensibly allusive; sometimes understanding is blocked by a single sentence or phrase.

Different obstacles have different causes, and only a full-scale commentary can pretend to touch upon them all. Nevertheless, a knowledge of certain aspects of Aristotle's intellectual life, an understanding of the style and literary genre of the *Ethics*, and a sympathetic insight into some of its philosophical presuppositions, may mitigate the perplexity which these obstacles occasion, and may increase the pleasure of the journey without taking away from the excitement and the challenge which it affords.

The sole function of my Introduction is to offer some aid

to that mitigatory end. I shall not attempt to extol the merits of the *Ethics*: a good wine needs no bush; and it is mere impertinence to advertise the rarest of vintages.

ARISTOTLE'S LIFE

Aristotle was born in 384 B.C. in the northern town of Stagira, far from the intellectual centre of Greece. His father, Nicomachus, was a physician attached to the court of Philip of Macedon, and a plausible speculation ascribes to paternal influence not only Aristotle's later connection with the Macedonian dynasty but also his powerful interest in, and love of, things scientific.

In 367 Aristotle moved south to Athens. Whether or not he was originally attracted there by the pull of Plato, he quickly became associated with the Academic circle, that brilliant band of philosophers, scientists, mathematicians, and politicians which gathered in Athens under the inspiring leadership of Plato. Scholars differ on the nature of Plato's Academy and dispute the extent of its similarity to a modern University or Institute for Advanced Study. It is tempting to see in *Ethics* IX.10 a sketch, somewhat idealized by the passage of time, of life in Plato's Academy. But however that may be, it is certain that in his early years at Athens, Aristotle studied alongside the Academicians and drank deeply from the Platonic springs. He soon made a name for himself as an industrious student, a vigorous polemicist, and an independent thinker of power and originality. We know that the study of rhetoric occupied him, and various pieces of evidence suggest an early professional interest in logic, metaphysics and ethics.

In 347 Plato died. In the same year Aristotle left Athens, where an upsurge of anti-Macedonian feeling may have made his emigration prudent. He settled for some years in the Eastern Aegean, first at Atarneus, then at Assos, and later at Mitylene. Hermias, the ruler of Atarneus, had close connections with the Athenian Academy, and was eager to foster learning in his eastern domain; his generous patronage established Aristotle and a few fellow exiles as a new university, and Aristotle later gave sentimental corroboration to their tie by marrying Hermias's niece and adopted daughter. It was here in the East that Aristotle first worked with Theophrastus, who was to become his successor and greatest pupil; together they embarked upon a series of zoological, biological and botanical studies which remained unrivalled for two millennia.

In 343 Aristotle was summoned by Philip of Macedon to take up the post of tutor to his son Alexander. The little we hear of these years is incurably romanticized. What studies Aristotle pursued is unknown, and what influence he had on his precocious charge is quite uncertain. It is pleasing to believe the old story that when Alexander embarked on his conquest of the East his expedition was equipped with natural historians who reported their discoveries back to Aristotle.

After a few years of royal tutoring Aristotle returned to his native Stagira where he remained until Macedon had extended its sway through Greece and he could at last travel south once more to Athens. There he set up his own school at the Lyceum. And from 334 to 323 he explored and discovered, argued, expounded and taught, mentally surveying the entire field of human knowledge – logic, metaphysics, theology, history, politics, ethics, aesthetics, psychology, anatomy, biology, zoology, botany, astronomy, meteorology, and the ancient equivalents of physics and chemistry. In these years he must have composed most of the treatises, philosophical and scientific, which we still possess, as well as the far more numerous volumes lost in the wastes of time.

In 323 Alexander died in Babylon. When the news reached Athens Aristotle, unwilling to share the fate of Socrates, left the city lest the Athenians put a second philosopher to death. He went to Chalcis, where he died a few months later. His will, which has survived, is a happy and humane document.

As an institution, the Lyceum lived on in diminishing glory for some 500 years after its founder's death; as a stimulus, a challenge, an inspiration, and a formative influence on subsequent thought, its power remains, scarcely abated.

It is not perhaps entirely idle to look for elements in Aristotle's eventful life which may have left their mark upon the *Ethics*. I single out four such features.

First, the shadow of Plato lies across the work. This is most evident in those several passages which explicitly reject or defend a Platonic thesis: thus I.6 criticizes Plato's view that Goodness is a single, self-subsistent, universal entity or Form; and VII.3 defends the Socratic position that it is impossible to perform an action which you know to be wrong. But Plato is also behind the *Ethics* in other, less immediately apparent ways; a reference to his dialogues will often illuminate a short argument (as a passage in the *Republic* illuminates the main argument in I.7) and sometimes determine a whole course of reasoning (as the *Philebus* determines much of the discussion of pleasure). Such allusions are, of course, regularly catalogued by the commentators.

Secondly, Aristotle was a giant polymath, whose life was largely devoted to the acquisition and dissemination of scientific knowledge. This may help to explain the prominent part played in the *Ethics* by the 'intellectual virtues' and the supreme status accorded to the 'contemplative' life, both of which features seem at first blush foreign to a work of moral philosophy. Again, on a different level, the methodological problems and theories suggested by the natural sciences are reflected in various and subtle ways in the practical science of ethics. One example of this is the question of *akribeia* or 'precision', of which I shall say more later; another is the leading part played by *endoxa*, or reputable opinions, in Aristotle's approach to practical principles.

Thirdly, the age Aristotle lived in was politically unstable, and his own life was constantly interrupted by external events. It is a plausible fancy to connect this to the authoritarianism of the *Ethics*: the 'good man' is the canon and measure of absolute excellence (1113a33), and it is a task of political science to ensure that the citizens of a state accommodate their lives to that canon as closely as their own inner capacities and the external pressures of the law can determine (see especially X.9). Political freedom is no more a pre-eminent *desideratum* for Aristotle than it was for Plato.

Fourthly, despite the imperial ambitions and successes of Philip and Alexander, Aristotle's world remained essentially that of the small city-state. The political unit in Greece was, by modern standards, minuscule: it is as though a small English county were a sovereign state, politically and economically independent, socially and culturally self-contained. Aristotle's *Politics* naturally exhibits the interests and preoccupations of a reflective inhabitant of such a state; and those passages in the *Ethics* which bear upon political theory must be read with these historical conditions in mind.

Written in a time of political upheaval, when the jealously individual states of Greece were becoming, perforce, members of a larger and less personal community; written by an old member of Plato's Academy who was at the same time a brilliant and self-confident scientist, the *Ethics* must from time to time betray its origins. Like all great works, it transcends the particular conditions of its conception; and like all great works it is misunderstood – mispraised or miscondemned – if it is not read with some general comprehension of those originative circumstances.

ARISTOTLE'S WRITINGS

Of Aristotle's vast *oeuvre*, known to us from the library catalogues of the Alexandrian age, only a fraction survives. That fraction is impressive enough, both in variety and in bulk: some thirty treatises, varying in length from short essays to substantial books, make up fifteen or so decent-sized volumes of text. Among the surviving treatises are two on ethics: the *Eudemian Ethics*, named after its editor Eudemus, and our *Nicomachean Ethics*, similarly named from Aristotle's son Nicomachus. In addition there are ethical asides in the

Rhetoric, the *Topics*, and the *de Motu Animalium*; and the *Protrepticus*, an early work of which substantial paraphrastic fragments survive, contains a quantity of moralizing. (The *Magna Moralia*, a third treatise on ethics included in the standard edition of Aristotle, was put together by a later compiler who drew heavily on Aristotle's genuine works.)

Modern scholarship has discussed at length the internal chronology of the Aristotelian *corpus*. It is now all but universally agreed that the *Eudemian Ethics* preceded the *Nicomachean*: our work, which I shall refer to baldly as the *Ethics*, represents Aristotle's more mature and settled thought. In most other respects, however, the chronological disputes have remained vexatiously inconclusive. A main reason for this can, I think, be found in the peculiar character of Aristotle's writings; since a rough understanding of that character is in any case indispensable to a student of the *Ethics*, I shall say a few words about it.

The ancients, who possessed more of Aristotle's works than we do, greatly admired his prose style. To the modern reader, particularly if he has approached Aristotle through the verdant plains of Plato's prose, that judgement sometimes seems mildly perverse: the treatises we possess show a certain rugged strength, and occasionally, for brief stretches, reveal a conscious elegance of style; but for the most part they are stark and abrupt: paragraphs are brusquely concatenated; arguments are enthymematic, taut, and sparsely expressed; and sentences are often concise, elliptical, and crammed with uncouth technical terms. (Translations are excusably inexact from this stylistic point of view.)

The ancient commentators divided Aristotle's works into the 'exoteric' and the 'esoteric' (cf. 1102a26). Although the precise sense of this distinction is disputed, it is fairly clear that the surviving treatises are all 'esoteric', and that a part at least of the significance of that description is that they were not intended for general circulation outside Aristotle's school, or for 'publication' in any ordinary sense of that term. Modern scholarship has gone a step further: Aristotle's treatises, as we have them, all stem from the lecture courses on philosophical and scientific subjects which he gave during his long teaching career – they are his lecture notes. The ancient editors doubtless indulged in some ordering and polishing; but what we now have before us is essentially what Aristotle had on the lectern in front of him when he addressed his pupils. Moreover, we may well suppose that these notes were not used once and then filed away; rather, they will have been taken up, year in year out, as the exigencies of lecturing dictated; and they will have been subject to a series of additions, corrections and refinements. (Philosophers may find something not vastly dissimilar in J. L. Austin's *Sense and Sensibilia*. That book, published after Austin's death, was put together from lecture notes which had evolved over some ten years; its editor describes in his Foreword a task which will not have been utterly different from that which faced Eudemus and Nicomachus.)

This account of the origin and nature of Aristotle's treatises in general, and of the *Ethics* in particular, has several far-reaching implications. First, it explains and excuses the stylistic quirks of the book: lecture notes are not customarily composed in a consistently polished prose style, nor adorned with literary embellishment; and it is misconceived to criticize for rough literary craftsmanship a work which was for the most part not worked up into literary form.

Secondly, the inconclusiveness of chronological research is explained: if the treatises are not datable publications but constantly evolving lectures, questions of their temporal interrelationships may often be simply inappropriate, and it may be a mere misunderstanding to ask whether treatise A was composed before or after treatise B.

Thirdly, if the *Ethics* represents a continually emended set of reflections rather than a fixed and considered system, we may expect to find in it inconcinnities of expression and argument, if not downright inconsistencies of thought. Scholars are seriously divided as to how far this expectation is satisfied. There is much in the conservative warning that when a critic sees an inconsistency in Aristotle others may only see a defect in the understanding of the critic. Nevertheless, in several parts of the *Ethics* it is a plausible hypothesis that we have twin versions of a single argument, stemming from different performances of the same lecture. A large-scale example is offered by the two discussions of pleasure in Books VII and X; a smaller case is provided by the different sets of introductory remarks in Book I.

A fourth implication is more important and less recognized than its predecessors. In the case of Plato the modern reader has, it is true, considerable and taxing problems of interpretation before him; but he is at least faced with a text which presents in a thoroughly explicit fashion the views and arguments which Plato wanted him to consider. The modern reader of Aristotle has a greater challenge: before he can attempt to understand and assess Aristotle's views – or rather, in the very course of his attempt – he must reconstruct them; he must, that is, endeavour to hear Aristotle's lecture voice while reading his lecture notes; and he must exercise his sympathy and his imagination to expand Aristotle's concise arguments and to illustrate Aristotle's bare abstractions. It is this extra challenge which makes Aristotle's treatises such exacting, and such exciting, reading: the general truth that philosophy must be read slowly and patiently, with frequent pause for intellectual breath, applies with particular force to Aristotle's writings. Anyone who intends to acquire more than a superficial knowledge of Aristotle's views must be prepared to sip the *Ethics* slowly: the vintage is old and strong; it is not for quaffing.

ARISTOTLE'S PHILOSOPHY

It is not my intention to offer here an exposition of Aristotle's ethical system, still less a reasoned assessment of it; rather, I shall try to accomplish three things: first, to set the *Ethics* in the context of Aristotle's general philosophical system; secondly, to sketch and illustrate an important logical distinction about which Aristotle was not fully clear; and thirdly, to air some notions about the connection between the *Ethics* and modern moral philosophy. My remarks, particularly in the third section, are not uttered in a didactic spirit: they are, for the most part, not statements of an established orthodoxy, but fairly tentative suggestions; and they should be read with an appropriate charity and scepticism.

The Aristotelian System

It is currently fashionable to deride the nineteenth century's attempts to systematize Aristotle's philosophy: they, like the scholastic constructions before them, are generally agreed to have imposed alien façades on an unsystematic text, falsifying the range and flexibility of Aristotle's thought, and disguising the tentative, aporematic nature of his philosophizing. Derision is often salutary but rarely definitive. The Aristotelian *corpus*, as I have already hinted, is by no means a rigid presentation of a finished and coherent system; but for all that it does, I think, possess a strong systematic framework: the laths of Aristotle's thought are not plastered over to a smooth synthetic finish; but they are held together by a firm timbering.

The timbering is easily described. Human knowledge, which will shortly be complete (and completely organized in a deductive arrangement), divides into different disciplines or 'sciences'. These 'sciences' group under three main heads: the theoretical, the practical, and the productive. The major divisions of theoretical science are theology, mathematics, and 'physics' or natural science; and the majority of Aristotle's surviving works, being concerned with natural science, fall therefore under the heading of theory. The *Ethics*, however, is a work of practical science. What that means is that the characteristic aim of studying ethics is not the acquisition of knowledge about action but action itself – we read the *Ethics*, according to Aristotle, not in order to know what good men are like, but in order to act as good men do (1095a5; 1103b25).

Ethics is only one of the practical sciences. Another is politics: at the beginning and at the end of the *Ethics* Aristotle stresses that his study is continuous with, and in a certain sense a subordinate part of, political science; Aristotle's *Politics* is, in a sense, the sequel to the *Ethics*. The details of the connection are hard to make out, but its general nature is readily discerned. Aristotle explicitly recognizes (what is, after all, a plain truth) that the practical sciences cannot easily be studied in isolation, either from one another or from the theoretical sciences: at the very crudest level, the student of ethics is unlikely to discover how a good man will act unless he has some knowledge of the general capacities and characteristics of human beings (see I.13). It is anthropology, or the science of human nature, which must provide that background knowledge; and one of the most familiar utterances of Aristotelian anthropology is the truism that man is a 'political animal' (1097b8–11; *Politics* 1253a2): distinctively human activity is carried on in a social setting. Political science thus studies, *inter alia*, the chief theatre in which the good man must act out his life; and in determining the design and purpose of the theatre it will of necessity take an interest in, and set limits upon, the types of drama that may be played out upon it.

Aristotle's thought makes up an impressive philosophical system which, though neither fully elaborated nor unyieldingly applied, is still sufficiently stable and sufficiently coherent to provide a framework for the *Ethics*. The frame is clearly visible at the extremities of the work and it appears less obtrusively at various points in the development of the argument.

Internally, too, the *Ethics* has a system of the same strong but loose nature: 'Our task is to become good men, or to achieve the highest human good. That good is happiness; and happiness is an activity of the soul in accordance with virtue (Book I). Virtue is therefore to be analysed, and the conditions for virtuous action determined (Books II–III); and the various virtues, "moral" and "intellectual", must be limned (Books IV–VI and VIII–IX). Pleasure, intimately tied to virtue by more than one cord, must also be anatomized (Books VII and X). And finally, the nature of happiness and the means of ensuring it can be laid down (Book X).' The key concepts here, which are not perfectly represented by the English words 'virtue' and 'happiness', will call for elucidation later on; but their structural inter-relations are immediately discernible, and it is these which provide the internal frame of the *Ethics*.

The *Ethics* does not fit that frame with perfect fidelity, as even a cursory reading will reveal; and the parenthetical references in my summary to the different Books of the work disguise as much as they discover. Nevertheless, the scheme does visibly lie behind the multiple and complex arguments of the *Ethics*; and it may serve as an Ariadne's thread to guide the reader through Aristotle's Daedalian edifice. (At all events, it is a useful corrective to the natural modern habit of reading the *Ethics* by book and chapter: the divisions on which this habit rests are not Aristotelian but the work of later booksellers and editors; and they sometimes mar rather than mark the structure of the argument.)

Ethics and Meta-ethics

Any work of moral philosophy is liable to contain judgements of two different sorts. It will contain, on the one hand, substantive moral judgements, to the effect that certain men or types of men, or actions or types of action, et cetera, are good or bad, right or wrong, virtuous or vicious, obligatory or impermissible, and so on. In short, it will offer opinion and advice on moral matters. A simple example from the beginning of the *Ethics* is Aristotle's recommendation that young men should not study political science (1095a2). On the other hand, a work of moral philosophy will contain judgements about such substantive moral judgements, to the effect that they are or are not factual or objective or prescriptive, et cetera; that the concepts they use are to be elucidated in such and such a way; that they are logically interrelated in such and such a manner, and so on. In short, it will contain adversions on what is sometimes called the 'logic' of moral discourse. A simple example from the beginning of the

Ethics is Aristotle's suggestion about the meaning of the term 'good' (1096b26–9).

It is convenient to have different names for these two different sorts of judgement: following an accepted custom, I shall call judgements of the first sort, *ethical* and judgements of the second sort, *meta-ethical*. An analogous distinction can, of course, be made in any other discipline or branch of study.

Most philosophical writings on morals contain, I think, a preponderance of meta-ethical judgements; indeed, it is tempting to regard as the specifically philosophical aspect of moral philosophy precisely this self-conscious study of the logic of moral discourse: if moral philosophers hope by their philosophizing to make us better men, their proprietary path to that goal is meta-ethical – the articulation and elucidation of our thought about moral matters will, they trust, lead us to judge well and to act rightly.

Aristotle's *Ethics* is no exception to this generalization, and the major portion of the work is, I think, properly construed as a contribution to meta-ethics. Aristotle himself, however, never expressly realized the distinction I have just roughly drawn between ethical and meta-ethical judgements; and that accounts for some uncertainties in his argument. I shall illustrate this by a fairly straightforward example.

More than once Aristotle emphasizes that the sciences cannot all aspire to an equal degree of 'precision' or *akribeia*: different subject matters make different demands, and the subject matter of ethics in particular allows only a modest amount of 'precision' (see especially I.3 and II.2; and also *Posterior Analytics* I.27 and *Metaphysics* II.3). This central notion of *akribeia* has aroused little scholarly comment, and it remains somewhat obscure. In the case of ethics at least the key concept seems to be that of generality: ethical judgements are lacking in precision because they hold only 'for the most part'. Mathematicians may truly advance theorems of the universal form 'Every F is G'; but moralists are restricted by the nature of their subject to generalizations of the form 'Most F's are G' or 'As a rule, F's are G'. (There is a very good illustration of this in IX.2.)

Why did Aristotle hold this view? He was inclined to believe that the biological sciences in general did not admit universally valid judgements, so that anthropology and human psychology would not furnish the moralist with anything stronger than generalizations; and he was also impressed by the seemingly infinite variety of human circumstances and situations. He must have inferred from this that any ethical proposition of the universal form 'Every F is G' ('Every courageous act is praiseworthy', 'Every promise is to be kept') would sooner or later be refuted by the occurrence of a situation in which, unusually but indisputably, an F failed to be G. To cater for this perpetual possibility the moralist falls back upon the phrase 'for the most part' or 'as a rule'; for 'As a rule, F's are G's' will survive a limited number of cases in which F's are not G's.

Reflection on the nature of law may have confirmed Aristotle in this belief. He insists that laws, though framed universally, cannot, or should not, be applied strictly in all cases: the virtue of 'equity' (*epieikeia*: V.13) is needed precisely to determine and adjudicate upon those situations in which the law's universality offends against the canons of justice (and equity, by its very nature, cannot frame universal rules for its own application).

It is worth underlining the fact that Aristotle is here adopting an extreme position, not unlike the one taken up by some existentialist thinkers: morals, he implies, cannot by any means be reduced to a set of universal principles; any principle that may be formulated is liable to exception, any universal moral judgement (strictly construed) is false. The most we can hope for is a group of roughly accurate generalizations – principles which will meet most ordinary situations but which are always liable to come unstuck. If they do come unstuck, we may abandon them for more satisfactory principles (if we can find any), or we may rely on some sort of 'moral intuition', or we may perhaps simply confess our incapacity to determine the moral issue. However that may be, we must not indulge in the vain fancy that a set of true and universal principles is somewhere waiting to be found: ethical absolutism, in that sense, is an illusion.

I cannot say anything here about the merits of such a view (it is clear that Aristotle himself had not thought out all its implications); rather, I want to use it as an illustration of a less exciting phenomenon.

In his introductory remarks on method in I.3 Aristotle asserts quite generally of his statements in the *Ethics* that they are to be taken implicitly as 'for the most part' propositions. In other words, the non-universality thesis is alleged to hold for all the matter in the *Ethics*, and thus in particular for the great quantity of meta-ethical judgements which it contains. But Aristotle's argument supports at most the view that there are no true universal *ethical* judgements; and that view does not imply that there are no true universal *meta-ethical* judgements. (Indeed, it implies that there is at least one true universal meta-ethical judgement – the judgement that all universal ethical judgements are false.) Nor is it easy to think of any independent reason for imagining that meta-ethics must be lacking in precision – or hard to think of reasons why it need not.

The injunction in I.3 is not a casual aside; yet no reader of the *Ethics* ever takes it *au pied de la lettre*. Aristotle doubtless ought to have said something to the effect that no substantive moral judgements can aspire to precision; but he did not say this, and he did not do so because he lacked a clear awareness of the distinction between ethics and meta-ethics.

Some judgements which are ethical rather than meta-ethical surely do attain precision; it is surely true that *every* generous man possesses a moral virtue, and that *every* murder is a wrongful act. Such judgements attain precision because, in a sense, they say nothing: they are tautologies, or analytic judgements – their subject terms already include the notion of goodness or badness (cf. 1107a9). 'Murder is wrong' is, in this respect, similar to 'Omnivores eat meat'. If I doubt the truth of 'Omnivores eat meat', then, assuming that I know what it is to eat meat, I show myself unacquainted with the sense of the term 'omnivore': omnivores are, one might say, meat-eaters by definition, since 'omnivore' means 'eater of anything'. (Contrast a doubt about the truth of 'Wallabies are meat-eaters': no explication of the meaning of 'wallaby' will do anything to resolve that.) Equally, if I doubt the truth of 'Murder is wrong' I show myself unacquainted with the sense of the term 'murder': murder is wrong by definition. (Contrast a doubt about the truth of 'Suicide is wrong'.)

Failure to distinguish between analytic and non-analytic ethical judgements is likely to march with failure to distinguish between meta-ethical and ethical judgements; for every ethical tautology or analytic judgement of the form 'Every F is G' can be paired off with (and is often helpfully replaced by) a meta-ethical judgement of the form 'The concept of F includes the concept of G'. Thus '(Every) murder is wrong' pairs with 'The concept of *murder* includes that of *wrongfulness*'. Being unclear about the distinction between ethical and meta-ethical judgements, Aristotle was also unclear about the distinction between analytic and non-analytic ethical judgements. I shall illustrate this claim by considering that most vulgarized notion of the *Ethics* – the Doctrine of the Golden Mean.

The Doctrine of the Mean (the epithet 'golden' is un-Aristotelian) regularly occurs in later writers as a piece of moral advice – a recipe or rule reminding us to 'observe the mean', to be moderate in all things and to avoid excess and deficiency. (If the Doctrine urges us not to drink too much wine, it equally urges us not to drink too little – that is something which the moralizers usually find it prudent to ignore.)

At its first appearance in the *Ethics*, in II.2, the Doctrine does indeed seem to claim the status of moral advice: the way to become, say, courageous is to shun some but not all dangers and to take a middle course in matters of fear; the way to become temperate is to shun some but not all objects of desire and to steer a middle course through temptation;

and, in general, the way to become virtuous is to observe the mean. Thus 'To be virtuous you must observe the mean' reads like a piece of advice, on all fours, logically speaking, with 'To act rightly you must pursue the general good'.

A closer inspection shows that the Doctrine will not bear the weight of advice. In II.6 Aristotle explains the notion of a mean or mid-point (*meson*, 'mean', is literally 'middle') by reference to continuous measurable quantities; but he warns us at once from a simple arithmetical interpretation of his Doctrine. In a reasonably obvious sense, 6 is the mean or mid-point between 2 and 10; but this sort of mean is the mean 'of the object' or the 'arithmetical' mean, and in matters of conduct it is not the mean 'of the object' but the mean 'relative to us' that counts. What, then, is the mean 'relative to us'? It is, it appears, whatever is neither too much for us nor too little for us. If I am offered a steak of any weight between half a pound and a pound and a half I shall not, in Aristotle's sense, follow the mean by plumping for a pound; rather, I must order the weight that happens to suit me, whatever it may be – I must choose what is neither too much for my system to take nor too little to sustain my physique. It follows (though Aristotle does not draw the inference) that the moralist's mean need not be the middle point of a continuum in any reasonable sense of 'middle': any point at all may turn out to be the 'mean' relative to me. I may 'observe the mean' with regard to exercise by doing absolutely nothing or by exercising for all I am worth; the 'mean' amount of port may, for me, be none.

Thus understood, the Doctrine of the Mean has no practical or advisory force: if you ask me how much cake you should help yourself to, and I reply 'Neither too much nor too little', your choice has hardly been eased. It is as though I were to hand a man a pack of cards and urge him to choose a middle one – adding that by 'middle' I meant 'middle relative to the chooser', and that any card in the pack may be middle in this sense.

The situation deteriorates further when we ask to what extent actions and emotions can be regarded as continuous measurable quantities. The *Eudemian Ethics* offers a short, weak argument for the thesis that they can be (1220b21–7); our *Ethics* offers nothing. An inspection of the virtues in Aristotle's list reveals that the notion of a continuum is at best only partially applicable: virtuous choice does not have its attention limited to a single dimension; and many of the dimensions it is required to consider do not lie as continua. A generous man will give the right share of his income to the right recipients: if his income is a measurable quantity, the potential recipients are not – picking the appropriate charities is not a matter of avoiding too many and too few.

The Doctrine of the Mean thus uses the term 'mean' as a metaphor; virtue is not, in any literal sense of the term, a matter of picking the mid-point. But this, I hasten to say, is no indictment of Aristotle; indeed it is implicit in his own exposition. For when he finds it necessary to state what the mean 'relative to us' is, he gives a perfectly clear account in which no trace of the literal sense of the term 'mean' hampers the analysis: to feel things 'when one should, and in the conditions and towards the people and for the end and in the way one should – that is the middle (*meson*) and best course' (1106b21; cf. 1109a25; b15). 'Act in accordance with the mean' thus becomes 'Act as you should act'; and such a sentence cannot give moral advice. (The sentence can, it is true, serve to remind someone that there *is* a proper way to act, that what he does is not a morally indifferent matter; but it will not serve to advise anyone on what that proper way is, or to pick out any one way as the right way.)

In an important paragraph Aristotle expressly recognizes that the Doctrine of the Mean is unhelpful in just this way: 'We have said that one should choose the mean . . . But although to say this is true, it is not at all explicit; for in all the other occupations about which there is a science it is true that one should exert oneself and relax neither too much nor too little, but to a mean extent and as the right principle dictates; but if you grasped only this you would know nothing more – e.g. you would not know *what* remedies to take if someone told you to take what medical science prescribes and as a medical man prescribes it' (1138b18–32). If I am puzzled about how I should act and you 'advise' me to observe the mean, then I 'know nothing more' than I did before; I am no better off, no better informed about the moral possibilities and demands of my situation.

The Doctrine of the Mean is incapable of advising because it enshrines an analytic truth. 'Acting virtuously requires observation of the mean' is analytic: once the metaphor of the mean is understood, it is clear that *observing the mean* is included in the concept of *acting virtuously*. And *acting viciously* includes, by the same token, the notion of *overdoing or underdoing* something. Thus stated, the Doctrine of the Mean is seen as a piece of meta-ethics; it teaches that it is part of the concepts of *virtue* and *vice* that virtues and vices come in triads – every virtuous disposition to do X in just the right way is flanked by two vicious dispositions, one to overdo X-ing and the other to underdo it. Such a theory, though unhelpful practically, might at least seem to be conceptually illuminating; unfortunately, as Aristotle's own analysis quickly reveals, the light fails: once the Doctrine is literally expressed it becomes platitudinous.

In the *Ethics* we can, I think, see Aristotle struggling with the logic and the sense of the Doctrine of the Mean: he becomes explicitly aware of its practical futility; and his discussions perhaps indicate an increasing disenchantment with its conceptual utility. Had Aristotle written a third ethical treatise, the celebrated Doctrine would not, I conjecture, have appeared in it.

The Ethics and Moral Philosophy

The *Ethics* hopes to make us into good men; having read it, we shall be better able to pursue the highest human good, and to help others in the same pursuit. It may, perhaps, seem either pedantic or imbecile to ask, in such circumstances, whether the *Ethics* is a work of moral philosophy or not. For surely, if there is such a subject as moral philosophy at all, it is precisely the subject which tells us what human goodness is and how to achieve it. Yet the matter is not quite so simple; and in this section I shall try to induce the suspicion that Aristotle's notion of ethics is not quite the same as our present notion of moral philosophy: if we ascribe to Aristotle the aims and interests of Kant or Mill or their modern successors, we shall be in danger of misunderstanding him.

(It is important not to be misled here by translated terminology. Aristotle refers to his book as *ta ēthika*: the title transliterates to 'The Ethics' but translates rather as 'Matters to do with Character'. Again, English translations abound with such phrases as 'moral virtue': but 'moral virtue' renders either *ēthikē aretē* (properly: 'excellence of character') or else the plain *aretē* ('excellence' – see below).)

It is a commonplace that not all ascriptions of goodness to men or to actions are ascriptions of moral goodness: good cricketers who hold good catches are not necessarily moral men performing moral acts. In one of his logical works, Aristotle takes the phrase 'good shoemaker' and points out that 'X is a good shoemaker' does not imply 'X is good' (*de Interpretatione* 11; cf. *Ethics* 1148b7–9, where Aristotle similarly observes that 'X is a bad doctor (actor)' does not imply 'X is bad'). We might perhaps be inclined to see in this point a recognition of the distinction between 'technical' goodness or expertise and moral goodness or goodness *simpliciter*: a man is a good shoemaker just insofar as he does well the things shoemakers professionally do; he is an expert in the technique of shoemaking. But a man who is good *simpliciter* or morally good is not, we might think, the possessor of any technique or expertise – moral goodness is not in that respect like the goodness of a shoemaker. Since 'the highest good' or 'the good for men', which forms the object of the *Ethics* (cf. 1094a18–b7), is surely goodness *simpliciter* or moral goodness, we may infer that the *Ethics* is not concerned with any skill or technique or expertise or accomplishment.

Unfortunately something is wrong with this argument, for Aristotle quite clearly would not have accepted the final conclusion which it draws. On the contrary, more than one

argument of some importance in the *Ethics* turns precisely
on the ignoring or rejecting of the distinction between
technical and moral goodness. Thus at 1097b24–1098a20 we
find the following argument: 'Just as a good lyre-player is
someone who performs well at the tasks which lyre-players
perform professionally or *qua* lyre-players, so a good man is
someone who performs well at the tasks which men perform
typically or *qua* men.' (See also 1101a1–6; 1106a36–b16.)
'Good man' is thus treated as logically similar to 'good lyre-
player': to be a good man is, so to speak, to be a professional
man, to have an expertise at being human; and in order to
achieve the highest human good towards which the *Ethics*
guides us we must exercise that expertise to the best of our
ability.

Many modern readers accept that passages such as these
prove Aristotle to have fudged the distinction between moral
and technical goodness; and they suppose that his analogy
with the lyre-player goes wrong at two different places.

First, they urge that the notion of 'what a man typically
does' is empty: shoemakers and lyre-players are indeed pro-
fessionals, with professional or typical tasks; but that is just
because 'shoemaker' and 'lyre-player' are words that are
defined in terms of certain tasks. 'Man', on the contrary, is
not defined in terms of any task or function. (There is no
verb 'man' analogous to 'cobble' or 'play the lyre'.) Nor is
there any other way of discovering some typically human
task.

This objection would not have impressed Aristotle: he
does think that 'man' can be defined in terms of a task or
function; and he is prepared to ground his definition in a
fairly sophisticated anthropology. (Moreover, he has at his
disposal a perfectly ordinary verb 'to man', *anthrōpeuesthai*:
1178b7.) The issue, in fact, is exceedingly complex. I shall
return to it briefly at a later stage in my argument. Here I
shall pass directly to the second objection to Aristotle's
account of the 'professional man'; for this, in effect, by-
passes any retort which he might fashion against the first.

Secondly, then, it is urged that, even if there is such a

thing as a typically human task, and even if a good man, in *one* sense, is a man who performs this task well; nevertheless, being a good man in *that* sense is not the same as being a *morally* good man. For let us suppose that the typical activity of the lion is to hunt, kill and consume its prey. Then we might write an *Ethics* for lions analysing those activities and offering instruction in their perfection; and in one sense our work would tell lions how to be good lions. But evidently it would not tell lions how to be moral lions – it would be no comfort to a modern Androcles to learn that his lion had read our treatise.

In general, 'X is a morally good F' and 'X performs well the activities typical of F's' are not equivalent to each other; the truth of the one does not imply the truth of the other. And there is no reason to think that in the particular case of man, 'X is a morally good man' is equivalent to 'X performs well the activities typical of men'.

Considerations such as these have led many to conclude that Aristotle's *Ethics* is founded on a serious confusion. The *Ethics* proposes to examine the morally good man; it expresses itself in terms of 'the good man'; and then it construes this phrase, by analogy with 'the good shoemaker', as an ascription of expertise or technical accomplishment. Thus moral goodness is treated as though it were a skill of some sort – a skill at being human; and such a treatment is wholly erroneous.

An alternative conclusion is both possible and preferable. Let us question the premiss that the *Ethics* proposes to examine the morally good man. This premiss is, after all, not explicit in Aristotle's text, which only introduces the 'moral' virtues at a later stage in the argument. If we were to drop it we might suppose that Aristotle is dealing, primarily, not with moral goodness but with human expertise or the technique of being a good man; the immediate aim of the *Ethics* is to make us 'good men' – not morally good men, but expert or successful human beings.

This suggestion has at least two merits. First, it remains fairly faithful to the letter of Aristotle's text; and secondly, it rids Aristotle of the gross confusion between moral and technical goodness which the traditional interpretation seems obliged to attribute to him. The suggestion immediately raises two fundamental questions. First, *is* there such a thing as human expertise? And secondly, what is the connection, in Aristotle's mind, between expertise and morality? how does the *Ethics* impinge upon moral philosophy? I shall sketch answers to these questions later on; for the moment they will be shelved.

The suggestion that the primary concern of the *Ethics* is human expertise rather than moral excellence has arisen from reflections upon I.7; consideration of I.2 may lead in the same direction.

I.2 reveals Aristotle as a 'eudaimonist' – a man who holds that happiness is the *summum bonum* or supreme end of life. This statement calls for three riders. First, the word 'happiness' translates the Greek *eudaimonia*; I abide, for the moment, by this stock translation, but I give notice that it will be questioned. Secondly, it is worth noting that happiness is not the same thing as pleasure: the man who follows the advice of the *Ethics* will, according to Aristotle, live an enjoyable life (e.g. 1099a7–21), but he will not live a life of pleasure, in the common sense of that phrase. Aristotle brusquely rejects the view that happiness consists in a constant succession of pleasures – such a view advocates a 'life suitable for cattle' (1095b20). If Aristotle is a eudaimonist, he is certainly not a hedonist.

Thirdly, eudaimonism does not maintain that happiness is the immediate aim of every action, but only that it is the ultimate aim. What this amounts to may be put, dramatically, as follows: Suppose you are doing X. I ask you why, and you reply, 'In order to achieve Y'. I then ask you why you are aiming at Y, and you say, 'In order to achieve Z'. Our conversation may go on as long as you please; but, Aristotle argues, if your doing X is a purposeful action and not a pointless frivolity, then there must eventually come a point at which you reject my questioning and say: 'I am not aiming at that in order to achieve any further aim – that is my ultimate aim' (see 1094a18–22). Aristotle also maintains that your penultimate line in every complete dialogue of this sort must be: 'In order to achieve happiness' (1095a18–22; 1097a25–b6).

All this may suggest that a moral philosophy is, after all, firmly embedded in the first Book of the *Ethics*, and in particular that Aristotle is offering a fairly refined species of Utilitarianism: the only ultimately good thing in the world is the happiness of sentient beings; and the only ultimate moral rule is one enjoining us to maximize the sum of that happiness. Aristotle is thus a precursor of the great English Utilitarians, Bentham and J. S. Mill.

This conclusion, however, is premature. Utilitarianism has no place in the *Ethics*; it is not assessed or even described, let alone recommended. Indeed, despite the political and social ambience of the *Ethics*, Aristotle shows a remarkable indifference to the effects of the good man's actions on his fellows; even where such eminently social virtues as generosity or munificence are under discussion, it is, one feels, the character of the virtuous man rather than the effects of his virtuous actions that excites Aristotle's interest.

Aristotle's eudaimonism in fact differs from classical Utilitarianism in one crucial respect which my exposition has so far deliberately suppressed. The happiness which Aristotle expects the virtuous agent to pursue is not, as the Utilitarians would have it, the general happiness of the sentient world, but rather the individual happiness of the agent himself. Happiness is to be my goal, not in the generous sense that I am to aim at a general increase in the commodity, but in the selfish sense that I am to seek the enlargement of my own portion of it. The good man is a producer of happiness – but of his own happiness and not, or at best incidentally, that of others. This theory, which might be called egoistic eudaimonism, is worlds away from the noble sentiments of Bentham and Mill; and it is, I think, well removed from anything that we might be tempted to think of as a system of morality.

There is a further vagueness in my description of Aristotle's eudaimonism which must be cleared up. The classical Utilitarians hold unambiguously that all agents *should* aim at happiness; and, in virtue of that 'should', the official utilitarian thesis is a species of *ethical* theory; for it prescribes what, morally speaking, is to be done. The Utilitarians regularly couple with this official thesis the different thesis that all agents *do*, and as a matter of psychological necessity are bound to, aim at their own happiness. This thesis is, in virtue of the word 'do', a *psychological* thesis; for it states what, psychologically speaking, is bound to be done. (I shall not enter into the question of the compatibility of these two utilitarian theses.)

In the light of this we may ask whether Aristotle's egoistic eudaemonism is an ethical or a psychological thesis. Aristotle is not perfectly clear on the subject; and his habitual talk of the 'ends' of action might have been designed to blur the distinction between ethics and psychology. Some passages strongly suggest a psychological thesis (e.g. 1097a15–24). Moreover, Aristotle holds that his thesis is platitudinous and almost universally accepted (1095a18); and though it is hardly a common belief that one *should* aim at one's own happiness, it is, I suppose, a part of common-sense 'realism' that men always *do* – 'in the last analysis' – act for their own happiness. On the other hand, the aim of the *Ethics* is expressly practical: its philosophy aims at changing the world, not at interpreting it; and we should therefore expect it to be concerned to advance a prescriptive 'should' rather than a descriptive psychological 'do'.

This ambiguity in Aristotle's thought can, I think, be resolved; and its resolution leads to a fuller understanding of Aristotle's task in the *Ethics*. Roughly, the position is this: It is a fact of human nature that men must act for their own happiness – that is to say, men always aim at what they *take* to be their own happiness; and since nature always arranges things for the best (1099b29), it is a reasonable and proper thing for men to behave in this way. But by and large men have incomplete or mistaken notions of what their happiness consists in; and they find, with dispiriting frequency, that it does not lie where they take it to lie. That fact gives scope for a prescriptive *Ethics*: Aristotle's prescriptions can serve a practical end by completing and correcting those ordinary notions of happiness; and thus they will ensure a more frequent and a more satisfactory achievement of the natural human end (see I.4) and at the same time enable even the morally fastidious to contemplate with approval our actions of enlightened self-love (see IX.8).

It is time to look more closely at the notion of *eudaimonia* or happiness. The recipe for happiness which the *Ethics* finally propounds has failed to please the palates of most intellectual gourmets; for it locates happiness in some sort of 'contemplation', and invites us to add felicity to our lives by taking thought. The invitation seems to some readers to presuppose an impossible ideal; and to others to evince a gross ignorance of elementary human psychology: perhaps 'contemplation' may make a few choice souls happy; but it surely is not the stuff and matter of the happiness to which most men aspire. If, as Aristotle urges (1179a20), we compare his theory with the 'facts of life', the theory totters.

This natural feeling of dissatisfaction with the chief thesis of the *Ethics* may be mitigated by a nicer attention to the Greek word *eudaimonia*. The stock translation, 'happiness', is by no means wholly absurd: it makes sense in most contexts of its occurrence, and it receives some degree of support on general semantic grounds. Yet it is far from adequate as a precise rendering of Aristotle's term. That is quickly shown in an abstract way: happiness, as the term is used in ordinary English, is a sort of mental or emotional state or condition; to call a man happy is (to put it very vaguely indeed) to say something about his general state of mind. *Eudaimonia*, on the other hand, is not simply a mental state: after setting out his analysis of *eudaimonia*, which I shall shortly comment on, Aristotle remarks that 'it agrees with our account that the *eudaimōn* lives well and acts well;

for it (i.e. *eudaimonia*) has been pretty well defined as a sort of well-living (*euzōia*) and well-acting (*eupraxia*)' (1098b21). To call a man *eudaimōn* is (to put it very vaguely indeed) to say something about how he lives and what he does. The notion of *eudaimonia* is closely tied, in a way in which the notion of happiness is not, to success: the *eudaimōn* is the man who makes a success of his life and actions, who realizes his aims and ambitions as a man, who fulfils himself.

This account helps, I think, to explain a curious argument in I.10–11 which tackles the strange question of whether a man's *eudaimonia* can be affected by what happens after his death and hence (in Aristotle's view) after the cessation of all his mental states. Clearly, this question is fatuous if asked of happiness: my happiness ends with the end of my life; in the absence of all mental states there can be no happy mental states. Equally clearly, the question is not obviously silly if asked of fulfilment or success; for in general my successes and failures are not terminated by the termination of my life: my plans and ambitions may be furthered or thwarted by the efforts of other men and the intercession of fortune; and often such interferences may continue in my absence and after my death. (In some matters, indeed, I cannot succeed until I am dead: my last testament publishes such *post mortem* plans.)

It will not, of course, do to replace 'happiness' by 'success' or 'fulfilment' as a translation of *eudaimonia*; the matter is far too complicated for any such simple remedy, and in what follows I shall continue to employ the word 'happiness', guarding it with a pair of inverted commas. But it is, I think, worth considering Aristotle's recipe for *eudaimonia* with the notion of success in mind. The *Ethics*, we are thus supposing, is not directly telling us how to be morally good men, or even how to be humanly happy: it is telling us how to live successful human lives, how to fulfil ourselves as men.

Aristotle's advocacy of his account of 'happiness' falls into two parts. First, in Book I, he identifies 'happiness' with the *summum bonum*, and proceeds to analyse the *summum bonum* as an 'activity of the soul in accordance with virtue'. Then, in Book X, he specifies that the activity in which 'happiness' principally consists is contemplation. By and large, it is fair to say that Book I does the analytic work of dissecting the concept of 'happiness', and Book X the substantive work of telling us how to ensure that the concept applies to us and to our lives. Aristotle, of course, does not distinguish the tasks in this way.

The arguments of both Books seem to lead to strange results. First, we might wonder why anyone should be tempted to think that 'happiness' is an *activity*, or that it is proper to the *soul*, or that it is intrinsically connected with *virtue*. Here again the stock (and scarcely avoidable) translations of Aristotle's technical vocabulary may mislead us.

First, in saying that 'happiness' is an activity or *energeia* Aristotle does not mean that the 'happy' man is a sort of intellectual athlete, forever engaged in mental press-ups. An activity is a doing only in that very broad sense of the word in which even dreamers and idlers may be said to be doing something. In general, *energeia* takes its sense from what it is contrasted with, and here the contrast is with a 'having' (*hexis*) – a disposition, capacity, ability or faculty (1098b30–1097a7; cf. 1098a6). Being 'happy', unlike, say, being intelligent, is not a matter of having some power or disposition; it is a matter of exercising one's powers and realizing one's dispositions.

Secondly, the term 'soul' must be divorced from its modern religious associations; nor may we think of any Cartesian substantial self, housed in an alien body and carrying on its own psychic activities. To have a soul or *psuchē* is, in Aristotle's view, simply to be alive or animate: 'activities of the soul' are things which living creatures by their nature can, and inanimate things by their nature cannot, do. Sticks and stones are disqualified from 'happiness' by the same decree that bars them from thought, perception, and reproduction: they are not endowed with life.

Thirdly, to act in accordance with virtue is not to play the saint. *Aretē*, 'virtue', is commonly used as the abstract noun for *agathos*, 'good'; and 'goodness' or 'excellence' are often better translations of the noun than 'virtue' is. In Aristotelian usage at least, the adjective *agathos* requires a substantive, explicit or implied, to lean upon: 'X is *agathos*' is elliptical for something of the form 'X is an *agathos* F'. Thus any *aretē* that X displays will be the *aretē* proper to some F; for to display an *aretē* is to be *agathos*, and to be *agathos* is to be an *agathos* F. For an F to 'act in accordance with virtue (i.e. with *its* virtue)' is, then, simply for it to perform well as an F, to do well whatever is the task typical of F's. (See especially 1106a15–25.)

If these three glosses are conjoined, then an 'activity of the soul in accordance with virtue' is revealed as an excellent performance of whatever task is typical of a living creature; and since we are concerned exclusively with human souls, we can specify the living creature as man.

Two further qualifications must be made to this account. First, if there is more than one typically human task, then we are interested in the best and most perfect of them. Secondly, the activity must take place 'in a complete life'. This phrase is, I think, best taken as an indication, admittedly exaggerated and inaccurate, that 'happiness' is essentially something that takes up time – a man cannot with propriety be called 'happy' in virtue of some brief or momentary state or event in his life; unlike pleasure or ecstasy, 'happiness' cannot be short-lived.

We may finally state Aristotle's account of *eudaimonia* in a less elevated idiom, and with some little polishing, as follows: A man is 'happy' if and only if, over some considerable period of time, he frequently performs with some success the most perfect of typically human tasks.

We are now brought back to one of the questions which were shelved earlier: what, if anything, is typical of humans? what do men do *qua* men? The celebrated Aristotelian answer is that man is a rational animal, and that his typical task is therefore rational activity. Now according to Aristotle, a man, or his soul, may be said to 'have reason' on two distinct counts (1103a1–10); and the notion of rational action is correspondingly two-fold: I act rationally either insofar as I base my actions in some way upon reasoning, or insofar as I indulge in some sort of ratiocinative exercises. Selling my shares in the expectation of a drop in the market, and following out the Euclidean proof of Pythagoras' theorem, are both rational acts, but rational in different ways: in the first case I might be said to be following or obeying my reason, in the second case to be exercising it.

The good man, or expert human, is thus an ace rationalist, either in that his actions are as a rule soundly based on excellent reasoning, or in that he indulges fairly often in fine excogitations. Aristotle's treatment of the 'moral virtues', or excellences of character (Books II–V and VIII–IX), provides, *inter alia*, a partial description of the mind of an ideal rationalist of the first variety. Aristotle's treatment of the 'intellectual virtues', or excellences of mind (Book VI), completes the description of the first sort of rationalist, and complements it with a description of the second sort. Book X then argues that the second rationalist is the better, and thus that it is rational activity of the second sort which is constitutive of true human 'happiness'.

Aristotle's analyses of the 'moral' virtues are, by and large, clear enough: we are left in no doubt about what we must do in order to qualify as men of good character. The case of the 'intellectual' virtues is less clear; and when, in Book X, Aristotle reveals that the sort of rational activity in which 'happiness' culminates is 'contemplation' or *theōria*, then both his argument and his conclusion are hard to follow and to understand. I shall say nothing here about the argument; but the conclusion calls for a gloss: what, after all, is 'contemplation'?

First, the Aristotelian contemplator is no monkish ascetic, denying the body for the good of his mind. Aristotle stresses that a moderate supply of 'external goods' is a precondition of 'happy' intellectual activity (e.g. 1099a32–b8; 1178a23–b7); and his contemplator is necessarily enjoying himself.

Secondly, Aristotelian contemplation is not, as we might be tempted to imagine, an exercise in discursive reasoning: it is not a matter of intellectual questing or research; it is not a matter of moving by logical inference from known premisses to hitherto unknown conclusions. As an argument for the thesis that the contemplator enjoys himself, Aristotle observes that 'it is reasonable that those who know have a more pleasant life than those who search' (1177a26); evidently, then, contemplators are not seekers after wisdom but possessors of it.

Thirdly, Aristotelian contemplation is to be distinguished from its fashionable Eastern homonym. Oriental meditation, if I understand aright, consists essentially in relaxing one's intellectual muscles and letting the mind roam at random over the vastnesses of eternity. Such an exercise is designed, in part at least, to gain new insight or knowledge; and to that extent it differs from the Aristotelian exercise. Moreover, it involves a voluntary surrender of intellectual control, whereas Aristotle clearly thinks of contemplation as a consciously directed activity.

The Aristotelian contemplator is a man who has already acquired knowledge; and what he is contemplating is precisely this knowledge already present in his mind. Contemplation is something like a review or survey of existing knowledge: the contemplator is engaged in the orderly inspection of truths which he already possesses; his task consists in bringing them forward from the recesses of his mind, and arranging them fittingly in the full light of consciousness. As a connoisseur of art with a penchant for impressionism might first purchase or procure a Manet and then gaze upon it; so an Aristotelian contemplator with a penchant for geometry will first read Euclid (or prove for himself the theorems which Euclid contains) and then gaze inwardly on the orderly array of theorems and deductions in his mind. He will pass in review the long concatenations of proofs which make up the *Elements*; he knows his Euclid already, but by contemplation he brings his knowledge once again to the forefront of his mind. In this way contemplation is a quasi-aesthetic appreciation of knowledge and truth.

A life of unbroken contemplation is something divine: no man can hope to live it for more than a portion of his time, and many men cannot aspire to it at all. All men for some of the time, and many men for all of the time, must therefore be contented with the performance of the second best of human tasks: incapable of constant rationality of the better sort, they must ensure their 'happiness' by recourse to the weaker variety of rational action. Now the man who follows or obeys his reason will, as I have said, act in accordance with the 'moral virtues' or excellences of character; this type of man will, according to Aristotle, be courageous, temperate, liberal, just and so on – in short, he will be precisely the sort of man we should ordinarily be prepared to hail as morally good. 'Happiness' for most men and for most of the time will thus consist in moral action and an upright life.

This, I think, enables us to answer the second of the questions which were earlier shelved: How does the *Ethics* impinge upon moral philosophy? The short answer is that it does so insofar as it argues that the expert man will for the most part be a moral man. But it is worth giving a slightly longer answer to the question.

Treatises of moral philosophy may simply tell us how to be morally good men. As such they have their utility, but it is of a limited sort: they will appeal only to those who already want or are prepared to be morally good; the rules of cricket are of no concern to those who have no interest in playing the game. Other treatises of moral philosophy attempt not merely to describe the moral life but also to provide men with a motive for living it. The first such treatise was Plato's *Republic*, with which Aristotle was intimately acquainted; and one strand in the *Ethics* is, I think, in this respect Platonic. The strand runs roughly as follows: 'Each man desires his own good, i.e. he desires the human good; hence he desires *eudaimonia*, and this, on analysis, turns out to be the excellent performance of typically human tasks. Anthropology and psychology reveal, first, that such tasks are kinds of rational activity, and secondly that the secondary kind of rational activity is all that most of us will attain. It is further seen that this sort of rational activity coincides fairly closely with what we are inclined to regard as moral activity. Thus anyone who has a correct and complete notion of what he desires and who acts (as he must) on his desires, will usually act morally.' We are all egoists; but the enlightened egoist will spend some of his time in contemplation, which is at worst harmless, and much of the rest of it in activities of a morally admirable variety. One task of the *Ethics* is to enlighten us egoists.

Such reflections may appear to make a nonsense of my earlier suggestion that Aristotle's *Ethics* is not exactly a work of moral philosophy. I do, of course, concede that the strand of thought I have just described is of a sort characteristic of ethical writings of the apologetic variety. Nonetheless, there is still substance to the claim that the *Ethics* is not primarily or directly about moral philosophy: first, the chief end of the *Ethics* is to discover and delineate the life and character not of the morally good man, but of the man who is an expert human, successful and fulfilled *qua* man; and secondly, the most perfect human fulfilment is found to lie not in moral action at all but in intellectual contemplation – morality is, so to speak, a *pis aller*; we should follow it only insofar as we cannot travel the high road of thought.

The account of 'happiness' which I have just ascribed to Aristotle will provoke questions and objections at a score of points; I shall end by mentioning one or two of these. It hardly needs to be said that the following paragraphs do not pretend to be more than outline sketches of a few possible criticisms and rejoinders.

First, it is often said that the introduction of 'virtue' or excellence into the account of 'happiness' is an error: after all, a man may achieve happiness without doing anything particularly well, and the vast majority of happy people have no outstanding excellences. There are also happy failures. If 'happiness' essentially involves success, however, this criticism collapses; for it is a simple analytic truth that I cannot succeed or fulfil myself as a man without doing something well – and hence that I cannot be *eudaimōn* or 'happy' without exercising some *aretē* or virtue.

Secondly, it is equally often argued that Aristotle's account is founded on the false presupposition that 'happiness' must be unique, and that there must be some single activity which for all men produces 'the' human good. Why, it is asked, may there not be several – even indefinitely many – such felicific activities? Just as different jokes make different men laugh, and different wines please different palates, so different types of men will be made happy by different types of activity.

Aristotle, indeed, might well have framed this objection for himself (cf. 1176a10–15); but he need not have been impressed by it. Different things may, it is true, make different men happy in the ordinary sense of the term. But if X and Y are both successful as F's, then there must be some one thing (or at least some fairly small disjunction of things) that accounts for both successes – namely, whatever amounts to performing well as an F. The presupposition of uniqueness, in other words, is guaranteed by the form of Aristotle's problem: there must be some one thing, or small disjunction of things, which constitutes human 'happiness', namely whatever it is which amounts to doing well as a man.

A third line of criticism is, I think, more telling. We might wonder whether Aristotle's view of human reason, and of human nature in general, is adequate and well rounded. It will occur to many readers that the life of the intellectual searcher is, despite Aristotle's contrary assertion, no less pleasant than that of the knower: the joys and excitements of the chase usually equal and often exceed those of the tranquil review, and it is by no means clear that contemplation is a better or more perfect activity than study and ratiocination. More generally, it is not unnatural to suppose that such features as affection and sympathy for other people, and sensibility to and appreciation of beautiful things, may claim a place alongside purely intellectual activity as pre-eminently human characteristics. If that is so, the 'happy' man will be a lover of men and an admirer of beauty as well as a contemplator of truth – a friend and an aesthete as well as a thinker. Human excellence, in short, runs in a broader and more amiable stream than Aristotle imagined.

In answer to this charge, Aristotle would doubtless have attempted to locate sympathy and sensibility on a lower level than contemplation, and he would appeal to his theory that the intellect or *nous*, which is the faculty of contemplation, is the most complete and perfect faculty of the soul and is, in a sense, identical with the real self of a man. I do not for my part believe that this answer can be sustained; but it certainly calls for a sober consideration, and any assault upon it would require a long and detailed examination of the arguments in Book X.

Finally, and most fundamentally, we might wonder whether everyone would, or should, care for 'happiness' on Aristotle's terms. Aristotle starts by noting that 'happiness' is the acknowledged aim of all men; and he tries to articulate this aim by his analysis of the notion of 'happiness'. But what if acquaintance with Aristotle's elucidation should cause men to change their aim? 'Aristotle', they may say, 'has shown us clearly what we were confusedly aiming at – and our new clear vision allows us to see the absurdity of our original aim: if "happiness" really consists in bouts of intellectual activity set in a life of moral rectitude, then we no longer want to be "happy" – let us set our sights on some other target:

> Let's be no stoics nor no stocks, I pray;
> Or so devote to Aristotle's ethics,
> As Ovid be an outcast quite abjured.'

Against such ignoble sentiments Aristotle deploys a bottomless contempt and a measure of abuse: men who prefer the sensual delights of Ovid to the austere pleasures advocated in the *Ethics* abjure their humanity and choose a bestial life. If they will not think as men, they cannot hope to act as men. 'Those great men', said Bishop Berkeley, 'Pythagoras, Plato, and Aristotle, the most consummate in politics, who founded states, or instructed princes, or wrote most accurately on public government, were at the same time the most acute at all abstracted and sublime speculations; the clearest light being ever necessary to guide the most important actions. And, whatever the world may say, he who hath not much meditated upon God, the human mind, and the *summum bonum*, may possibly make a thriving earthworm, but will most indubitably make a sorry patriot and a sorry statesman.'

Such splendid pronouncements must make a powerful impression on the mind; yet they will not convince the world if the world chooses to be stubborn. They state, magnificently, the unworthiness of the man who rejects his Aristotelian humanity; yet they do not present any argument to prove his rejection foolish, imprudent, or irrational. A stubborn and intemperate world may still ask why it should aim at an unexciting human excellence if it finds bestial excellence more engaging; and a stubborn and sober world may still ask why it should aim at an unsatisfying human excellence if it finds a decent satisfaction in the excellence of an artist or a craftsman or a man of affairs. If, as I believe, the *Ethics* does not answer the stubborn world on these points, it has at least the signal merit of presenting the questions starkly to our judgements.

JONATHAN BARNES

Oriel College
Oxford

BIBLIOGRAPHY
(revised 1983)

THE main purpose of this bibliography is to offer potential philosophical explorers a guide through the luxuriant jungle of Aristotelian literature; in the hope that it will also serve the needs of interested tourists and sight-seers I have asterisked a few of the more accessible and enjoyable items. The order of the list bears a rough correspondence to the order of the narrative in the Introduction.

The standard English version of Aristotle's works is the 'Oxford Translation':

1   J. A. SMITH and W. D. ROSS (eds.), *The Works of Aristotle*, translated into English, Oxford, 1910–52.

There is a highly serviceable abridgement of |1| in:

*2   R. MCKEON (ed.), *The Basic Works of Aristotle*, New York, 1941.

The classic edition of the Greek text is 'Bekker's Aristotle':

3   I. BEKKER (ed.), *Aristotelis Opera*, Berlin, 1831.
As a text this is largely superseded; but references to Aristotle's works are, by a convenient custom, still standardly keyed to Bekker: thus '*EN* 1097b24' refers to that sentence of the *Ethics* which occupies line 24 of column b of page 1097 of |3|.

The evidence for Aristotle's life, which I briefly sketch in the Introduction, is collected and exhaustively analysed in:

4   I. DÜRING, *Aristotle in the Ancient Biographical Tradition*, Göteborg, 1957.

The influence of Plato on Aristotle's thought is variously assessed in |9|, |10| and |11|. A number of papers on Aristotle's scientific aims and achievements are assembled in the first volume of:

*5   J. BARNES, M. SCHOFIELD and R. SORABJI (eds.), *Articles on Aristotle*, 4 vols., London, 1975–9.

The general historical background is described in Book VI of:

5   N. G. L. HAMMOND, *A History of Greece*, Oxford, 1959:

and an account of the social and political life of a Greek city
state can be found in:

7   A. H. M. JONES, *Athenian Democracy*, Oxford, 1957.

The original *corpus* of Aristotle's writings is fully discussed
by:

8   P. MORAUX, *Les Listes anciennes des ouvrages d'Aristote*. Louvain, 1951.

Argument about the nature and the chronology of the treatises has, for half a century, revolved around:

9   W. W. JAEGER, *Aristotle*, trans. R. Robinson. Oxford,
1948[2]; first published Berlin, 1923.

Two stimulating recent contributions to the debate are:

10   W. D. ROSS, 'The Development of Aristotle's Thought', *Pro-
ceedings of the British Academy*, 1957, reprinted in |5|, vol. I;

*11 G. E. L. OWEN, 'The Platonism of Aristotle', *Proceedings of
the British Academy*, 1965, reprinted in |5|, vol. I.

On the evolution of Aristotle's ethics see Chapters IV
and IX of |9|; Chapter I of vol. I of |24|; and:

12   J. D. MONAN, *Moral Knowledge and its Methodology in Aristotle*.
Oxford, 1968;

13   C. J. ROWE. *The Eudemian and Nicomachean Ethics: a study
in the development of Aristotle's thought*. Proceedings of the
Cambridge Philological Society. suppl. 3, Cambridge,
1971;
and also:

14   H. FLASHAR, 'The Criticism of Plato's Theory of Ideas in
Aristotle's Ethics', in |5|, vol. II.

There is an excellent account of the nature and style of
the *Ethics* in vol. I. Chapter II of |24|.

Of the many general introductions to Aristotle's thought I
single out:

15   G. E. R. LLOYD, *Aristotle*. Cambridge, 1968;
*16 J. L. ACKRILL. *Aristotle the Philosopher*. Oxford, 1981;
*17 J. BARNES. *Aristotle*. Oxford, 1982.

The best account of Aristotle's system of the sciences is that
given in the introduction to:

18   H. H. JOACHIM. (ed.), *Aristotle on Coming-to-be and Passing-
away*. Oxford, 1922.

Or Aristotle's anthropology see:

19 S. R. L. CLARK, *Aristotle's Man*, Oxford, 1975

For the connection between ethics and politics see Appendix A to vol. II of |29|; and:

20 D. J. ALLAN, 'Individual and State in the *Ethics* and *Politics*', in *La Politique d'Aristote*, Entretiens Hardt XI, Vandoeuvres, 1964.

Papers on Aristotle's method in science and philosophy are collected in vol. I of |5| and in:

21 S. MANSION (ed.), *Aristote et les Problèmes de Méthode*, Louvain, 1961;
see especially:

*22 G. E. L. OWEN, '*Tithenai ta Phainomena*', in |21 |, reprinted in |5|, vol. I.

Some account of the method of the *Ethics* can be found in |12|; see also:

23 D. J. ALLAN, 'Quasi-mathematical Method in the *Eudemian Ethics*', in |21 |;

23a J. BARNES, 'Aristotle and the Methods of Ethics', *Revue Internationale de Philosophie*, 1980.

The fullest and in many respects most helpful commentary on the *Ethics* is in French:

24 R. A. GAUTHIER and J. Y. JOLIF, *Aristote: l'Éthique à Nicomaque*, Louvain, 1970².

English readers will still find much of value in three older commentaries:

25 A. GRANT, *The Ethics of Aristotle*, London, 1885⁴;
26 J. A. STEWART, *Notes on the Nicomachean Ethics of Aristotle*, Oxford, 1892;
27 J. BURNET, *The Ethics of Aristotle*, London, 1900.
For the *Eudemian Ethics* see:
27a M. J. WOODS, *Aristotle's Eudemian Ethics Books I, II and VIII*, Oxford, 1982.
For the *Protrepticus* see:
28 A. H. CHROUST, *Aristotle: Protrepticus*, Notre Dame, 1964;
and for the *Politics*:
29 W. L. NEWMAN (ed.), *The Politics of Aristotle*, Oxford, 1887.

An invaluable companion to the *Ethics* which discusses most of the important points with both scholarly and philosophical penetration is provided by:

*30   W. F. R. HARDIE, *Aristotle's Ethical Theory*, Oxford, 1980[2].
      See also:

31   J. M. COOPER, *Reason and the Human Good in Aristotle*, Cambridge, Mass., 1975.

Several of the best papers on the *Ethics* are collected in vol
II of |5|, in:

31a   J. J. WALSH and H. L. SHAPIRO (eds.), *Aristotle's Ethics*,
      Belmont, 1967; and in:

*32   A. O. RORTY (ed.), *Essays on Aristotle's Ethics*, Berkeley, 1980.

I turn now to studies of particular doctrines of, or passages
in, the *Ethics*.

   The main issues of Books I and X about goodness and
happiness are dealt with by:

33   W. F. R. HARDIE, 'The Final Good in Aristotle's *Ethics*',
      Philosophy, 1965, reprinted in: *Aristotle*, ed. J. M. E.
      Moravcsik, New York, 1967;

34   J. L. ACKRILL, 'Aristotle on *Eudaimonia*', *Proceedings of the
      British Academy*, 1974, reprinted in |32|;

35   T. H. IRWIN, 'The Metaphysical and Psychological Basis
      of Aristotle's Ethics', in |32|.

   Aristotle's notion of goodness is defended by:

*36   S. HAMPSHIRE, 'Ethics – a Defence of Aristotle', in his
      Freedom of Mind, Oxford, 1972.
      See also:

37   B. A. O. WILLIAMS, 'Aristotle on the Good – a formal
      sketch', *Philosophical Quarterly*, 1962;

38   K. V. WILKES, 'The Good Man and the Good for Man in
      Aristotle's Ethics', *Mind*, 1978, reprinted in |32|.

   The criticism of the Platonic 'Form of the Good' in I.6
has occasioned a quantity of comment; among the best
contributions are |14| and:

39   D. J. ALLAN, 'Aristotle's Criticism of Platonic Doctrine
      concerning Goodness and the Good', *Proceedings of the Aris-
      totelian Society*, 1963–4;

40   L. A. KOSMAN, 'Predicating the Good', *Phronesis*, 1968;

*41   J. L. ACKRILL, 'Aristotle on "Good" and the Categories',
      in *Islamic Philosophy and the Classical Tradition*, eds. S. M.
      Stern, A. Hourani and V. Brown, Oxford, 1972, reprinted
      in |5| vol. II.

Aristotle's account of happiness is treated by:

42   J. LÉONARD, *Le Bonheur chez Aristote*, Brussels, 1948.
He is made a hedonist by:

43   H. A. PRICHARD, 'The meaning of *agathon* in the *Ethics* of Aristotle', *Philosophy*, 1935, reprinted in *Aristotle*, ed. J. M. E. Moravcsik, New York, 1967.
Against this see:

44   J. L. AUSTIN, 'Agathon and *Eudaimonia* in the *Ethics* of Aristotle', in *Aristotle*, ed. J. M. E. Moravcsik, New York, 1967; see also:

45   J. MCDOWELL, 'The Role of *Eudaimonia* in Aristotle's Ethics', in |32|;

*46   A. J. P. KENNY, 'Happiness', *Proceedings of the Aristotelian Society*, 1965–6, reprinted in |5| vol. II;

47   T. NAGEL, 'Aristotle on *Eudaimonia*', *Phronesis*, 1972, reprinted in |32|;

48   P. DEFOURNY, 'Contemplation in the Ethics of Aristotle', in |5| vol. II.

Books II–IV analyse the 'moral' virtues. Some of the background to this analysis is examined by:

49   W. W. JAEGER, 'Aristotle's Use of Medicine as a Model of Method in his Ethics', *Journal of Hellenic Studies*, 1957;
and the analysis itself is discussed by:

50   H. W. B. JOSEPH, *Essays in Ancient and Modern Philosophy*, Oxford, 1935;

*51   W. F. R. HARDIE, 'Aristotle's Doctrine that Virtue is a "Mean" ', *Proceedings of the Aristotelian Society*, 1964–5, reprinted in |5| vol. II;

52   W. W. FORTENBAUGH, 'Aristotle and the Questionable Mean-Dispositions', *Transactions of the American Philological Association*, 1968;

53   W. W. FORTENBAUGH, 'Aristotle: Emotion and Moral Virtue', *Arethusa*, 1969;

54   J. O. URMSON, 'Aristotle's Doctrine of the Mean', *American Philosophical Quarterly*, 1973, reprinted in |32|.
See on the acquisition of virtue:

55   M. F. BURNYEAT, 'Aristotle on Learning to be Good', in |32|.
On some individual virtues see:

56   D. F. PEARS, 'Courage as a Mean', in |32|;

57   W. F. R. HARDIE, ' "Magnanimity" in Aristotle's *Ethics*',
     Phronesis, 1978.

     The special virtue of justice is analysed in Book V; there
     are helpful notes in:
58   H. JACKSON, *Peri Dikaiosunēs -- the Fifth Book of the Nicoma-
     chean Ethics of Aristotle*, Cambridge, 1879.
     Aristotle's analysis is discussed by: ·
59   M. HAMBURGER, *Morals and Law: the Growth of Aristotle's
     Legal Theory*. New Haven, 1951;
60   R. BAMBROUGH, 'Aristotle on Justice, a Paradigm of Philo-
     sophy', in *New Essays on Plato and Aristotle*, ed. R. Bam-
     brough, London, 1965;
61   B. WILLIAMS, 'Justice as a Virtue', in [32];
62   K. MARC-WOGAU, 'Aristotle's Theory of Corrective Justice
     and Reciprocity', in his *Philosophical Essays*, Lund, 1967;
*63 M. I. FINLEY, 'Aristotle and Economic Analysis', *Past and
     Present*, 1970, reprinted in [5] vol. II;
64   F. ROSEN, 'The Political Context of Aristotle's Categories
     of Justice', *Phronesis*, 1975.

     On the special virtue of friendship (Books VIII and IX)
     see:
65   A. W. H. ADKINS, 'Friendship and Self-sufficiency in
     Homer and Aristotle', *Classical Quarterly*, 1963;
66   J. ANNAS, 'Plato and Aristotle on Friendship and Altru-
     ism', *Mind*, 1977;
67   J. M. COOPER, 'Aristotle on Friendship', *Philosophical
     Review*, 1977, reprinted in [32].

     Many of the difficulties in Book VI are eased by:
68   L. H. G. GREENWOOD, *Aristotle: Nicomachean Ethics Book Six*,
     Cambridge, 1909.
     The 'intellectual' virtues, which the book dissects, have
     received scanty attention from scholars, with the exception
     of 'practical wisdom' or *phronēsis*. Some of the problems
     raised by this notion are examined in:
*69 D. J. ALLAN, 'Aristotle's Account of the Origins of Moral
     Principles', *Actes du XIe Congrès internationale de Philosophie*,
     vol. XII, Brussels, 1953, reprinted in [5] vol. II;
70   R. DEMOS, 'Some Remarks on Aristotle's Doctrine of

Practical Reason', *Philosophy and Phenomenological Research*, 1961–2;

71   P. AUBENQUE, *La Prudence chez Aristote*, Paris, 1963;

72   R. SORABJI, 'Aristotle on the Role of Intellect in Virtue', *Proceedings of the Aristotelian Society*, 1973–4;

73   D. WIGGINS, 'Deliberation and Practical Reason'. *Proceedings of the Aristotelian Society*, 1975–6.

See also, on a related topic:

74   G. RYLE, 'On Forgetting the Difference between Right and Wrong', in *Essays in Moral Philosophy*, ed. A. I. Melden, Seattle, 1958.

Virtuous and vicious action depend on a certain state of mind in the agent; Aristotle's subtle remarks on the mental preconditions of action are found in Books III, VI, and VII. Modern discussions of this topic tend to circle around the problem of free will; for Aristotle's attitude to this issue see:

75   P. M. HUBY, 'The First Discovery of the Freewill Problem', *Philosophy*, 1967;

76   W. F. R. HARDIE, 'Aristotle and the Freewill Problem', *Philosophy*, 1968.

Aristotle's general account of voluntariness is placed in its historical setting by:

77   R. SORABJI, *Necessity, Cause and Blame*, London, 1980;

78   A. W. H. ADKINS, *Merit and Responsibility*, Oxford, 1960;

79   H. D. P. LEE, 'The Legal Background of Two Passages in the *Nicomachean Ethics*'. *Classical Quarterly*, 1937.

It is examined philosophically by:

80   F. A. SIEGLER, 'Voluntary and Involuntary', *Monist*, 1968;

*81   D. J. FURLEY, Aristotle and Epicurus on Voluntary Action', in his *Two Studies in the Greek Atomists*, Princeton, 1967, partly reprinted in [5] vol. II.

See also Chapter I of:

*82   J. GLOVER, *Responsibility*, London, 1970;

83   A. KENNY, *Aristotle's Theory of the Will*, London, 1979; and

84   V. HAKSAR, 'Aristotle and the Punishment of Psychopaths', *Philosophy*, 1964.

There is a stimulating and original account of intention or *or hairesis* by:

*85   G. E. M. ANSCOMBE. 'Thought and Action in Aristotle', in
       New Essays on Plato and Aristotle, ed. R. Bambrough, London,
       1965, reprinted in |32| and in |5| vol. II;

85a   J. L. ACKRILL, 'Aristotle on Action', in |32|.

Intentional action is in some sense governed by the 'practical syllogism': on the difficult passages in which Aristotle
describes this sort of reasoning see:

86   D. J. ALLAN, 'The Practical Syllogism', *Autour d'Aristote*,
       Louvain, 1955;

87   T. ANDO, *Aristotle's Theory of Practical Cognition*, Kyoto, 1958;
and also |95| and |96|. Aristotle's remarks here have
sparked off some exciting modern papers; see especially
paragraphs 32–44 of:

88   G. E. M. ANSCOMBE, *Intention*, Oxford, 1963[2];

89   G. E. M. ANSCOMBE, 'Two Kinds of Error in Action', *Jour-
       nal of Philosophy*, 1963;

90   A. J. P. KENNY, 'Practical Inference', *Analysis*, 1966;

*91   R. M. HARE, 'Practical Inferences', in his *Practical Inferences*,
       London, 1971;

92   D. WIGGINS, 'Deliberation and Practical Reason', in |32|.

If deliberation enjoins an action, and the agent is able to
perform it, it might seem that acting would automatically
follow; yet we appear to be faced in ordinary life by cases of
'back-sliding' or *akrasia*, in which a man in full possession of
his powers acts against his reasoned decisions. Among the
many attempts to elucidate Aristotle's dark discussion of
akrasia are:

93   J. COOK WILSON, *On the Structure of Book 7 of the Nicomachean
       Ethics*, Oxford, 1912[2];

*94   R. ROBINSON, 'Aristotle on Acrasia', in his *Essays in Greek
       Philosophy*, Oxford, 1969, reprinted in |5| vol. II;

95   J. J. WALSH. *Aristotle's Conception of Moral Weakness*, New
       York, 1963;

96   A. J. P. KENNY, 'The Practical Syllogism and Incontin-
       ence', *Phronesis*, 1966;

97   D. WIGGINS, 'Weakness of Will, Commensurability, and
       the Objects of Deliberation and Desire', in |32|.
The most controversial, and in many ways the most Aristotelian, contribution to the modern discussion of back-
ing is that in Chapter V of:

98   R. M. HARE, *Freedom and Reason*, Oxford, 1963;
see also:

99   D. DAVIDSON, 'How is Weakness of the Will Possible?' in *Moral Concepts*, ed. J. Feinberg, Oxford, 1969.

Various reasons make pleasure a central concern to the *Ethics*. Most of the problems raised by the dual accounts of pleasure in Books VII and X are dealt with by:

100   A. J. FESTUGIÈRE, *Aristote – le Plaisir*, Paris, 1946².

Issues of a more philosophical nature are raised by:

101   J. O. URMSON, 'Aristotle on Pleasure', in *Aristotle*, ed. J. M. E. Moravcsik, New York, 1967;

102   G. E. L. OWEN, 'Aristotelian Pleasures', *Proceedings of the Aristotelian Society*, 1971–2, reprinted in [5] vol. II;

103   J. C. B. GOSLING, 'More Aristotelian Pleasures', *Proceedings of the Aristotelian Society*, 1973–4;
and in Chapter VI of:

*104   A. J. P. KENNY, *Action, Emotion and Will*, London, 1963.
See also:

105   J. C. B. GOSLING and C. C. W. TAYLOR, *The Greeks on Pleasure*, Oxford, 1982.

Modern philosophers have been particularly interested in Aristotle's key distinction between an activity or *energeia* and a change or *kinēsis* (see 1174a13–b9); the more Aristotelian of the essays on this subject include: Chapter VIII of [104], and:

*106   J. L. ACKRILL, 'Aristotle's Distinction between *Energeia* and *Kinēsis*', in *New Essays on Plato and Aristotle*, ed. R. Bambrough, London, 1965;

107   C. C. W. TAYLOR, 'States, Performances, and Activities', *Proceedings of the Aristotelian Society*, supp. vol. 1965;

108   T. PENNER, 'Verbs and the Identity of Actions', in *Ryle*, eds. O. P. Wood and G. Pitcher, London, 1971.

There is an ever increasing outpouring of books and articles on the *Ethics*; these publications are often of the highest philosophical calibre, and illustrate well how the *Ethics* continues to stimulate and to help modern students of philosophy. Anyone wishing to keep abreast of this tide of thought may have recourse to such bibliographical periodicals as *L'Année Philologique* and *A Philosopher's Index*

CONTENTS

I THE OBJECT OF LIFE

II MORAL GOODNESS

III MORAL RESPONSIBILITY
TWO VIRTUES

IV OTHER MORAL VIRTUES

V JUSTICE

VI INTELLECTUAL VIRTUES

VII CONTINENCE AND INCONTINENCE
THE NATURE OF PLEASURE

VIII THE KINDS OF FRIENDSHIP

IX THE GROUNDS OF FRIENDSHIP

X PLEASURE AND THE LIFE OF HAPPINESS

THE ETHICS

The figures and letters printed on the page-heads refer to the corresponding pages, columns (left or right) and lines of Bekker's Greek text, which are regularly used for giving exact references to Aristotle's writings. Throughout this translation the point at which each new column or page begins is indicated by an asterisk *.

I

THE OBJECT OF LIFE

*Every rational activity aims at some end or good. One end
(like one activity) may be subordinate to another*

i. *Every art and every investigation, and similarly every
action and pursuit,[1] is considered to aim at some good.
Hence the Good has been rightly defined as 'that at which
all things aim'. Clearly, however, there is some difference
between the ends at which they aim: some are activities and
others results distinct from the activities. Where there are
ends distinct from the actions, the results are by nature
superior to the activities. Since there are many actions, arts
and sciences, it follows that their ends are many too – the
end of medical science is health; of military science, victory;
of economic science,[2] wealth. In the case of all skills of this
kind that come under a single 'faculty'[3] – as a skill in making
bridles or any other part of a horse's trappings comes under
horsemanship, while this and every kind of military action
comes under military science, so in the same way other skills
are subordinate to yet others – in all these the ends of the
directive arts are to be preferred in every case to those of the
subordinate ones, because it is for the sake of the former that
the latter are pursued also. It makes no difference whether
the ends of the actions are the activities themselves or something apart from them, as in the case of the sciences we have
mentioned.

If, then, our activities have some end which we want for
its own sake, and for the sake of which we want all the other
ends – if we do not choose everything for the sake of something else (for this will involve an infinite progression, so
that our aim will be pointless and ineffectual) – it is clear
that this must be the Good, that is the supreme good. Does

1. *proairesis* seems to be used here quite generally, but see Glossary.
2. i.e. household or property management.
3. For *dunamis* see Glossary.

it not follow, then, that a knowledge of the Good is of great importance to us for the conduct of our lives? Are we not more likely to achieve our aim if we have a target? If this is so, we must try to describe at least in outline what the Good really is, and by which of the sciences or faculties[1] it is studied.

The science that studies the supreme Good for man is politics

ii.   Presumably this would be the most authoritative and directive science. Clearly this description fits the science of politics; for it is political science that prescribes what subjects are to be *taught in states, and which of these the different sections of the community are to learn, and up to what point.[2] We see also that under this science come those faculties which are most highly esteemed; e.g. the arts of war, of property management, and of public speaking. But if politics makes use of the other sciences, and also lays down what we should do and from what we should refrain, its end must include theirs; and this end must be the good for man. For even if the good of the community coincides with that of the individual, it is clearly a greater and more perfect thing to achieve and preserve that of a community; for while it is desirable to secure what is good in the case of an individual, to do so in the case of a people or a state is something finer and more sublime.

Such, then, is the aim of our investigation; and it is a kind of political science.[3]

Politics is not an exact science

iii.   Our account of this science will be adequate if it achieves such clarity as the subject-matter allows; for the

1. Here 'faculty' (*dunamis*) means 'art' or 'practical science'.
2. Or perhaps 'up to what age'.
3. A. seems to regard ethics not as a species of politics but as a sort of introduction to it.

same degree of precision is not to be expected in all discussions, any more than in all the products of handicraft. Instances of morally fine and just conduct – which is what politics investigates – involve so much difference and variety that they are widely believed to be such only by convention and not by nature. Instances of goods involve a similar kind of variety, for the reason that they often have hurtful consequences. People have been destroyed before now by their money, and others by their courage. Therefore in discussing subjects, and arguing from evidence, conditioned in this way, we must be satisfied with a broad outline of the truth; that is, in arguing about what is for the most part so from premises which are for the most part true we must be content to draw conclusions that are similarly qualified. The same procedure, then, should be observed in receiving our several types of statement; for it is a mark of the trained mind never to expect more precision in the treatment of any subject than the nature of that subject permits; for demanding logical demonstrations from a teacher of rhetoric is clearly about as reasonable as accepting mere plausibility from a mathematician.

The student should have some general knowledge and experience of life

Since in every case a man judges rightly what he understands, and of this only is a good critic, *it follows that while in a special field the good critic is a specialist, the good critic in general is the man with a general education. That is why a young man is not a fit person to attend lectures on political science, because he is not versed in the practical business of life from which politics draws its premises and subject-matter. Besides, he tends to follow his feelings, with the result that he will make no headway and derive no benefit from his course, since the object of it is not knowledge but action. It makes no difference whether he is young in age or youthful in character; the defect is due not to

lack of years but to living, and pursuing one's various aims,
under sway of the feelings; for to people like this knowledge
becomes as unprofitable as it is for the incontinent.[1] On the
other hand for those who regulate their impulses and act in
accordance with principle[2] a knowledge of these subjects
will be of great advantage.

So much by way of introductory remarks about the
student, the proper attitude towards instruction, and the
proposed course.

The end is no doubt happiness, but views of happiness differ

iv.   To resume. Since all knowledge and every pursuit aims
at some good,[3] what do we take to be the end of political
science – what is the highest of all practical goods? Well, so
far as the name goes there is pretty general agreement. 'It
is happiness', say both ordinary and cultured people; and
they identify happiness with living well or doing well[4]. But
when it comes to saying in what happiness consists, opinions
differ, and the account given by the generality of mankind
is not at all like that of the wise. The former take it to be
something obvious and familiar, like pleasure or money or
eminence, and there are various other views; and often the
same person actually changes his opinion: when he falls ill
he says that it is health, and when he is hard up that it is
money. Conscious of their own ignorance, most people are
impressed by anyone who pontificates and says something
that is over their heads. Some,[5] however, have held the
view that over and above these particular goods there is
another which is good in itself and the cause of whatever
goodness there is in all these others. It would no doubt be

1. Those who know what is right but fail to do it; cf. 1145b8ff.
2. The difficult word *logos*; see Glossary.
3. Cf. 1094a1ff.
4. The Greek phrases are ambiguous, connoting both prosperity and
right conduct.
5. Plato and his followers in the Academy.

rather futile to examine all these opinions; enough if we consider those which are most prevalent or seem to have something to be said for them.[1]

Learners must start from beliefs that are accepted or at least familiar

We must not overlook the difference that it makes whether we argue *from* or *to* first principles. Plato too used very properly to raise this question, inquiring whether the procedure was from or to first principles – just as *on a race-track they run either from the judges' stand to the far end, or in the reverse direction.[2] We must start from what is known. But things are known in two senses: known to us and known absolutely. Presumably *we* must start from what is known to us. So if anyone wants to make a serious study of ethics,[3] or of political science generally, he must have been well trained in his habits. For the starting-point is the *fact*; and if this is sufficiently clear there will be no need to ascertain the reason why. Such a person can easily grasp the first principles[4] if he is not in possession of them already; but one who has neither of these qualifications had better take to heart what Hesiod says:[5]

> That man is best who sees the truth himself;
> Good too is he who listens to wise counsel.
> But who is neither wise himself nor willing
> To ponder wisdom is not worth a straw.

1. For the phrase *logon echein* see note on 1102b32.
2. According as the race is one length of the stadium or two ('there and back').
3. 'Fine and just things'.
4. Moral values.
5. *Works and Days* 291–4.

*The three types of life. Neither pleasure nor public honour
seems to be an adequate end; the contemplative life will be
considered later*

v.   But let us resume from the point at which we digressed.
To judge by their lives, the masses and the most vulgar
seem – not unreasonably – to believe that the Good or
happiness is pleasure. Accordingly they ask for nothing
better than the life of enjoyment. (Broadly speaking, there
are three main types of life: the one just mentioned, the
political, and thirdly the contemplative.[1]) The utter
servility of the masses comes out in their preference for a
bovine existence; still, their view obtains consideration
from the fact that many of those who are in positions of
power share the tastes of Sardanapalus.[2] Cultured people,
however, and men of affairs identify the Good with honour,
because this is (broadly speaking) the goal of political life.
Yet it appears to be too superficial to be the required answer.
Honour is felt to depend more on those who confer than on
him who receives it; and we feel instinctively that the Good
is something proper to its possessor and not easily taken
from him. Again, people seem to seek honour in order to
convince themselves of their own goodness; at any rate it is
by intelligent men, and in a community where they are
known, and for their goodness, that they seek to be honoured; so evidently in their view goodness is superior to
honour. One might even be inclined to suppose that goodness rather than honour is the end pursued in public life.
But even this appears to be somewhat deficient as an end,
because the possession of goodness is thought to be compatible
even with being asleep, or with leading a life of inactivity,
and also *with incurring the most atrocious suffering and
misfortune; and nobody would call such a life happy – unless
he was defending a paradox.[3] So much for these views:

1. Cf. Plato, *Republic* 581c; the division is attributed to Pythagoras.

2. An Assyrian king of legendary sensuality.

3. A *thesis*, i.e. a paradoxical generalization by a leading philosopher;
cf. *Topics* 104b19ff., where examples are quoted.

they have been fully treated in current discussions.[1] The
third type of life is the contemplative, and this we shall
examine later.[2]

As for the life of the business man, it does not give him
much freedom of action. Besides, wealth is obviously not
the good that we are seeking, because it serves only as a
means; i.e. for getting something else. Hence the earlier
suggestions might be supposed to be more likely ends,
because they are appreciated on their own account; but
evidently they too are inadequate, and many attacks on
them have been published.[3]

There cannot be a universal good such as Plato held to be the culmination of his Theory of Forms

vi. Perhaps we had better examine the universal,[4] and
consider critically what is meant by it; although such a
course is awkward, because the Forms were introduced by
friends of ours. Yet surely it would be thought better, or
rather necessary (above all for philosophers) to refute, in
defence of the truth, even views to which one is attached;
since although both are dear, it is right to give preference to
the truth.

Those who introduced this theory did not posit Ideas of
classes in which they recognized degrees of priority (which
also accounts for their not attempting to construct a Form
in the case of numbers).[5] But things are called good both

---

1. Apparently at a popular level.   2. In Book X.
3. Following the reading of the best MSS with Bernays and Gauthier.
4. A.'s Greek does not at once make it clear that he means the concept of a universal *good*. See Appendix C.
5. The classes in question appear to be developing series, i.e. groups
whose members follow a serial order, each after the first being in some
sense a development of the one before it; and therefore depending on it
and implying it, but not coordinate with it. The natural numbers constitute such a series. A. means that the Platonists did not set up a Form
of Number, although they recognized Forms of separate numbers –
Unity, Twoness, Threeness, etc.

in the category of substance and in that of quality and in that of relation; and what exists in its own right, viz. substance, is by nature prior to what is relative (for this is a sort of offshoot or attribute of that which exists); so that there cannot be any common Idea in these cases.[1]

Again, things are called good in as many senses as they are said to exist; for they are so called in the category of Substance (e.g. God or mind) and in Quality (the virtues) and in Quantity (what is moderate) and in Relation (what is useful) and in Time (opportunity) and in Place (habitat) and so on. Clearly, then, there cannot be a single universal common to all cases, because it would be predicated not in all the categories but in one only.

Again, since of the things that come under one Idea there is one single science, there would be some one science of all good things; but in fact there are more than one even of those that fall under one category: e.g. of opportunity, because in war it is the concern of military but in disease the concern of medical science; and of moderation, which in diet is the concern of medical science but in exercise the concern of physical training.[2]

One might raise the question: What on earth do they mean by speaking of a thing-itself?[3] – assuming that the definition of man is *one and the same both in man and in man-himself; for *qua* man they will not differ at all, and if they do not, neither will what is good and the good-itself differ *qua* good. Nor will the Good be any more good by being eternal, if a long-lasting white thing is no whiter than an ephemeral one. On this point the Pythagoreans (followed apparently by Speusippus) seem to have a more plausible doctrine, for they place unity in their column of

1. For the doctrine of the Categories see Appendix D.
2. Opportunity: good or right time; moderation: good or right amount.
3. This use of the pronoun *auto*, 'self', was introduced by Plato to designate the form or essential nature of anything (but he used it as a separate word, not as a prefix).

goods.[1] But we must leave the discussion of this to another occasion.[2]

To the arguments that we have been using the objection presents itself that their[3] statements do not apply to *every* good: that only those goods that are pursued or esteemed in their own right are called good in virtue of one Form; those that are merely in some sense productive or conservative of these, or preventative of their contraries, are called good because of them and in a different sense. Clearly, then, things can be called good in two senses: some as good in their own right, and others as means to secure these. Let us, then, separate the things that are good in themselves from those that are merely useful, and consider whether they are called good in virtue of one Idea. What sort of things can one posit as good in themselves? Everything that is pursued even when considered in isolation – intelligence, for example, and sight, and some pleasures and honours? for these are things which, even if we do pursue them on account of something else, nevertheless might be classed as good in themselves. Or nothing else at all except the Idea? – then the class will be purposeless. If on the other hand the things that we have mentioned are also among those good in themselves, the definition of good will have to be recognizably the same in them all, just as that of white is in snow and chalk.[4] But when it comes to honour and intelligence and pleasure, their definitions are different and distinct in respect of goodness. Therefore good is not a common characteristic corresponding to one Idea.

But in what sense, then, are these things called good?

1. Instead of asserting that there is a universal good, i.e. that goodness is one, they said that unity is a good – no doubt on the ground that it is determinate, which plurality is not (cf. *Metaphysics* 986a22ff.); see Appendix A.

2. Cf. *Met.* 1028b21ff., 1072b30ff., 1091a29–b3, b13–1092a17; but he may be thinking of his (now lost) work *On the Pythagoreans*.

3. The Platonists'.

4. The Greek word means 'white lead', which is not a common example of whiteness in English.

71

because they do not seem to be accidental homonyms.[1] Is it that all goods derive from or contribute to one good? Or is it rather that they are good by analogy: as sight is good in the body, so is intuition in the mind, and so on? But perhaps this subject should be dismissed here, since a detailed examination of it would be more appropriate for another branch of philosophy.[2] Similarly too with the Idea of the Good; for even if the goodness that is predicated in common is some one thing or has a separate existence of its own, clearly it cannot be realized in action or acquired by man. Yet it is precisely that sort of good that we are looking for now. It may perhaps be thought that we had better gain knowledge of the Good *as a means of attaining to those goods that *can* be acquired and realized in practice; because if we have it as a pattern we shall gain a better knowledge of the things that are good *for us*, and so knowing, obtain them. The argument has a certain plausibility, but it seems to clash with the procedure of the ⟨practical⟩ sciences; for all these, though aiming at some good and seeking to supply its deficiency, neglect knowledge of it.[3] Yet that all craftsmen should ignore such a potent aid and not even try to secure it is not reasonable. And there is another problem. What advantage in his art will a weaver or a joiner get from knowledge of this good-itself? Or how will one who has had a vision of the Idea itself become thereby a better doctor or general? As a matter of fact it does not appear that the doctor even studies health in this way; his concern is the health of a human being, or perhaps rather of a particular patient, because what he treats is the individual. So much for our discussion of this topic.

1. Things that have nothing in common except their name.
2. i.e. metaphysics. No such examination has reached us.
3. i.e. of the ultimate good.

What is the Good for man? It must be the ultimate end or
object of human life: something that is in itself completely
satisfying. Happiness fits this description

vii.   Let us now turn back again to the good which is the
object of our search, and ask what it can possibly be; because it appears to vary with the action or art. It is one thing
in medicine and another in strategy, and similarly in all
the other sciences. What, then, is the good of each particular one? Surely it is that for the sake of which everything
else is done. In medicine this is health; in strategy, victory;
in architecture, a building – different things in different
arts, but in every action and pursuit it is the *end*, since it is
for the sake of this that everything else is done. Consequently
if there is any one thing that is the end of all actions, this
will be the practical good – or goods, if there are more than
one. Thus while changing its ground the argument has
reached the same conclusion as before.[1]

We must try, however, to make our meaning still clearer.
Since there are evidently more ends than one, and of these
we choose some (e.g. wealth or musical instruments or tools
generally) as means to something else, it is clear that not
all of them are final ends, whereas the supreme good is
obviously something final. So if there is only one final end,
this will be the good of which we are in search; and if
there are more than one, it will be the most final of these.
Now we call an object pursued for its own sake more final
than one pursued because of something else, and one which
is never choosable because of another more final than those
which are choosable because of it as well as for their own
sakes; and that which is always choosable for its own sake
and never because of something else we call final without
any qualification.

Well, happiness more than anything else is thought to be
just such an end, *because we always choose it for itself,
and never for any other reason. It is different with honour,

1. In the first two chapters.

73

pleasure, intelligence and good qualities[1] generally. We do choose them partly for themselves (because we should choose each one of them irrespectively of any consequences); but we choose them also for the sake of our happiness, in the belief that they will be instrumental in promoting it. On the other hand nobody chooses happiness for *their* sake, or in general for any other reason.

The same conclusion seems to follow from another consideration. It is a generally accepted view that the perfect good is self-sufficient. By self-sufficient we mean not what is sufficient for oneself alone living a solitary life,[2] but something that includes parents, wife and children, friends and fellow-citizens in general; for man is by nature a social being. (We must set some limit to these, for if we extend the application to grandparents and grandchildren and friends of friends it will proceed to infinity; but we must consider this point later.[3]) A self-sufficient thing, then, we take to be one which by itself makes life desirable[4] and in no way deficient; and we believe that happiness is such a thing. What is more, we regard it as the most desirable of all things, not reckoned as one item among many; if it were so reckoned, happiness would obviously be more desirable by the addition of even the least good, because the addition makes the sum of goods greater, and the greater of two goods is always more desirable. Happiness, then, is found to be something perfect and self-sufficient, being the end to which our actions are directed.

1. Or 'virtues'.

2. The Greek word (*autarkēs*) normally carries the sense of independence.

3. In chs. ix and x, and in Book IX. ch. x.

4. Here and in the following lines the meaning is really 'choosable', *hairetos*.

But what is happiness? If we consider what the
function of man is, we find that happiness is a
virtuous activity of the soul

But presumably to say that happiness is the supreme good
seems a platitude, and some more distinctive account of it
is still required. This might perhaps be achieved by grasping
what is the function of man. If we take a flautist[1] or a
sculptor or any artist – or in general any class of men who
have a specific function or activity – his goodness and
proficiency is considered to lie in the performance of that
function; and the same will be true of man, assuming that
man has a function. But is it likely that whereas joiners and
shoemakers have certain functions or activities, man as
such has none, but has been left by nature a functionless
being? Just as we can see that eye and hand and foot and
every one of our members has some function, should we not
assume that in like manner a human being has a function
over and above these particular functions? What, then, can
this possibly be? Clearly life is a thing shared also by plants,
and we are looking for man's *proper* function; so we must
*exclude from our definition the life that consists in nutri-
tion and growth. Next in order would be a sort of sentient
life; but this too we see is shared by horses and cattle and
animals of all kinds. There remains, then, a practical life of
the rational[2] part. (This has two aspects: one amenable to
reason, the other possessing it and initiating thought.)[3] As
this life also has two meanings, we must lay down that we
intend here life determined by activity, because this is
accepted as the stricter sense.[4] Now if the function of man is
an activity of the soul in accordance with, or implying, a

1. The Greek *aulos* was not a flute but a reed instrument.
2. See note on 1102b32.
3. This comment is irrelevant here; it anticipates the discussion in
1102b25ff.
4. The other being life as a *state*, implying no more than the possession
of reason. See Appendix E.

rational principle; and if we hold that the function of an individual and of a good individual of the same kind – e.g. of a harpist and of a good harpist, and so on generally – is generically the same, the latter's distinctive excellence being attached to the name of the function (because the function of the harpist is to play the harp, but that of the good harpist is to play it well); and if we assume that the function of man is a kind of life, viz., an activity or series of actions of the soul, implying a rational principle; and if the function of a good man is to perform these well and rightly; and if every function is performed well when performed in accordance with its proper excellence: if all this is so, the conclusion is that the good for man is an activity of soul in accordance with virtue, or if there are more kinds of virtue than one, in accordance with the best and most perfect kind.

There is a further qualification: in a complete lifetime. One swallow does not make a summer; neither does one day. Similarly neither can one day, or a brief space of time, make a man blessed[1] and happy.

This sketch can be elaborated later, but great precision is not to be expected

This may stand as an outline account of the Good; for presumably we should first rough out a sketch and then fill in the details afterwards. When the outline has been satisfactorily drawn, it may be supposed that anybody can carry on the work and fill in the detail;[2] and that in such a case time is a good source of invention or cooperation. In fact this is how progress in the arts has been made; for anyone can fill in the gaps. But we must still remember the caution given above,[3] and not look for the same degree of

1. *makarios*: see Glossary.
2. The metaphor is taken from architecture or large-scale sculpture, in which the master supplies only the overall design.
3. 1094b19ff.

exactness in all our studies, but only for as much as the
subject-matter in each case allows, and so far as is appropriate to the investigation. For example, a carpenter's
interest in the right angle is different from a geometrician's:
the former is concerned with it only so far as it is useful for
his work, but the other wants to know what it is or what its
properties are, because his gaze is set on the truth. We
ought to follow this procedure in other studies as well, in
order to prevent the swamping of main by side issues.

We must not even demand *to know the explanation in
all cases alike; there are some in which it is quite enough if
the *fact* itself is exhibited, e.g. in the case of first principles;
the fact is primary and a starting-point.[1] Some starting-
points are grasped by induction, some by perception,[2]
some by a kind of habituation, others in other ways. We
must try to investigate each type in accordance with its
nature. We must also make a point of formulating them
correctly, because they have a great importance for the
understanding of what follows. By common consent the
beginning is more than half the whole task,[3] and throws a
flood of light on many of the aspects of the inquiry.

Our view of happiness is supported by popular beliefs

viii.   We must examine our principle not only as reached
logically, from a conclusion and premises, but also in the
light of what is commonly said about it; because if a statement is true all the data are in harmony with it, while if it
is false they soon reveal a discrepancy.

1. The same Greek word *archē* means 'beginning' or 'starting-point'
and 'first principle'. In every science a first principle is primary because
it is the cause or ground of all that follows from it, while being itself
indemonstrable because there is no higher principle to which it can be
referred.

2. *aisthēsis* usually means 'sensation', but it can, and probably does
here, convey the sense of direct perception or intuition, which perceives
the truth immediately.

3. The phrase is proverbial.

Now goods have been classified[1] under three heads, as (*a*) external, (*b*) of the soul, and (*c*) of the body. Of these we say that goods of the soul are good in the strictest and fullest sense, and we rank actions and activities of soul as goods of the soul; so that according to this view, which is of long standing and accepted by philosophers, our definition will be correct. We are right, too, in saying that the end consists in certain actions or activities, because this puts it among goods of the soul and not among external goods. Our definition is also supported by the belief that the happy man lives and fares well; because what we have described is virtually a kind of good life or prosperity.[2] Again, our definition seems to include all the required constituents of happiness; for some think that it is virtue, others prudence,[3] and others wisdom;[4] others that it is these, or one of these, with the addition of pleasure, or not in total separation from it; and others further include favourable external conditions. Some of these views are popular beliefs of long standing; others are those of a few distinguished men. It is reasonable to suppose that neither group is entirely mistaken, but is right in some respect, or even in most.

Now our definition is in harmony with those who say that happiness is virtue, or a particular virtue; because an activity in accordance with virtue implies virtue. But presumably it makes no little difference whether we think of the supreme good as consisting in the *possession* or in the *exercise* of virtue: in a state of mind or in an activity. For it is possible for the *state* *to be present in a person without effecting any good result (e.g. if he is asleep or quiescent in some other way), but not for the *activity*: he will necessarily act, and act well. Just as at the Olympic Games it is not the best-looking or the strongest men present that are crowned with wreaths, but the competitors (because it is from them that the winners come), so it is those who *act* that rightly win the honours and rewards in life.

1. By Plato: *Euthydemus* 279A–B, *Philebus* 48E, *Laws* 743E.
2. The Greek phrase can mean 'acting well' or 'faring well'.
3. *phronēsis*: see Glossary.   4. *sophia*: see Glossary.

Moreover, the life of such people is in itself pleasant. For pleasure is an experience of the soul,[1] and each individual finds pleasure in that of which he is said to be fond. For example, a horse gives pleasure to one who is fond of horses, and a spectacle to one who is fond of sight-seeing. In the same way just acts give pleasure to a lover of justice, and virtuous conduct generally to the lover of virtue. Now most people find that the things which give them pleasure conflict, because they are not pleasant by nature; but lovers of beauty find pleasure in things that are pleasant by nature, and virtuous actions are of this kind, so that they are pleasant not only to this type of person but also in themselves. So their life does not need to have pleasure attached to it as a sort of accessory, but contains its own pleasure in itself. Indeed, we may go further and assert that anyone who does not delight in fine actions is not even a good man; for nobody would say that a man is just unless he enjoys acting justly, nor liberal unless he enjoys liberal actions, and similarly in all the other cases. If this is so, virtuous actions must be pleasurable in themselves. What is more, they are both good and fine, and each in the highest degree, assuming that the good man is right in his judgement of them; and his judgement is as we have described.[2] So happiness is the best, the finest, the most pleasurable thing of all; and these qualities are not separated as the inscription at Delos[3] suggests:

> Justice is loveliest, and health is best,
> But sweetest to obtain is heart's desire.

All these attributes belong to the best activities; and it is these, or the one that is best of them, that we identify with happiness.

Nevertheless it seems clear that happiness needs the addition of external goods, as we have said;[4] for it is dif-

---

1. Of the conscious self.   2. In the preceding lines.
3. On the entrance to the temple of Leto. The lines (which are quoted at the beginning of the *Eudemian Ethics*) are also found, slightly altered, in Theognis 225f., and paraphrased in Sophocles (*Creusa*), fr. 326.
4. 1098b26.

ficult if not impossible to do fine deeds without any re-sources.[1] Many can only be done *by the help of friends, or wealth, or political influence. There are also certain advan-tages, such as good ancestry or good children, or personal beauty, the lack of which mars our felicity; for a man is scarcely happy if he is very ugly to look at, or of low birth, or solitary and childless; and presumably even less so if he has children or friends who are quite worthless, or if he had good ones who are now dead. So, as we said, happiness seems to require this sort of prosperity too; which is why some identify it with good fortune, although others identify it with virtue.

How is happiness acquired?

ix. From this springs another problem. Is happiness something that can be learnt, or acquired by habituation, or cultivated in some other way, or does it come to us by a sort of divine dispensation, or even by chance? Well, in the first place, if anything is a gift of the gods to men, it is reasonable that happiness should be such a gift, especially since of all human possessions it is the best. This point, however, would perhaps be considered more appropriately by another branch of study.[2] Yet even if happiness is not sent by a divine power, but is acquired by moral goodness and by some kind of study or training, it seems clearly to be one of our most divine possessions; for the crown and end of goodness is surely of all things the best: something divine and blissful. Also on this view[3] happiness will be something widely shared; for it can attach, through some form of study or application, to anyone who is not handicapped by some incapacity for goodness. And, assuming that it is better to win happiness by the means described than by

1. The Greek word carries a metaphor; see Appendix I.
2. i.e. what A. calls 'first philosophy': a combination of theology and metaphysics.
3. That it is acquired by human effort.

chance, it is reasonable that this should in fact be so, since it is natural for nature's effects to be the finest possible, and similarly for the effects of art and of any ⟨other⟩ cause,[1] especially those of the best kind.[2] That the most important and finest thing of all should be left to chance would be a gross disharmony.

The problem also receives some light from our definition, for in it happiness has been described[3] as a kind of virtuous activity of soul; whereas all the other goods either are necessary pre-conditions of happiness or naturally contribute to it and serve as its instruments. This will agree with what we said at the outset:[4] we suggested that the end of political science is the highest good; and the chief concern of this science is to endue the citizens with certain qualities, namely virtue and the readiness to do fine deeds. Naturally, therefore, we do not speak of an ox or a horse or any other animal as happy, because none of them *can take part in this sort of activity. For the same reason no child is happy either, because its age debars it as yet from such activities; if children are so described, it is by way of congratulation on their future promise. For, as we said above,[5] happiness demands not only complete goodness but a complete life. In the course of life we encounter many reverses and all kinds of vicissitudes, and in old age even the most prosperous of men may be involved in great misfortunes, as we are told about Priam in the Trojan poems.[6] Nobody calls happy a man who suffered fortunes like his and met a miserable end.

1. i.e. efficient cause.   2. Of cause, viz. mind or intelligence.
3. 1098a16.   4. 1094a27ff.   5. 1098a18ff.
6. i.e. the epics about the Trojan War; cf. *Iliad* xxii. 37–78, xxiv. 160ff., and for the account of Priam's death (derived from the lost *Iliu Persis*) Virgil, *Aeneid* ii. 506–58.

Is it only when his life is completed that a man can rightly be called happy?

x. Ought we, then, to go further and call no man happy so long as he is alive? Must we, in Solon's phrase, 'look to the end'?[1] And if we *are* bound to lay down this rule, is a man really happy after he is dead? Surely this is an utter paradox, especially for us who define happiness as a kind of activity. On the other hand if we deny that a dead man is happy – if Solon's words mean something else, namely that only when a man is dead can one safely congratulate him on being immune from evil and misfortune – even this admits of some dispute; for it is popularly believed that some good and evil – such as honours and dishonours, and successes and disasters of his children and descendants generally – can happen to a dead man, inasmuch as they can happen to a live one without his being aware of them. But this too entails a difficulty. Suppose that a man has lived an exceptionally happy life right into old age, and has ended it in like manner: many changes of fortune may befall his descendants, some of whom may be good and enjoy such a life as they deserve, and others just the opposite; and they may of course be separated from their ancestors by any number of generations. It would surely be absurd, then, if the dead man changed with their changes of fortune, and became at one time happy and then in turn miserable; but it would also be absurd for the experiences of the descendants to have no effect, even for a limited period, upon their ancestors.[2]

But let us return to the difficulty that we raised earlier;[3] because perhaps that will throw light on our present problem. If we must 'look to the end' and only then call a man happy, not because he *is* but because he *was* so before,

1. Herodotus i. 32.
2. These are only popular beliefs; for A.'s own conclusion see ch. xi below.
3. 1100a10ff.

surely it will be absurd if when a man *is* happy the fact
cannot be truly stated of him – for the reason that we are
*unwilling to call the living happy because of the changes of
fortune, and because we have assumed that happiness is a
permanent thing and not at all liable to change, whereas
fortune's wheel often turns upside down for the same people!
For clearly, supposing that we follow the guidance of his
fortunes, we shall often call the same man by turns happy
and miserable, representing the happy man as a sort of
'chameleon; a castle set on sand'.[1] Probably it is not right
at all to follow the changes of a man's fortunes, because
success and failure in life do not depend on these; they are
merely complements, as we said,[2] of human life. It is virtuous activities that determine our happiness, and the opposite
kind that produce the opposite effect.

Our examination of this problem bears out our definition,
because no other human operation has the same permanence as virtuous activities (they are considered to be more
persistent even than the several kinds of scientific knowledge); and of these themselves the most highly esteemed
are more persistent ⟨than the rest⟩, because it is in them
that the truly happy most fully and continuously spend their
lives: this seems to be the reason why we do not forget
them.[3] We conclude, then, that the happy man will have
the required quality,[4] and in fact will be happy throughout
his life; because he will spend all his time, or the most time
of any man, in virtuous conduct and contemplation. And
he will bear his fortunes in the finest spirit and with perfect sureness of touch, as being 'good in very truth' and
'foursquare without reproach'.[5]

Yet the accidents of fortune are many, and they vary in
importance. Little pieces of good luck (and likewise of the
opposite kind) clearly do not disturb the tenor of our life.
On the other hand many great strokes of fortune, if favourable, will make life more felicitous (since they tend naturally

1. A quotation from an unknown poet.   2. 1099a31ff.
3. Cf. 1140b28.   4. i.e. permanence in happiness.
5. Simonides, fr. 3, quoted and discussed by Plato, *Protagoras* 339B.

of themselves to add to its attractions, and also they can be used in a fine and responsible way); but if they fall out adversely they restrict and spoil our felicity, both by inflicting pain and by putting a check on many of our activities. Nevertheless even here, when a man bears patiently a number of heavy disasters, not because he does not feel them but because he has a high and generous nature, his nobility shines through. And if, as we said,[1] the quality of a life is determined by its activities, no man who is truly happy can become miserable; because he will never do things that are hateful and mean. For we believe that the truly *good and wise man bears all his fortunes with dignity, and always takes the most honourable course that circumstances permit; just as a good general uses his available forces in the most militarily effective way, and a good shoemaker makes the neatest shoe out of the leather supplied to him, and the same with all the other kinds of craftsmen. And if this is so, the happy man can never become miserable – although he cannot be entirely happy if he falls in with fortunes like those of Priam.[2] Nor indeed can he be variable and inconstant; for he will not be dislodged from his happiness easily nor by ordinary misfortunes – only by a succession of heavy blows, and from these he will not quickly recover his happiness; if he does so at all, it will only be at the end of a long interval in which he has attained great and splendid achievements.

We are now in a position to define the happy man as 'one who is active in accordance with complete virtue, and who is adequately furnished with external goods, and that not for some unspecified period but throughout a complete life'. And probably we should add 'destined both to live in this way and to die accordingly'; because the future is obscure to us, and happiness we maintain to be an *end* in every way utterly final and complete.[3] If this is so, then we shall describe those of the living who possess and will

1. b9f. above.
2. Cf. 1100a8ff.
3. Both meanings are conveyed by the word *teleios*.

84

continue to possess the stated qualifications as supremely happy – but with a human happiness.[1]

So much for our systematic treatment of this subject.

Are the dead affected by the fortunes of those who survive them?

xi. The notion that the dead are not affected at all by the fortunes of their descendants or any of those whom they love seems unduly heartless and contrary to accepted beliefs. But experiences are so many and exhibit such a variety of differences, some touching us more closely than others, that it would obviously be a long or rather an endless task to distinguish between them in detail; a general account in broad outline may perhaps be sufficient.

Since, then, a man's own misfortunes sometimes have a powerful influence upon his life, and sometimes seem comparatively trivial; and the same applies also to the misfortunes of all his friends alike; although it makes a difference whether a particular misfortune befalls people while they are alive or after they are dead – a far greater difference than it makes in a tragedy whether the crimes and atrocities are committed beforehand or carried out during the action; then we must take into our reckoning this difference too; or rather, perhaps, the fact that it is questionable whether the departed have any *participation in good or its opposite. For the probable inference from what we have been saying is that if any effect of good or evil reaches them at all, it must be faint and slight, either in itself or to them – or if not that, at any rate not of such force and quality as to make the unhappy happy or to rob the happy of their felicity. So it appears that the dead are affected to some extent by the good fortunes of those whom they love, and similarly by their misfortunes; but that the effects are not of such a kind or so great as to make the happy unhappy, or to produce any other such result.

1. Subject to human imperfection.

Is happiness to be praised as a means or valued as an end?

xii.   Now that we have decided these questions let us consider whether happiness is something that is *praised* or something that is *valued* (for it is clearly not a mere potentiality).[1] Well, everything that we praise seems to be praised because it has a certain quality and stands in a certain relation to something else; for we praise the just man and the brave man, and in general the good man and virtue, because of the actions and effects that they produce; and we praise the strong and swift-footed and every other such type of man because he has a certain natural quality and stands in a certain relation to something good and worthwhile. This is evident also from the consideration of praise addressed to the gods: it is obviously absurd that the gods should be referred to our standards, yet this follows from the fact that (as we said) praise involves reference to something else. But if praise belongs to what is relative, clearly the best things call not for praise but for something greater and better, as in fact we find; because we call the gods 'happy' or 'blessed',[2] a term which we apply also to such men as most closely resemble the gods. Similarly too with *things* that are good. No one praises happiness as he praises justice; he calls it 'blessed', as being something better and more divine. Eudoxus[3] too is held to have made a good point in supporting the claim of pleasure to supremacy; he thought that the fact of its not being praised, although it is a good, is evidence that it is superior to the goods that are praised, as God and the Good are also, because they are the standards to which all other goods are referred. For praise is

---

1. i.e. whether it is a relative or an absolute good; it is not something like wealth that can serve a good or a bad purpose.

2. Instead of praising them. To theists such as Christians and Jews the idea of praising God is so natural that the ancient Greeks' avoidance of it seems strange.

3. See Index of Names, and cf. 1172b9ff.

concerned with goodness,[1] because this enables men to do
fine deeds; while encomia are directed towards achievements, physical and non-physical alike. However, the
detailed examination of this subject is presumably more
appropriate for those who have made a special study of
encomia. For us it is clear, from what *has been said already,
that happiness is one of those things that are precious and
perfect. This view seems to be confirmed by the fact that it
is a first principle, since everything else that any of us do, we
do for its sake; and we hold that the first principle and
cause of what is good is precious and divine.[2]

To understand what moral goodness is we must study the soul of man

xiii.   Since happiness is an activity of the soul in accordance
with perfect virtue, we must examine the nature of virtue;
for perhaps in this way we shall be better able to form a view
about happiness too. Besides, the true statesman is thought
of as a man who has taken special pains to study this subject; for he wants to make his fellow-citizens good and law-
abiding people (we have an example of this in the lawgivers of Crete and Sparta,[3] and any others who have shown
similar qualities). And if this investigation is a part of
political science, clearly our inquiry will be in keeping with
the plan that we adopted at the outset.

The goodness that we have to consider is human goodness, obviously; for it was the good *for man* or happiness *for
man* that we set out to discover. But by human goodness is
meant goodness not of the body but of the soul, and happiness

1. In the widest sense. Praise is for A. an appreciation of quality in
the agent, and an encouragement to maintain and improve that quality;
an encomium is a tribute to services already rendered. See *Rhetoric*
1367b21ff.

2. This is the logical end of Book I; ch. xiii is introductory to the
discussion in Book II.

3. Cf. *Politics* II. vi and vii.

also we define as an activity of the soul. This being so, it is evident that the statesman ought to have some acquaintance with psychology, just as a doctor who intends to treat the eye must have a knowledge of the body as a whole. Indeed the statesman's need is greater than the doctor's, inasmuch as politics is a better and more honourable science than medicine.[1] But the best kind of doctors take a good deal of trouble to acquire a knowledge of the body; so the statesman too must study the soul, but with a view to politics, and only so far as is sufficient for the questions that we are investigating; for to explore its nature in greater detail would presumably be too laborious for our present purpose.

The several faculties of the soul distinguished

Some aspects of psychology are adequately treated in discourses elsewhere,[2] and we should make use of the results: e.g. that the soul is part rational and part irrational[3] (whether these are separate like the parts of the body or anything else that is physically divisible, or whether like the convex and concave aspects of the circumference of a circle they are distinguishable as two only in definition and thought, and are by nature inseparable, makes no difference for our present purpose). Of the irrational soul one part seems to be common, viz. the vegetative: I mean the cause of nutrition and growth; because one can assume such a faculty of soul in everything that receives *nourishment, even in embryos; and this same faculty too in the fully developed creature, because this is more reasonable than to suppose that the latter has a different one. Thus the excellence of this faculty is evidently common and not confined to man; because this part or faculty seems to be most active in sleep, when the good and the bad are least easy to distinguish

1. Because politics is the supreme practical science (1094a26ff.).
2. Whether the reference is to A.'s own popular courses or to views expressed by others (e.g. at the Academy) is uncertain; cf. 1140a3.
3. Cf. 1098a3ff., and see note on b33 below.

(hence the saying 'for half their lives the happy are no different from the wretched'). This is a natural consequence, because sleep is a suspension of that function[1] of the soul by which it is distinguished as good and bad – except that to a certain limited extent some of the stimuli[2] reach the soul; this is what makes the dreams of decent people better than those of the ordinary man. But enough of this subject; we may dismiss the nutritive soul, because of its very nature it has no part in human goodness.

But there seems to be another element[3] of the soul which, while irrational, is in a sense receptive of reason. Take the types of man which we call continent and incontinent. They have a principle – a rational element in their souls – which we commend, because it urges them in the right direction and encourages them to take the best course; but there is also observable in them another element, by nature irrational, which struggles and strains against the rational. Just as in the case of the body paralysed limbs, when the subject chooses to move them to the right, swing away in the contrary direction to the left, so exactly the same happens in the case of the soul; for the impulses of the incontinent take them in the contrary direction. 'But in bodies we see what swings away, whereas in the case of the soul we do not.' Probably we should believe nevertheless that the soul too contains an irrational element which opposes and runs counter to reason – in what sense it is a separate element does not matter at all. But this too, as we said,[4] seems to be receptive of reason; at any rate in the continent man it is obedient to reason, and is presumably still more amenable in the temperate and in the brave man, because in them it is in complete harmony with the rational principle.

1. Sensation or consciousness.

2. From sensation or imagination, i.e. the impression left in the mind by an earlier sensation.

3. The word is *phusis* (see Glossary), but here it seems to be virtually a synonym for *dunamis*, 'faculty'.

4. 1102b13f. above.

Evidently, then, the irrational part of the soul also consists of two parts. The vegetative has no association at all with reason, but the desiderative and generally appetitive part does in a way participate in reason, in the sense that it is submissive and obedient to it (this is the sense of *logon echein* in which we speak of 'taking account' of one's father or friends, not that in which we speak of 'having an account' of mathematical propositions).[1] That the irrational part is in some way persuaded by reason is indicated by our use of admonition, and of reproof and encouragement *of all kinds. If, however, one should speak of the appetitive part of the soul as rational too, it will be the rational part that is divided in two: one rational in the proper sense of the word and in itself, the other in the sense that a child pays attention to its father.

Virtue, too, is divided into classes in accordance with this differentiation of the soul. Some virtues are called intellectual and others moral; Wisdom and Understanding and Prudence are intellectual, Liberality and Temperance are moral virtues. When we are speaking of a man's *character*[2] we do not describe him as wise or understanding, but as patient or temperate. We do, however, praise a wise man on the ground of his state of mind; and those states that are praiseworthy we call virtues.

1. The phrase *logon echein* 'to have a *logos*' can mean 'to have an explanation' or 'reason', or (more mildly) 'to have something to be said for it'; also 'to have a ratio', 'to have an account' (to give of oneself) or 'to take account' (of somebody or something). See Glossary.

2. The word is *ēthos* (now widely used in English); from its adjective *ēthikos* comes our word ethics.

II

MORAL GOODNESS

*Moral virtues, like crafts, are acquired by practice
and habituation*

i. Virtue, then, is of two kinds, intellectual and moral.
Intellectual virtue owes both its inception and its growth
chiefly to instruction, and for this very reason needs time
and experience. Moral goodness, on the other hand, is the
result of habit, from which it has actually got its name, being
a slight modification of the word *ethos*.[1] This fact makes it
obvious that none of the moral virtues is engendered in us
by nature, since nothing that is what it is by nature can be
made to behave differently by habituation. For instance, a
stone, which has a natural tendency downwards, cannot
be habituated to rise, however often you try to train it by
throwing it into the air; nor can you train fire to burn
downwards; nor can anything else that has any other
natural tendency be trained to depart from it. The moral
virtues, then, are engendered in us neither *by* nor *contrary to*
nature; we are constituted by nature to receive them, but
their full development in us is due to habit.

Again, of all those faculties with which nature endows us
we first acquire the potentialities, and only later effect their
actualization. (This is evident in the case of the senses. It
was not from repeated acts of seeing or hearing that we
acquired the senses but the other way round: we had these
senses before we used them; we did not acquire them as the
result of using them.) But the virtues we do acquire by first
exercising them, just as happens in the arts. Anything that
we have to learn to do we learn by the actual doing of it:
people become builders by building and instrumentalists
by playing instruments. Similarly we become *just by

1. The words *ēthos* 'character' and *ethos* 'custom' show different
grades of the same root *eth-*.

performing just acts, temperate[1] by performing temperate ones, brave by performing brave ones. This view is supported by what happens in city-states.[2] Legislators make their citizens good by habituation; this is the intention of every legislator, and those who do not carry it out fail of their object. This is what makes the difference between a good constitution and a bad one.

Again, the causes or means that bring about any form of excellence are the same as those that destroy it, and similarly with art; for it is as a result of playing the harp that people become good and bad harpists. The same principle applies to builders and all other craftsmen. Men will become good builders as a result of building well, and bad ones as a result of building badly. Otherwise there would be no need of anyone to teach them: they would all be *born* either good or bad. Now this holds good also of the virtues. It is the way that we behave in our dealings with other people that makes us just or unjust, and the way that we behave in the face of danger, accustoming ourselves to be timid or confident, that makes us brave or cowardly. Similarly with situations involving desires and angry feelings: some people become temperate and patient from one kind of conduct in such situations, others licentious and choleric from another. In a word, then, like activities produce like dispositions. Hence we must give our activities a certain quality, because it is their characteristics that determine the resulting dispositions. So it is a matter of no little importance what sort of habits we form from the earliest age – it makes a vast difference, or rather all the difference in the world.

1. Or 'self-controlled'; see Glossary s.v. *sōphrosunē*.
2. The word is *polis*; see Glossary.

In a practical science, so much depends on particular
circumstances that only general rules can be given

ii. Since the branch of philosophy on which we are at
present engaged is not, like the others, theoretical in its
aim – because we are studying not to know what goodness
is, but how to become good men, since otherwise it would
be useless[1] – we must apply our minds to the problem of how
our actions should be performed, because, as we have just
said,[2] it is these that actually determine our dispositions.

Now that we should act according to the right principle
is common ground and may be assumed as a basis for discussion (the point will be discussed later, both what 'the
right principle' is, and how it is related to the other virtues).[3]
But we must first agree *that any account of conduct must
be stated in outline and not in precise detail, just as we said
at the beginning[4] that accounts are to be required only in
such a form as befits their subject-matter. Now questions of
conduct and expedience have as little fixity about them as
questions of what is healthful;[5] and if this is true of the
general rule, it is still more true that its application to
particular problems admits of no precision. For they do
not fall under any art or professional tradition, but the
agents are compelled at every step to think out for themselves what the circumstances demand, just as happens in
the arts of medicine and navigation. However, although
our present account is of this kind, we must try to support
it.[6]

1. Being a practical science.   2. b22f.   3. 1144b26ff.
4. 1094b11ff.   5. Both vary with circumstances.
6. By giving it as much precision as possible.

*A cardinal rule: right conduct is incompatible with
excess or deficiency in feelings and actions*

First, then, we must consider this fact: that it is in the
nature of moral qualities that they are destroyed by
deficiency and excess, just as we can see (since we have to
use the evidence of visible facts to throw light on those that
are invisible) in the case of ⟨bodily⟩ health and strength.
For both excessive and insufficient exercise destroy one's
strength, and both eating and drinking too much or too
little destroy health, whereas the right quantity produces,
increases and preserves it. So it is the same with temperance, courage and the other virtues. The man who shuns
and fears everything and stands up to nothing becomes a
coward; the man who is afraid of nothing at all, but marches
up to every danger, becomes foolhardy. Similarly the man
who indulges in every pleasure and refrains from none
becomes licentious;[1] but if a man behaves like a boor[2] and
turns his back on every pleasure, he is a case of insensibility.
Thus temperance and courage are destroyed by excess and
deficiency and preserved by the mean.[3]

*Our virtues are exercised in the same kinds of action as
gave rise to them*

But besides the fact that the virtues are induced and
fostered as a result, and by the agency, of the same sort of
actions as cause their destruction, the activities that flow
from them will also consist in the same sort of actions. This
is so in all the other more observable instances, e.g. in that
of ⟨bodily⟩ strength. This results from taking plenty of
nourishment and undergoing severe training, and it is the
strong man that will be best able to carry out this pro-

1. *akolastos.*
2. *agroikos*, a person of undeveloped taste and appreciation.
3. i.e. by observance of the mean.

94

gramme. So with the virtues. It is by refraining from
pleasures that we become temperate, and it is when we
have become temperate that we are most able to abstain
from pleasures. Similarly *with courage; it is by habituating
ourselves to make light of alarming situations and to face
them that we become brave, and it is when we have become brave that we shall be most able to face an alarming
situation.

*The pleasure or pain that actions cause the agent may serve
as an index of moral progress, since good conduct consists
in a proper attitude towards pleasure and pain*

iii.   The pleasure or pain that accompanies people's acts
should be taken as a sign of their dispositions. A man who
abstains from bodily pleasures and enjoys the very fact of
so doing is temperate; if he finds it irksome he is licentious.
Again, the man who faces danger gladly, or at least without
distress, is brave; the one who feels distressed is a coward.
For it is with pleasures and pains that moral goodness is
concerned. Pleasure induces us to behave badly, and pain
to shrink from fine actions. Hence the importance (as
Plato says[1]) of having been trained in some way from
infancy to feel joy and grief at the right things: true education is precisely this. If the virtues are concerned with
actions and feelings, and every feeling and every action is
always accompanied by pleasure or pain, on this ground
too virtue will be concerned with pleasures and pains. The
fact that punishments are effected by their means[2] is further
evidence, because punishment is a kind of remedial treatment, and such treatment is naturally effected by contraries.[3] Again, as we said above,[4] every state of the soul attains
its natural development in relation to, and in the sphere of,

1. *Laws* 653A–C; cf. *Republic* 401E–402A.
2. By pains or deprivation of pleasures.
3. Chills by warmth, fevers by cooling, etc.
4. a28 ff.

those conditions by which it is naturally made better or worse. Now when people become bad it is because of pleasures and pains, through seeking (or shunning) the wrong ones, or at the wrong time, or in the wrong way, or in any other manner in which such offences are distinguished by principle. This is why some thinkers[1] actually define the virtues as forms of impassivity or tranquillity. But they are wrong in speaking absolutely instead of adding 'in the right (or wrong) manner and at the right time' and any other due qualifications.

We have decided, then, that this kind of virtue disposes us to act in the best way with regard to pleasures and pains, and contrariwise with the corresponding vice. But we may obtain further light on the same point from the following considerations.

There are three factors that make for choice, and three that make for avoidance: the fine, the advantageous, and the pleasant, and their contraries, the base, the harmful, and the painful. Now with regard to all these the good man tends to go right and the bad man to go wrong, especially about pleasure. This is common to all animals, and accompanies all objects of choice, *for clearly the fine and the advantageous are pleasant too. Consciousness of pleasure has grown up with all of us from our infancy, and therefore our life is so deeply imbued with this feeling that it is hard to remove all trace of it. Pleasure and pain are also the standards by which – to a greater or lesser extent – we regulate our actions. Since to feel pleasure and pain rightly or wrongly has no little effect upon conduct, it follows that our whole inquiry must be concerned with these sensations. Heraclitus says[2] that it is hard to fight against emotion, but harder still to fight against pleasure; and the harder course is

1. Probably Speusippus and his followers, but Democritus had held the view before (Diogenes Laertius ix. 45).

2. Fragment 85, quoted by Plutarch, *Coriolanus* 22: 'It is hard to fight against *thūmos*, for what it wants it buys at the price of life.' Here *thūmos* no doubt means 'heart' or 'desire', but when Aristotle wrote it would more naturally have meant 'emotion' or 'temper'.

always the concern of both art and virtue, because success
is better in the face of difficulty. Thus on this ground too
the whole concern of both morality and political science
must be with pleasures and pains, since the man who treats
them rightly will be good and the one who treats them
wrongly will be bad.

We may take this as a sufficient statement that virtue is
concerned with pains and pleasures; that the actions that
produce it also increase it, or if differently performed, destroy it; and that the actions that produce it also constitute
the sphere of its activity.

*Acts that are incidentally virtuous distinguished from those
that are done knowingly, of choice, and from a virtuous
disposition*

iv.   A difficulty, however, may be raised as to how we can
say that people must perform just actions if they are to become just, and temperate ones if they are to become temperate; because if they do what is just and temperate, they
are just and temperate already, in the same way that if they
use words or play music correctly they are already literate or
musical. But surely this is not true even of the arts. It is
possible to put a few words together correctly by accident, or
at the prompting of another person; so the agent will only
be literate if he does a literate act in a literate way, viz. in
virtue of his own literacy. Nor, again, is there an analogy
between the arts and the virtues. Works of art have their
merit in themselves; so it is enough for them to be turned
out with a certain quality of their own. But virtuous acts are
not done in a just or temperate way merely because *they* have
a certain quality, but only if the agent also acts in a certain
state, viz. (1) if he knows what he is doing, (2) if he chooses
it, and chooses it for its own sake, and (3) if he does it from
a fixed and permanent disposition. Now these – knowledge
*excepted – are not reckoned as necessary qualifications for
the arts as well. For the acquisition of virtues, on the other

97

hand, knowledge has little or no force; but the other requirements are not of little but of supreme importance, granted that it is from the repeated performance of just and temperate acts that we acquire virtues. Acts, to be sure, are called just and temperate when they are such as a just or temperate man would do; but what makes the agent just or temperate is not merely the fact that he does such things, but the fact that he does them in the way that just and temperate men do. It is therefore right to say that a man becomes just by the performance of just, and temperate by the performance of temperate, acts; nor is there the smallest likelihood of any man's becoming good by not doing them. This is not, however, the course that most people follow: they have recourse to their principle,[1] and imagine that they are being philosophical and that in this way they will become serious-minded – behaving rather like invalids who listen carefully to their doctor, but carry out none of his instructions. Just as the bodies of the latter will get no benefit from such treatment, so the souls of the former will get none from such philosophy.

In order to define virtue we must decide to what class or genus it belongs. It is not a feeling or a faculty, but a disposition

v.   We must now consider what virtue is. Since there are three kinds of modification that are found in the soul, viz. feelings, faculties and dispositions,[2] virtue must be one of these three. By feelings I mean desire, anger, fear, daring, envy, joy, friendliness, hatred, longing, jealousy, pity, and in general all conditions that are attended by pleasure or pain. By faculties I mean those susceptibilities in virtue of which we are said to be capable of the feelings in question, e.g. capable of anger or sorrow or pity. By dispositions I mean conditions in virtue of which we are well or ill disposed in respect of the feelings concerned. We have, for instance, a

1. Or 'theory'; see Glossary under *logos*.
2. See Glossary under *pathos, dunamis* and *hexis*.

bad disposition towards anger if our tendency is too strong or too weak, and a good one if our tendency is moderate. Similarly with the other feelings.

Now neither the virtues nor the vices are feelings, because we are not called good or bad on the ground of our feelings, but we are so called on the ground of our virtues and vices; nor are we either praised or blamed for our feelings (a man is not praised for being frightened or angry, nor is he blamed just for being *angry; it is for being angry in a particular way); but we *are* praised and blamed for our virtues and vices. Again, when we are angry or frightened it is not by our choice;[1] but our virtues are expressions of our choice, or at any rate imply choice. Besides, we are said to be moved in respect of our feelings, but in respect of our virtues and vices we are said to be not moved but disposed in a particular way. By the same line of reasoning they are not faculties either. We are not called good or bad, nor are we praised or blamed, merely because we are *capable* of feeling. Again, what faculties we have, we have by nature; but it is not nature that makes us good or bad (we mentioned this point above[2]). So if the virtues are neither feelings nor faculties, it remains that they are dispositions.

We have now stated what virtue is generically.

But what is its differentia? Any excellence enables its
possessor to function; therefore this is true
of human excellence, i.e. virtue

vi.   But we must not only make the simple statement that it is a disposition; we must also say what *kind* of disposition. Let us assert, then, that any kind of excellence renders that of which it is the excellence *good*, and makes it perform its function *well*. For example, the excellence of the eye makes both the eye and its function good (because it is through the excellence of the eye that we see well). Similarly the excellence of a horse makes him both a fine horse and good at

1. *proairesis*; see Glossary.   2. 1103a 18ff.

running and carrying his rider and facing the enemy. If this rule holds good for all cases, then *human* excellence will be the disposition that makes one a good man and causes him to perform his function well. We have already explained[1] how this will be; but it will also become clear in another way if we consider what is the specific nature of virtue.

This is confirmed by the doctrine of the Mean

In anything continuous and divisible it is possible to take a part which is greater or less than, or equal to, the remainder; and that in relation either to the thing divided or to us. The equal part is a sort of mean between excess and deficiency; and I call mean in relation to the *thing* whatever is equidistant from the extremes, which is one and the same for everybody; but I call mean in relation to *us* that which is neither excessive nor deficient, and this is *not* one and the same for all. For example, if ten is 'many' and two 'few' of some quantity, six is the mean if one takes it in relation to the thing, because it exceeds the one number and is exceeded by the other by the same amount; and this is the mean by arithmetical reckoning. But the mean in relation to *us* is not to be obtained in this way. Supposing that *ten pounds of food is a large and two pounds a small allowance for an athlete, it does not follow that the trainer will prescribe six pounds; for even this is perhaps too much or too little for the person who is to receive it – too little for Milo[2] but too much for one who is only beginning to train. Similarly in the case of running and wrestling. In this way, then, every knowledgeable person avoids excess and deficiency, but looks for the mean and chooses it – not the mean of the thing, but the mean relative to us.

If, then, every science[3] performs its function well only when it observes the mean and refers its products to it

1. 1103b10ff.
2. A prodigiously strong wrestler from Croton in S. Italy.
3. He means *practical* science, as is evident from the context.

(which is why it is customary to say of well-executed works that nothing can be added to them or taken away, the implication being that excess and deficiency alike destroy perfection, while the mean preserves it) – if good craftsmen, as we hold, work with the mean in view; and if virtue, like nature, is more exact and more efficient than any art, it follows that virtue aims to hit the mean. By virtue I mean moral virtue since it is this that is concerned with feelings and actions, and these involve excess, deficiency and a mean. It is possible, for example, to feel fear, confidence, desire, anger, pity, and pleasure and pain generally, too much or too little; and both of these are wrong. But to have these feelings at the right times on the right grounds towards the right people for the right motive and in the right way is to feel them to an intermediate, that is to the best, degree; and this is the mark of virtue. Similarly there are excess and deficiency and a mean in the case of actions. But it is in the field of actions and feelings that virtue operates; and in them excess and deficiency are failings, whereas the mean is praised and recognized as a success: and these are both marks of virtue. Virtue, then, is a mean condition, inasmuch as it aims at hitting the mean.

Again, failure is possible in many ways (for evil, as the Pythagoreans[1] represented it, is a form of the Unlimited, and good of the Limited), but success is only one. That is why the one is easy and the other difficult; it is easy to miss the target and difficult to hit it. Here, then, is another reason why excess and deficiency fall under evil, and the mean state under good;

For men are bad in countless ways, but good in only one.[2]

A provisional definition of virtue

So virtue is a purposive disposition, lying in a mean *that is relative to us and determined by a rational principle, and

1. See Appendix A.   2. The source of the quotation is unknown.

by that which a prudent man would use to determine it.[1] It is a mean between two kinds of vice, one of excess and the other of deficiency; and also for this reason, that whereas these vices fall short of or exceed the right measure in both feelings and actions, virtue discovers the mean and chooses it. Thus from the point of view of its essence and the definition of its real nature, virtue is a mean; but in respect of what is right and best, it is an extreme.

But the rule of choosing the mean cannot be applied to some actions and feelings, which are essentially evil

But not every action or feeling admits of a mean; because some have names that directly connote depravity, such as malice, shamelessness and envy, and among actions adultery, theft and murder. All these, and more like them, are so called[2] as being evil in themselves; it is not the excess or deficiency of them that is evil. In their case, then, it is impossible to act rightly; one is always wrong. Nor does acting rightly or wrongly in such cases depend upon circumstances – whether a man commits adultery with the right woman or at the right time or in the right way, because to do anything of that kind is simply wrong. One might as well claim that there is a mean and excess and deficiency even in unjust or cowardly or intemperate actions. On that basis there must be a mean of excess, a mean of deficiency, an excess of excess and a deficiency of deficiency. But just as in temperance and courage there can be no mean or excess or deficiency, because the mean is in a sense an extreme, so there can be no mean or excess or deficiency in the vices that we mentioned; however done, they are wrong. For in general neither excess nor deficiency admits of a mean, nor does a mean admit of excess and deficiency.

1. It is purposive as being a deliberately cultivated and exercised state of the appetitive faculty; and the mean is determined not merely by a general principle but by the application of it to particular circumstances by a man of good character and intelligence; cf. ch. ix. below.

2. Or 'are censured'.

The doctrine of the mean applied to particular virtues

vii.   But a generalization of this kind is not enough; we must apply it to particular cases. When we are discussing actions, although general statements have a wider application, particular statements are closer to the truth. This is because actions are concerned with particular facts, and theories must be brought into harmony with these. Let us, then, take these instances from the diagram.[1]

In the field of Fear and Confidence[2] the mean is Courage; *and of those who go to extremes the man who exceeds in fearlessness has no name to describe him (there are many nameless cases), the one who exceeds in confidence is called Rash, and the one who shows an excess of fear and a deficiency of confidence is called Cowardly. In the field of Pleasures and Pains – not in all, especially not in all pains – the mean is Temperance,[3] the excess Licentiousness; cases of defective response to pleasures scarcely occur, and therefore people of this sort too have no name to describe them, but let us class them as Insensible. In the field of Giving and Receiving Money the mean is Liberality, the excess and deficiency are Prodigality and Illiberality; but these show excess and deficiency in contrary ways to one another: the prodigal man goes too far in spending and not far enough in getting, while the illiberal man goes too far in getting money and not far enough in spending it. This present account is in outline and summary, which is all that we need at this stage; we shall give a more accurate analysis later.[4]

But there are other dispositions too that are concerned with money. There is a mean called Magnificence (because the magnificent is not the same as the liberal man: the one

1. Or 'table'; see p. 104, where the Greek names of the several virtues and vices are shown.

2. These should be regarded (for the understanding of A.'s general theory) as forming a single continuum with extremes Rashness and Cowardice; the reference to Fearlessness may be ignored.

3. Generally 'self-control' is a better rendering.

4. 1115a4–1138b14.

TABLE OF VIRTUES AND VICES

SPHERE OF ACTION OR FEELING	EXCESS	MEAN	DEFICIENCY
Fear and Confidence	Rashness *thrasutēs*	Courage *andreia*	Cowardice *deilia*
Pleasure and Pain	Licentiousness *akolasia*	Temperance *sōphrosunē*	Insensibility *anaisthēsia*
Getting and Spending (minor)	Prodigality *asōtia*	Liberality *eleutheriotēs*	Illiberality *aneleutheria*
Getting and Spending (major)	Vulgarity *apeirokalia, banausia*	Magnificence *megaloprepeia*	Pettiness *mikroprepeia*
Honour and Dishonour (major)	Vanity *chaunotēs*	Magnanimity *megalopsūchia*	Pusillanimity *mikropsūchia*
Honour and Dishonour (minor)	Ambition *philotīmia*	Proper ambition	Unambitiousness *aphilotīmia*
Anger	Irascibility *orgilotēs*	Patience *prāotēs*	Lack of spirit *aorgēsia*
Self-expression	Boastfulness *alazoneia*	Truthfulness *alētheia*	Understatement *eirōneia*
Conversation	Buffoonery *bōmolochia*	Wittiness *eutrapelia*	Boorishness *agroikia*
Social Conduct	Obsequiousness *areskeia* Flattery *kolakeia*	Friendliness *philia*(?)	Cantankerousness *duskolia* (*duseris*)
Shame	Shyness *kataplēxis*	Modesty *aidōs*	Shamelessness *anaischuntia*
Indignation	Envy *phthonos*	Righteous indignation *nemesis*	Malicious enjoyment *epichairekakia*

deals in large and the other in small outlays); the excess is Tastelessness and Vulgarity, the deficiency Pettiness. These are different from the extremes between which liberality

lies; how they differ will be discussed later.[1] In the field of
Public Honour and Dishonour the mean is Magnanimity,
the excess is called a sort of Vanity, and the deficiency
Pusillanimity. And just as liberality differs, as we said,[2]
from magnificence in being concerned with small outlays,
so there is a state related to Magnanimity in the same way,
being concerned with small honours, while magnanimity is
concerned with great ones; because it is possible to aspire to
⟨small⟩ honours in the right way, or to a greater or less
degree than is right. The man who goes too far in his aspira-
tions is called Ambitious, the one who falls short, Unambitious; the one who is a mean between them has no name.
This is true also of the corresponding dispositions, except
that the ambitious man's is called Ambitiousness. This is
why the extremes lay claim to the intermediate territory. We
ourselves sometimes call the intermediate man ambitious and
sometimes unambitious; that is, we sometimes *commend
the ambitious and sometimes the unambitious. Why it is
that we do this will be explained in our later remarks.[3]
Meanwhile let us continue our discussion of the remaining
virtues and vices, following the method already laid down.

In the field of Anger, too, there is excess, deficiency and
the mean. They do not really possess names, but we may
call the intermediate man Patient and the mean Patience;
and of the extremes the one who exceeds can be Irascible
and his vice Irascibility, while the one who is deficient can
be Spiritless and the deficiency Lack of Spirit.

There are also three other means which, though different,
somewhat resemble each other. They are all concerned with
what we do and say in social intercourse, but they differ in
this respect, that one is concerned with truthfulness in such
intercourse, the other two with pleasantness – one with
pleasantness in entertainment, the other with pleasantness
in every department of life. We must therefore say something
about these too, in order that we may better discern that in
all things the mean is to be commended, while the extremes
are neither commendable nor right, but reprehensible.

1. 1122a20–b18.   2. Just above.   3. 1125b11–25.

Most of these too have no names; but, as in the other cases, we must try to coin names for them in the interest of clarity and to make it easy to follow the argument.

Well, then, as regards Truth the intermediate man may be called Truthful and the mean Truthfulness; pretension that goes too far may be Boastfulness and the man who is disposed to it a Boaster, while that which is deficient[1] may be called Irony and its exponent Ironical. As for Pleasantness in Social Entertainment, the intermediate man is Witty, and the disposition Wit; the excess is Buffoonery and the indulger in it a Buffoon; the man who is deficient is a kind of Boor and his disposition Boorishness. In the rest of the sphere of the Pleasant – life in general – the person who is pleasant in the right way is Friendly and the mean is Friendliness; the person who goes too far, if he has no motive, is Obsequious; if his motive is self-interest, he is a Flatterer. The man who is deficient and is unpleasant in all circumstances is Cantankerous and Ill-tempered.

There are mean states also in the sphere of feelings and emotions. Modesty is not a virtue, but the modest man too is praised. Here too one person is called intermediate and another excessive – like the Shy man who is overawed at anything. The man who feels too little shame or none at all is Shameless, and the intermediate man is Modest. *Righteous Indignation is a mean between Envy and Spite, and they are all concerned with feelings of pain or pleasure at the experiences of our neighbours. The man who feels righteous indignation is distressed at instances of undeserved good fortune, but the envious man goes further and is distressed at *any* good fortune, while the spiteful man is so far from feeling distress[2] that he actually rejoices.

However, we shall have occasion to continue this discussion elsewhere.[3] After that we shall treat of Justice, distinguishing its two kinds – because the word is used in more

1. By understating the truth; in fact 'understatement' is often a better equivalent than 'irony'.

2. At their *bad* fortune, because the Greek work means literally 'rejoicing at misfortune'.   3. In Book V.

senses than one – and explain in what way each of them is a mean.[1] [We shall also treat similarly of the rational virtues.][2]

The mean is often nearer to one extreme than to the other,
or seems nearer because of our natural tendencies

viii.   Thus there are three dispositions, two of them vicious (one by way of excess, the other of deficiency), and one good, the mean. They are all in some way opposed to one another: the extremes are contrary both to the mean and to each other, and the mean to the extremes. For just as the equal is greater compared with the less, and less compared with the greater, so the mean states (in both feelings and actions) are excessive compared with the deficient and deficient compared with the excessive. A brave man appears rash compared with a coward, and cowardly compared with a rash man; similarly a temperate man appears licentious compared with an insensible one and insensible compared with a licentious one, and a liberal man prodigal compared with an illiberal one and illiberal compared with a prodigal one. This is the reason why each extreme type tries to push the mean nearer to the other: the coward calls the brave man rash, the rash man calls him a coward; and similarly in all other cases. But while all these dispositions are opposed to one another in this way, the greatest degree of contrariety is that which is found between the two extremes. For they are separated by a greater interval from one another than from the mean, just as the great is further from the small, and the small from the great, than either is from the equal. Again, some extremes seem to bear a resemblance to a mean; e.g. rashness seems like courage, and prodigality like liberality; but between the extremes there is always the maximum

1. 1115a4ff.
2. The words in square brackets were almost certainly added by another hand; A. never calls the intellectual virtues 'rational', nor did he regard them as mean states. The intellectual virtues are discussed in Book VI.

dissimilarity. Now contraries are by definition as far distant as possible from one another;[1] hence the further apart things are, the more contrary they will be. In some cases it is the *deficiency, in others the excess, that is more opposed to the mean; for instance, the more direct opposite of courage is not the excess, rashness, but the deficiency, cowardice; and that of temperance is not the deficiency, insensibility, but the excess, licentiousness. This result is due to two causes. One lies in the nature of the thing itself. When one extreme has a closer affinity and resemblance to the mean, we tend to oppose to the mean not that extreme but the other. For instance, since rashness is held to be nearer to courage and more like it than cowardice is, it is cowardice that we tend to oppose to courage, because the extremes that are further from the mean are thought to be more opposed to it. This is one cause, the one that lies in the *thing*. The other lies in ourselves. It is the things towards which we have the stronger natural inclination that seem to us more opposed to the mean. For example, we are naturally more inclined towards pleasures, and this makes us more prone towards licentiousness than towards temperance; so we describe as more contrary to the mean those things towards which we have the stronger tendency. This is why licentiousness, the excess, is more contrary to temperance.[2]

Summing up of the foregoing discussion, together with three practical rules for good conduct

ix.   We have now said enough to show that moral virtue is a mean, and in what sense it is so: that it is a mean between two vices, one of excess and the other of deficiency, and that it is such because it aims at hitting the mean point in feelings and actions. For this reason it is a difficult business to be good; because in any given case it is difficult to find the mid-point[3] – for instance, not everyone can find the centre of a

1. Cf. *Metaphysics* 1018a25ff.
2. sc. 'than insensibility is' (1109a3f.).   3. Or 'mean'.

circle; only the man who knows how. So too it is easy to get angry – anyone can do that – or to give and spend money; but to feel or act towards the right person to the right extent at the right time for the right reason in the right way – that is not easy, and it is not everyone that can do it. Hence to do these things well is a rare, laudable and fine achievement.

For this reason anyone who is aiming at the mean should (1) keep away from that extreme which is more contrary to the mean, just as Calypso advises:

> Far from this surf and surge keep thou thy ship.[1]

For one of the extremes is always more erroneous than the other; and since it is extremely difficult to hit the mean, we must take the next best course, as they say, and choose the lesser of the evils; and this *will be most readily done in the way that we are suggesting. (2) We must notice the errors into which we ourselves are liable to fall (because we all have different natural tendencies – we shall find out what ours are from the pleasure and pain that they give us), and we must drag ourselves in the contrary direction; for we shall arrive at the mean by pressing well away from our failing – just like somebody straightening a warped piece of wood. (3) In every situation one must guard especially against pleasure and pleasant things, because we are not impartial judges of pleasure. So we should adopt the same attitude towards it as the Trojan elders did towards Helen, and constantly repeat their pronouncement;[2] because if in this way we relieve ourselves of the attraction, we shall be less likely to go wrong.

To sum up: by following these rules we shall have the best chance of hitting the mean. But this is presumably difficult, especially in particular cases; because it is not easy to deter-

1. In our text of Homer these words are spoken not by Calypso (the nymph who detained Odysseus on her island) but by Odysseus himself quoting the enchantress Circe's advice to steer closer to Scylla (the lesser evil) than to Charybdis (*Odyssey* xii. 219f.).

2. As a sort of charm or spell. The elders paid tribute to her beauty, but said that she ought to be sent back to Greece, for fear of the consequences for Troy if she remained (*Iliad* iii. 156–60).

mine what is the right way to be angry, and with whom, and on what grounds, and for how long. Indeed we sometimes praise those who show deficiency, and call them patient, and sometimes those who display temper, calling them manly. However, the man who deviates only a little from the right degree, either in excess or in deficiency, is not censured – only the one who goes too far, because he is noticeable. Yet it is not easy to define by rule for how long, and how much, a man may go wrong before he incurs blame; no easier than it is to define any other object of perception. Such questions of degree occur in particular cases, and the decision lies with our perception.[1]

This much, then, is clear: in all our conduct it is the mean that is to be commended. But one should incline sometimes towards excess and sometimes towards deficiency, because in this way we shall most easily hit upon the mean, that is, the right course.

1. e.g. a person of good character *feels* that he is getting too angry; he does not, in a particular case, refer to a general principle of ethics.

III

MORAL RESPONSIBILITY – TWO VIRTUES

Actions are voluntary, involuntary or non-voluntary

i. Since moral goodness is concerned with feelings and actions, and those that are voluntary receive praise and blame, whereas those that are involuntary receive pardon and sometimes pity too, students of moral goodness must presumably determine the limits of the voluntary and involuntary. Such a course is useful also for legislators with a view to prescribing honours and punishments.

Actions are regarded as involuntary when they are performed under compulsion *or through ignorance. An act is compulsory when it has an external origin of such a kind that the agent or patient contributes nothing to it; e.g. if a voyager were to be conveyed somewhere by the wind or by men who had him in their power. But sometimes the act is done through fear of something worse, or for some admirable purpose; e.g. if a tyrant who has a man's parents and children in his power were to order him to do something dishonourable on condition that if he did it their lives would be spared, and if he did not they would be put to death : in these cases it is debatable whether the actions are involuntary or voluntary. A similar difficulty occurs with regard to jettisoning cargo in bad weather. In general no one willingly throws away his property; but if it is to save the lives of himself and everyone else, any reasonable person will do it. Such actions are mixed, although they seem more like voluntary than involuntary ones; because at the time that they are performed they are matters of choice, and the end of an action varies with the occasion; so the terms voluntary and involuntary should be used with reference to the time when the actions are performed. Now in cases like the above the agent acts voluntarily; because the movement of the limbs that are the instruments of action has its origin in the agent himself, and where this is so it is in his power either to act or not. Therefore such actions are voluntary; but considered absolutely they are presumably involuntary, because nobody would choose to do anything of this sort in itself. Sometimes people are actually praised for such actions, when they endure some disgrace or suffering as the price of great and splendid results; but if the case is the other way round, they are blamed, because to endure the utmost humiliation to serve no fine or even respectable end is the mark of a depraved nature. In some cases, however, the action, though not commended, is pardoned: viz. when a man acts wrongly because the alternative is too much for human nature, and nobody could endure it. But presumably there are some things such that a man cannot be compelled to do them – that he must sooner die than do, though he suffer the most dreadful fate. Indeed the reasons that 'compelled' Alcmaeon in Euripides' play to kill his mother seem absurd.[1] Yet it is sometimes difficult to decide what sort of advantage is to be chosen at what sort of price, or what fate endured for the sake of what advantage; and it is still harder to abide by one's decisions. For the expected consequences are usually unpleasant, and what people are forced to do is discreditable; which is why agents are praised or blamed according to *whether they have yielded to compulsion or not.

What sort of acts, then, ought we to call compulsory? Surely we should call them compulsory without qualification when the cause is external and the agent contributes nothing to it; whereas acts that are in themselves involuntary but are preferable at a given time and at a given cost, and that have their origin in the agent, although they are involuntary in themselves, nevertheless are voluntary at the given time and cost. They are more like voluntary acts, because actions belong to the sphere of particulars, and here

1. This seems a little unfair. He claimed to be obeying the solemn charge (reinforced by a curse if he disobeyed) of his father Amphiaraus, who (being a seer) knew that the expedition against Thebes, which his wife Eriphyle had treacherously persuaded him to join, would be fatal for him.

the particular acts are voluntary. But what sort of acts are
to be preferred, and to what alternatives, and at what cost
to the agent, is not an easy point to decide; because the
differences in particular cases are many.

If it were argued that pleasurable and admirable things
have a compulsive effect (because they bring external pressure to bear on us), it would make all acts compulsory; because every act of every agent is done for the sake of such
objects. Also, to act under compulsion and against one's will
is painful, but to act for a pleasurable or admirable object is
pleasant. Also it is absurd for the agent to lay the blame on
external factors and not on himself for falling an easy prey
to them, and to attribute his fine acts to himself, but his disgraceful ones to the attractions of pleasure. It seems likely,
then, that an act is compulsory ⟨only⟩ when its originating
cause is external, and receives no contribution from the
person under compulsion.

Every act done through ignorance is non-voluntary, but it
is involuntary only when it causes the agent subsequent pain
and repentance. For if a man has done any act through
ignorance and is not in the least upset about it, although he
has not acted voluntarily (not knowing what he was doing),
he has not acted involuntarily either, since he feels no pain.
Thus when a man repents of an act done through ignorance,
he is considered to have acted involuntarily: but a man who
does not repent of such an act is another case, so he may be
said to have acted non-voluntarily; since he is different, it is
better that he should have a name of his own.

Also it seems that there is a distinction between acting
through ignorance and acting *in* ignorance. When a man is
drunk or in a rage his actions are considered to be the result
not of ignorance but of one of the said conditions; but he acts
not knowingly but *in* ignorance. As a matter of fact, every
bad man is ignorant of what he ought to do and refrain from
doing, and it is just this sort of fault that makes people unjust and generally bad. An act is not properly called involuntary if the agent is ignorant of his own advantage; for
what makes an act involuntary is not ignorance in the

choice (this is a cause of wickedness), nor ignorance of the universal[1] (for this people are blamed), but *particular* ignorance, i.e. of the *circumstances and objects of the action; for it is on these that pity and pardon depend, because a man who acts in ignorance of any such detail is an involuntary agent.

It will probably not be a bad thing, then, to determine the nature and number of these particular circumstances. They are (1) the agent, (2) the act, (3) the object or medium of the act, and sometimes also (4) the instrument (e.g. a tool), (5) the aim (e.g. saving life), and (6) the manner (e.g. gently or roughly). Now nobody in his right mind could be ignorant of *all* these circumstances. Obviously he cannot be ignorant of (1) the agent either – how can he fail to know himself? But he may not realize (2) what he is doing; as people say that they were 'carried away while speaking',[2] or 'did not know it was a secret' (as in the case of Aeschylus and the Mysteries[3]), or like the man who let off the catapult[4] 'because he wanted to show how it worked'. Or (3) a person might actually think, like Merope,[5] that his son was an enemy; or (4) that a sharp-pointed spear had a button on it, or that a stone was a piece of pumice,[6] or (5) one might kill someone with a dose of a drug intended to save his life, or (6) hit one's opponent when one meant only to seize his hand, as in finger wrestling.[7] All these particular circumstances of an action admit of ignorance, and anyone who is ignorant of any of them is considered to have acted involuntarily, especially in the case of the most important of

1. i.e. moral principle.

2. Or perhaps 'got flustered'; the other interpretation, of a slightly different reading, 'the remark escaped them', seems to lack sound support.

3. He was accused of revealing secret rites in his plays, but was acquitted.

4. Not, of course, a hand catapult, but a large siege engine.

5. A character in the (lost) *Cresphontes* of Euripides.

6. And therefore not a lethal missile (?).

7. i.e. wrestling at arm's length – but the Greek word may mean 'sparring'.

them, which are supposed to be the circumstances of the act and its effect.[1] Further, for an act to be called involuntary in virtue of this sort of ignorance, the agent must also feel distress and repentance for having done it.

If an involuntary act is one performed under compulsion or as a result of ignorance, a voluntary act would seem to be one of which the originating cause lies in the agent himself, who knows the particular circumstances of his action. It is probably wrong to say that acts due to temper or desire are involuntary; for on this view in the first place the capacity for voluntary action will not extend to any animal other than man, or even to children; and secondly, when we act from desire or temper are none of our actions voluntary? Or are our fine actions done voluntarily and our discreditable ones involuntarily? Surely this is a ridiculous distinction, since the cause[2] is one and the same; and it is presumably absurd to describe as involuntary acts to which we are rightly attracted. There are some things at which we actually ought to feel angry, and others that we actually ought to desire – health, for instance, and learning. Also what is involuntary is considered to be disagreeable, and what accords with our desire pleasant. Besides, what difference is there in point of voluntariness between wrong actions that are calculated and wrong actions that are due to temper? Both are to be avoided; *and the irrational feelings are considered to be no less part of human nature than our considered judgements. It follows that actions due to temper or desire are also proper to the human agent. Therefore it is absurd to class these actions as involuntary.

Moral conduct implies choice, but what is choice? It must be distinguished from desire, temper, wish and opinion

ii.   Now that we have determined the limits of the voluntary and the involuntary, our next task is to discuss choice;[3]

1. The text is rather uncertain.   2. Viz. desire.
3. *proairesis*: see Glossary.

because it is felt to be very closely related to moral goodness, and to be a better test of character than actions are.

Now choice is clearly a voluntary thing, but the two words have not the same connotation: that of 'voluntary' is wider; for both children and animals have a share in voluntary action, but not in choice; and we call actions done on the spur of the moment voluntary, but not the result of choice.

Those who identify it with desire or temper or wish or some kind of opinion[1] seem to do so mistakenly. Choice is not shared with man by irrational creatures as desire and temper are. Moreover, the incontinent[2] man acts from desire but not from choice, while contrariwise the continent[2] man acts from choice but not from desire. Again, a desire can be contrary to choice, but not to another desire.[3] Again, desire is concerned with what is pleasurable and painful, but choice with neither.[4] Still less is choice to be identified with temper; for acts due to temper[5] are thought to involve choice less than any others. Nor, again, is choice wish, although it is obvious that there is a close connection between them. There is no choice of impossibilities, and anyone who professed to choose one would be thought silly; but one can wish for what is impossible, e.g. immortality. Also one can wish for results which one could not possibly bring about oneself, e.g. the success of a particular actor or athlete; but nobody *chooses* things like that – only what he thinks could be achieved by his own efforts. Again, wish is more concerned with the end, and choice with the means: e.g. we wish to be healthy, but choose things that will make us healthy; and we actually say 'we wish to be happy', but to say 'we choose to be happy' is incongruous, because in general choice seems to be concerned with acts that lie in our own power. Neither can it be opinion, for opinion seems

1. The Greek words are *epithūmia, thūmos, boulēsis* and *doxa.*
2. *akratēs* and *enkratēs.*
3. The same person cannot feel contrary desires at the same time.
4. It is concerned only with practicable means to an end.
5. Being unpremeditated.

to cover everything – things eternal[1] or impossible no less
than those that lie in our own power. Besides, opinions are
distinguished by being true or false, not good or bad, which
is rather the distinction between kinds of choice. Probably,
then, *no one even suggests that choice is the same as
opinion in general; but neither is it the same as any particular opinion; for our characters are determined by our
choice of what is good or evil, not by our opinion about it.
Again, when we choose, it is to take or avoid something
good or bad; but when we form an opinion, it is of what a
thing is, or whom it benefits or how; but we do not really
form an opinion of taking or avoiding. Again, a choice is
more properly praised for choosing the right object than for
being correct in itself; but an opinion is praised for being in
accordance with the truth. Also we choose what we know
very well to be good, but we form opinions about things that
we do not really know to be good. It seems, too, that the same
people are not equally good at choosing the best actions and
forming the best opinions; some are comparatively good at
forming opinions, but through a moral defect fail to make
the right choices. Whether the forming of an opinion is
prior to, or simultaneous with, an act of choice is immaterial;
what we are investigating is not that, but whether choice is
the same as a kind of opinion.

If, then, choice is none of the things that we have mentioned, what is it? what is its specific quality? Obviously
what is chosen is voluntary, but not everything that is voluntary is chosen. Well, is it the result of previous deliberation? For choice implies a rational principle,[2] and
thought. The name, too, seems to indicate something that is
chosen *before* other things.[3]

1. Cf. 1112a21ff. below.   2. *logos*: see Glossary.
3. The prefix *pro-* in the word *proairesis* is a preposition meaning
'before'.

If Choice involves Deliberation, what is the sphere of the latter?

iii.   Do people deliberate about all issues – i.e. is everything an object of deliberation? – or are there some things that do not admit of it? (Presumably we should call an object of deliberation what might be deliberated by a reasonable person, not by a fool or a madman.) Surely nobody deliberates about eternal facts, such as the order of the universe or the incommensurability of the diagonal with the side of a square; nor about eternal regular processes, whether they have a necessary or a natural or some other kind of cause[1] – such as the solstices, or the risings of the sun; nor about irregular happenings like droughts and heavy rainstorms; nor about chance occurrences, like the finding of a treasure; for none of these results could be effected by our agency. What we deliberate about is practical measures that lie in our power; this is the class of things that actually remains, for the accepted types of cause are nature, necessity and chance, and also mind and human agency of all kinds.[2] Not even all human affairs are objects of deliberation; thus no Spartan deliberates about the best form of constitution for the Scythians;[3] each of the various groups of human beings deliberates about the practical measures that lie in its own power. Deliberation is not concerned *with those branches of knowledge that have precise rules of their own (e.g. writing, for we do not hesitate over the way in which a word should be written[4]). The effects about which we deliberate are those which are produced by our agency but not always in the same way;[5] e.g. the practice of medicine and of finance, and of navigation – which calls for more

1. 'Necessary' causes are those of physical, 'natural' those of biological phenomena.
2. A traditional analysis accepted by A.
3. Because it does not concern him and he can do nothing about it.
4. Or if we do it is from ignorance or forgetfulness.
5. i.e. by the same means or the same use of them.

deliberation than physical training does, inasmuch as it has not been reduced to such a precise system; and similarly also with the other occupations. The arts call for more deliberation than the sciences, because we feel less certain about them. Thus the field of deliberation is 'that which happens for the most part, where the result is obscure and the right course not clearly defined'; and for important decisions we call in advisers, distrusting our own ability to reach a decision.

Deliberation is about means, not ends

We deliberate not about ends but about means. A doctor does not deliberate whether to cure his patient, nor a speaker whether to persuade his audience, nor a statesman whether to produce law and order; nor does anyone else deliberate about the end at which he is aiming. They first set some end before themselves, and then proceed to consider how and by what means it can be attained. If it appears that it can be attained by several means, they further consider by which it can be attained best and most easily. If it can only be achieved by one means, they consider how it will be brought about by this, and then by what other means this will be brought about, until they arrive at the first cause, which is the last in the order of discovery (because the process of deliberation by the method described is like the investigation or analysis of a geometrical problem – it seems that not every investigation is a kind of deliberation, e.g. those of mathematics are not; but every deliberation is an investigation – and the last step in the analysis is the first in the process[1]). If they then encounter an impossibility – e.g. if money is needed and cannot be provided – they give up; but

1. The analytical method of solving a problem consists in assuming the required solution and then considering what conditions must be satisfied to prove it valid. Then if X is valid if A is, and A if B is, and B if C is, and C is something that we can prove (or supply), C, the last step in the analysis, is the first in the process of solution.

if the thing appears possible, they set about doing it. By possible I mean those things that can be done by our agency (for the results of our friends' actions are in a sense results of our own, because the originating cause is in us). The question[1] is sometimes what tools to use, and sometimes what use to make of them; similarly in other activities it is sometimes what means to use, and sometimes how to use it or how to secure it.

It seems, then, as we have said,[2] that the originating cause of actions is a man, and the field of deliberation is what is practicable for the agent; and that the actions are for the sake of something else. The object of deliberation, then, cannot be the end, but must be the means to ends. Nor again is deliberation concerned with particular facts, *such as 'is it a loaf?' or 'is it properly cooked?'; these are matters for sense-perception. And if one is to deliberate in every case, the process will go on to infinity.

The object of deliberation and the object of choice are the same, except that the latter has already been determined; it has been selected as the result of deliberation. In every case a man stops inquiring how to act when he has traced the starting-point of action back to himself, i.e. to the dominant part[3] of himself; for it is this that makes the choice. This is evident also from the ancient constitutions as portrayed by Homer – the kings proclaimed to the people what they had already chosen to do.

Definition of choice

Since, therefore, an object of choice is something within our power at which we aim after deliberation, choice will be a deliberate appetition of things that lie in our power. For we first make a decision as the result of deliberation, and then direct our aim in accordance with the deliberation.

1. For a craftsman.   2. Not exactly, but cf. 1112a30–34, b27f.
3. The rational element in the soul; cf. 1139a18ff., and 1168b23–1169a6.

This may serve as an outline account of choice, and the sort of objects with which it is concerned, and the fact that it is a choice of means towards an end.

The object of wish is in one sense the good, in another the apparent good

iv. We have already said that wish is concerned with the end;[1] but some think that its object is the good, and others that it is the *apparent* good. Now for those who hold that the object of wish is the good it follows that if a person chooses wrongly, what he wishes is not an object of wish (because if it is wishable it must be good; but it may in fact have been bad); while on the other hand for those who hold that what is wished is the *apparent* good it follows that nothing is by nature wishable, but that what any individual thinks is good is wishable for him – and different people have different and, it may be, contrary views.

If these consequences are unacceptable, perhaps we should say that absolutely and in truth the object of wish is the good, but for the individual it is what seems good to him; so for the man of good character[2] it is the true good, but for the bad man it is any chance thing. It is just the same as it is with physical conditions. What is wholesome for those who are in good health is what is really wholesome; but what is wholesome for invalids is something different (and similarly with things bitter and sweet, hot and heavy, and every other kind of object). For the man of good character judges every situation rightly; i.e. in every situation what appears to him is the truth. Every disposition has its own appreciation of what is fine and pleasant; and probably what makes the man of good character stand out furthest is the fact that he sees the truth in every kind of situation: he is a sort of standard and yardstick of what is fine and pleasant. Most people seem to owe their deception

1. 1111b26.   2. *spoudaios*.

to pleasure, which appears to them to be a good *although it is not; consequently they choose what is pleasant as a good, and avoid pain as an evil.

Actions that we initiate ourselves, whether they are good or bad, are voluntary

v.   Since, while the end is an object of wish, the means to it are objects of deliberation and choice, the actions that are related to the means will be performed in accordance with choice, and voluntarily. But the exercise of moral virtues is related to means. Therefore virtue lies in our power, and similarly so does vice; because where it is in our power to act, it is also in our power not to act, and where we can refuse we can also comply. So if it is in our power to do a thing when it is right, it will also be in our power not to do it when it is wrong; and if it is in our power not to do it when it is right, it will also be in our power to do it when it is wrong. And if it is in our power to do right and wrong, and similarly not to do them; and if, as we saw,[1] doing right or wrong is the essence of being good or bad, it follows that it is in our power to be decent or worthless.[2] The saying

None would be evil, or would not be blessed,[3]

seems to be partly false and partly true; because nobody is unwilling to be blessed, but wickedness is voluntary. Otherwise we must dispute what we have just been saying, and assert that man is *not* the originator or begetter of his own actions as he is of his children. But if it is manifestly true that he *is*, and we cannot refer our actions to any other sources than those that are in ourselves, then the actions whose sources are in us are themselves in our power, i.e. voluntary.

1. cf. 1103a 31ff.

2. It is only for variety that A. uses different adjectives; the change is not significant.

3. The (unknown) author probably meant 'wretched' rather than 'evil', so the quotation is used rather unscrupulously.

This is borne out by the common use of rewards and punishments

This view seems to be supported by the practice both of the various groups privately and of the legislators themselves; for they impose punishments and penalties upon malefactors (except where the offence is committed under duress or in unavoidable ignorance), and bestow honours on those who do fine actions; which implies that their object is to encourage the latter and restrain the former. But nobody is encouraged to do an act which is neither in our power nor voluntary; it is assumed that there is no point in our being persuaded not to get hot or feel pain or hunger or anything else of that sort, because we shall feel them just the same.

Responsibility for the results of bad moral states

Indeed they punish the offender for his very ignorance, if he is thought to be responsible for it. E.g. penalties are doubled[1] for committing an offence in a state of drunkenness, because the source of the action lay in the agent himself: he was capable of not getting drunk, and his drunkenness was the cause of his ignorance. They also punish ignorance of any point of law that ought to be known and is not difficult *to ascertain. Similarly too in all other cases where the offenders' ignorance is considered to be due to negligence, on the ground that it was in their power not to be ignorant, because they were capable of taking care.

'Well, probably he is the sort of person that doesn't take care.' But people get into this condition through their own fault, by the slackness of their lives; i.e. they make themselves unjust or licentious by behaving dishonestly or spending their time in drinking and other forms of dissipation; for in every sphere of conduct people develop qualities corresponding to the activities that they pursue. This is evident

1. e.g. by Pittacus (for whom see 1167a32); cf. *Politics* 1274b19.

from the example of people training for any competition or undertaking: they spend all their time in exercising. So to be unaware that in every department of conduct moral states are the result of corresponding activities is the mark of a thoroughly unperceptive person.

A bad moral state, once formed, is not easily amended

Again, it is unreasonable to suppose that a man who acts unjustly or licentiously does not wish to be unjust or licentious; and if anyone, without being in ignorance, acts in a way that will make him unjust, he will be voluntarily unjust; but it does not follow that he can stop being unjust, and be just, if he wants to – no more than a sick man can become healthy, even though (it may be) his sickness is voluntary, being the result of incontinent living and disobeying his doctors. There was a time when it was open to him not to be ill; but when he had once thrown away his chance, it was gone; just as when one has once let go of a stone, it is too late to get it back – but the agent was responsible for throwing it, because the origin of the action was in himself. So too it was at first open to the unjust and licentious persons not to become such, and therefore they are voluntarily what they are; but now that they have become what they are, it is no longer open to them not to be such.

Even physical defects, if voluntarily incurred, are culpable

It is not only vices of the soul that are voluntary; physical defects too are voluntarily incurred by some people, and we blame them for it. Nobody blames those who are naturally ugly, but we do blame those who become so through lack of exercise and care for their appearance. Similarly too in the case of physical weakness and disability. Nobody would criticize a person who is blind by nature or as a result of disease or injury – he would more likely be an object of

pity – but anyone would blame a person whose blindness
is due to heavy drinking or some other self-indulgence. Thus
physical defects for which we are responsible are blamed,
but those for which we are not responsible are not blamed.
And if this is so, then in the case of moral defects too those
that are blamed will be ones for which we are responsible.

*It may be objected that moral discernment is a gift of
nature and cannot be acquired otherwise*

But suppose that somebody says 'Everyone aims at what
appears to him to be good, but over this appearance people
have no control. How the end appears to each individual
*depends on the nature of his character, whatever this may
be. Then if the individual is in a manner responsible for his
moral state, he will also be in a manner himself responsible
for his view of what is good; but if he is *not* responsible for
the former, then no wrongdoer is responsible for doing
wrong; he does it through ignorance of the end, because
he thinks that by this conduct he will achieve what is best
for him. His aiming at the end is not a matter of his choosing;
he must be born with it as a sort of ⟨moral⟩ vision to enable
him to judge correctly and choose what is truly good. A man
of good natural disposition is one who is well endowed in
this way, for he will possess as a natural gift the finest and
most important thing in the world, which cannot be had or
learnt from another; and to be well and rightly endowed in
this respect will be to have true and perfect goodness of disposition.'

Even so, virtue will be no more voluntary than vice

Now if this is a true statement of the facts, how will virtue be
more voluntary than vice? The end is envisaged and decided upon in the same way – whether through natural
ability or otherwise – by both good and bad; and it is with

reference to this end that they perform all their other actions, of whatever kind. So whether (a) the individual's view of the end – whatever it may be – is *not* supplied by nature, but depends partly on himself, or (b) the end *is* the gift of nature, but virtue is voluntary because the good man performs voluntarily all the means towards the end – in either case vice will be no less voluntary; because the bad man has just as much ⟨scope for⟩ independence in his *actions*, even if not in his choice of the end. So if, as is asserted, our virtues are voluntary (because we ourselves are in a sense partly responsible for our dispositions, and it is because we have a certain moral quality that we assume the end to be of a certain kind), our vices will be voluntary too; the cases are similar.

We have now given a general account of the virtues, stating in outline what their genus is, viz. that they are mean states and dispositions;[1] and that they of themselves enable their possessor to perform the same sort of actions as those by which they are acquired;[2] and that they are under our control and are voluntary;[3] and act as the right principle prescribes.[4] But our dispositions are not voluntary in the same sense that our actions are. Our actions are under our control from beginning to end, because we are aware of the individual stages, but we only control the beginning of our *dispositions; the individual stages of their development, as in the case of illness, are unnoticeable. They are, however, voluntary in the sense that it was originally in our power to exercise them in one way or the other.

Now to discuss the virtues one by one

Let us now resume our discussion of the virtues, taking them one by one, and explaining what each is, and with what sort of objects it is concerned, and in what way. At the same time it will become clear how many virtues there are.

1. 1105b19–1106a13.   2. 1104a27–b3.   3. 1113b3–1114b25.
4. 1103b31ff.

Courage: the right attitude towards feelings of fear and confidence. What we ought and ought not to fear

vi.   Let us begin with courage. It has already[1] been shown that it is a mean state in relation to feelings of fear and confidence. Obviously the things that we fear are fearful, and such things are, broadly speaking, evils; which is why some people define fear as an expectation of evil. Well, we do fear all evils – e.g. disgrace, poverty, sickness, friendlessness, death – but not all of these are considered to be the concern of the courageous man, because there are some of them that it is right and honourable to fear, and shameful not to fear, e.g. disgrace. The man who is afraid of it is upright and decent,[2] and the man who is not afraid of it is shameless; but he is sometimes called courageous by a transference of meaning, because he has a point of similarity to a courageous man: the latter is also a sort of fearless person.

Probably one ought not to fear poverty or disease, nor in general anything that is not the result of vice, or one's own fault; but a person who feels no fear about these things is not courageous either (although he too[3] is called so by analogy), because some people who are cowardly in the perils of war are liberal with their money and face the loss of it with equanimity. And surely a man is not a coward if he dreads brutality towards his wife and children, or envy, or anything of this kind; nor is he brave if he is undismayed at the prospect of a flogging.

What, then, are the terrors with which the courageous man is concerned? Surely the greatest, because nobody is better able to endure dreadful experiences. Now the most fearful thing of all is death; for it is the end, and it is assumed that for the dead there is no good or evil any more. But it may be thought that even death does not in all its forms afford scope for courage; e.g. death at sea, or in illness. Death in what circumstances, then? Surely in the

---

1. 1107a33ff.   2. *aidēmōn*: see Glossary.
3. Like the shameless man.

noblest; and this describes deaths in warfare, where the danger is greatest and most glorious. This is borne out by the honours paid to the fallen both in city-states and at the courts of monarchs. So in the strict sense of the word the courageous man will be one who is fearless in the face of an honourable death, or of some sudden threat of death; and it is in war that such situations chiefly occur. Of course the courageous man will be fearless *on the sea too (or in out-breaks of disease); but not in the same way as a seaman is, because the landsmen have given up all hope of being saved, and are revolted by the thought of such a death, but the sea-men have high hopes because of their experience. Also courage can be shown in situations that give scope for stout resistance or a glorious death; but in a disaster of this kind[1] there is no place for either.

Degrees of fear and fearfulness

vii.   What is terrible is not the same for all persons. There is a kind of thing that we describe as beyond human endur-ance, and this is fearful to any reasonable person; but things within the limits of human endurance differ in the magni-tude and intensity of the fear that they inspire (and similarly with things that inspire confidence). The courageous man, however, is undaunted, so far as is humanly possible; he will fear what it is natural for man to fear, but he will face it in the right way and as principle directs, for the sake of what is right and honourable;[2] for this is the end of virtue. But it is possible to fear these things too much or too little, and also to fear what is not fearful as if it were. One kind of error is to be afraid of the wrong thing, another to be afraid in the wrong way, and another at the wrong time, or with some other such qualification (and similarly with things that inspire confidence). The man who faces and fears (or similarly feels confident about) the right things for the right reason and in the right way and at the right time is cour-

1. The loss of a ship.   2. *kalos*: see Glossary.

ageous (for the courageous man feels and acts duly, and as principle directs); and the end of every activity is that which accords with the disposition corresponding to that activity. This is true of the courageous man. His courage is a noble thing, so its end is of the same kind, because the nature of any given thing is determined by its end. Thus it is for a right and noble motive that the courageous man faces the dangers and performs the actions appropriate to his courage.

Excessive fearlessness, rashness, and cowardice

The person who carries fearlessness too far has no distinctive name (we have noted above[1] that many types are nameless), but if he were afraid of nothing – not even of an earthquake or inundation, as they say of the Celts[2] – he would be a maniac or insensate. The man who exceeds in confidence about things that are fearful is rash. The rash man is considered to be both a boaster and a pretender to courage; at any rate he wishes to *seem* as the courageous man really *is* in his attitude towards fearful situations, and therefore imitates him where he can.[3] Hence such people are usually cowardly as well as rash, because while they make a show of confidence when circumstances permit, they cannot face anything fearful.

The man who exceeds in fearing is a coward. He fears the wrong things and in the wrong way, and all the other similar qualifications attach to him. *He also shows a deficiency in confidence; but he is more easily identified by his excessive reaction in cases of pain. Thus the coward is a despondent sort of person, because he is afraid of everything; whereas the courageous man is in the opposite case, because confidence is the mark of optimism.

Thus the coward, the rash man and the courageous man are all concerned with the same things, but differ in their attitudes towards them. The two former show excess and

1. 1107b2.　　　　2. Cf. *Eudemian Ethics* 1229b28 and Strabo vii. 293.
3. i.e. where there is no real danger.

deficiency, but the other has the right disposition and observes the mean. Rash people are impetuous, eager before danger arrives but shifty when it is actually present; whereas courageous ones are keen at the time of action but calm beforehand.

So, as we have said,[1] courage is a mean state in relation to things conducive to confidence or fear in the circumstances described;[2] it feels confidence or faces danger because this is a fine thing to do, or it is a disgrace not to do it. But to kill oneself to escape from poverty or love[3] or anything else that is distressing is not courageous but rather the act of a coward, because it shows weakness of character to run away from hardships, and the suicide endures death not because it is a fine thing to do but in order to escape from suffering.

Five dispositions that resemble courage

(1) Civic courage

viii. Such, then, is the nature of courage; but the name is also applied to five other kinds of behaviour under five heads.

Civic courage comes first because it is very like courage proper; for citizens[4] are considered to face their dangers not only because of the legal penalties and the disgrace, but also because of the honours. This is why those peoples are thought bravest among whom cowards are despised and brave men held in honour. Homer represents such characters, e.g. Diomede and Hector:

> Polydamas will be the first to cast reproach at me;[5]

and Diomede says:[6]

1. 1107a33ff, 1115a6ff.   2. i.e. in war: 1115a29ff.
3. Presumably unrequited or otherwise hopeless love.
4. As citizen soldiers.
5. *Iliad* xxii. 100. Hector is picturing what will happen if he declines Achilles' challenge.
6. *Iliad* viii. 148. Diomede (son of Tydeus) is reluctant to retire, because Hector may claim to have put him to flight.

> For one day Hector will proclaim among the host of Troy
> 'The son of Tydeus by my hand . . .'

This courage has the closest resemblance of all to courage as
described above,[1] because its ground is a moral virtue: a
proper sense of shame, and a desire for something noble
(that is, honour), and avoidance of reproach, which is a
disgrace. And one might place in the same rank those who
are compelled to face death by their commanders; but they
are inferior inasmuch as they do so not through shame but
through fear, and what they shun is not dishonour but pain.
Their officers compel them as Hector does:[2]

> That man of you that I shall mark skulking behind the lines –
> He shall not save his carcase from the dogs . . .

The same policy is followed by those who line their men up
in front of them[3] and beat them if they *give ground, and
those who post their men in front of trenches and other such
obstacles – they are all using compulsion. But one ought to
be brave not under compulsion but because it is a fine
thing.

(2) *Experience of risk*

Experience of particular kinds of risk is regarded as a form
of courage (this is why Socrates thought that courage is a
kind of knowledge[4]). This sort of courage is shown by different types of person in different kinds of danger, but in the
dangers of war it is shown by soldiers.[5] It is accepted that
there are many false alarms in war, of which these men are
very well aware from their own observation; and so they
appear to be brave, because other people do not know how
groundless the alarms are. Then their experience makes
them highly proficient in causing damage without suffering

1. Chs. vi. and vii.
2. An inaccurate quotation; cf. *Iliad* ii. 391–3 and xv.348–51.
3. Or 'give their men orders' (to stand firm).
4. Cf. Plato, *Laches* 195 and 199, *Protagoras* 350 and 360, and *Meno* 88;
but none of these passages quite justifies A.'s sweeping statement.
5. Professional mercenaries as distinct from citizen soldiers.

it, because they can use their weapons, and they carry the sort of arms that will be most effective both for attack and for defence.[1] So they are like armed fighting against un-armed men, and trained athletes against ordinary people; because in contests of this kind the best fighters are not the bravest men, but those who are strongest and fittest physic-ally. On the other hand when the danger is extreme and they are inferior in numbers and equipment it is the pro-fessional soldiers that turn coward; they are the first to flee, while the citizen troops die at their posts – as happened in the fighting at the temple of Hermes.[2] This is because to the latter running away is a disgrace, and death is preferable to saving their lives in such a way; but the others originally accepted the risk in the belief that they had the advantage, and when they find out their mistake they flee, because they fear death more than dishonour. But the courageous man is not like that.

(3) *Spirit or mettle*

Spirit[3] is also referred to courage, for those who act with spirit, like beasts charging those who have wounded them, are also considered to be courageous, because the courage-ous too are spirited (for spirit is very bold in the face of danger): hence Homer's phrases 'into their spirit he put strength' and 'rage he aroused and spirit' and 'bitter rage about his nostrils' and 'up boiled his blood';[4] for all these seem to indicate the rousing and impulse of the spirit. Courageous people act for a fine motive, and their spirit is an accessory; but beasts act under the influence of pain: it is because they have been injured or frightened; this is shown

1. In the fourth century light-armed mercenaries often defeated the hoplites or heavily-armed citizen infantry.

2. When Coronea was attacked in 353 B.C. the citizens, though deserted by their allies, shut themselves up in the town and resisted to the death.

3. *thūmos*: see Glossary.

4. Inaccurate quotations from *Iliad* xiv.151 or xvi.529, v.470 and *Odyssey* xxiv.318; the last is not in our text of Homer but occurs in Theocritus xx.15.

by the fact that in a forest [or marsh] they do not attack.[1]
Thus it does not mean that beasts are courageous simply because, impelled by pain and anger, they rush into danger,
blind to the risks they run; if this were so, even donkeys
would be brave when they are hungry, because they refuse
*to stop grazing even if you beat them.[2] (Adulterers, too, are
led on by their lust to do many reckless things.) The quasi-
courage that is due to spirit seems to be the most natural,
and if it includes deliberate choice and purpose it is considered to be courage.[3] Human beings, too, feel pain when
they get angry, and pleasure when they retaliate; but those
who fight for these reasons, although they may be good
fighters, are not courageous, because they are acting not
from a fine motive, nor on principle, but from feeling. Still,
they bear a close resemblance to the courageous.

(4) *Sanguineness or optimism*

Nor, indeed, are sanguine people courageous. It is because
they have often defeated many enemies that they are confident in danger. They are very similar to the courageous in
that both are confident; but whereas the courageous are
confident for the reasons stated above,[4] the sanguine are
confident because they think they are the best soldiers and
cannot lose (this is how people behave when they get drunk:
they become sanguine); but when the result does not turn
out as expected, they run away. But as we saw,[5] it is the
mark of a courageous man to face things that are terrible to
a human being, and that he can see are such, because it is a
fine act to face them and a disgrace not to do so. This is why
it is thought to be a better proof of courage to remain calm
and undismayed in sudden alarms than in those that are
foreseen: the action proceeds more directly from the moral
state, because it is less the result of preparation. One may
choose to face a foreseeable danger after calculation and re-

1. Because they have a chance to escape.
2. Cf. Homer, *Iliad* xi.557ff.
3. It does not fulfil all the conditions; cf. 1115b17–24.
4. 1115b 10–24ff.   5. Cf. previous note.

flection, but one faces sudden dangers only in virtue of the formed state of character.

(5) *Ignorance*

Those who act in ignorance, too, appear to be courageous. They are not far different from the sanguine, but they are inferior inasmuch as they have no self-confidence such as the sanguine have. Hence while the sanguine stand firm for a time, those who are under a misapprehension, if they find out or suspect that the situation is different from what they supposed, run away. This is just what happened to the Argives when they fell in with the Spartans under the impression that they were Sicyonians.[1]

We have now described the different kinds of courage and supposed courage.

Courage in relation to pleasure and pain

ix.   Courage is concerned with grounds for confidence and fear, but not to the same degree with both; it is more concerned with what is fearful, because the man who is composed in the thick of dangers and meets them in the right spirit is more truly courageous than the one who behaves similarly in encouraging circumstances. Indeed, as we have said,[2] people are called courageous for enduring pain. Hence courage implies the presence of pain, and it is rightly praised, because it is harder to bear pain than to abstain from pleasure. It may, of course, *be thought that the *end* of an act which involves courage is pleasant, but that this fact is obscured by the attendant circumstances, just as happens in athletic contests. The end or purpose of the boxers, i.e. the wreath and the honours, is pleasant; but it hurts to take punches if you are made of flesh and blood – it is painful, and so is all their laborious training. And because these hardships are so many, their object, being small ⟨by

1. At the battle of the Long Walls at Corinth, 392 B.C. (Xenophon, *Hellenica* IV.iv.10).

2. Not explicitly, but cf. 1115a17–24, b7–13, 1116a1.

comparison⟩, seems to entail no pleasure. Now if it is like this in the case of courage, death and wounds will be painful to the courageous man, and he will not willingly endure them; but endure them he will, because that is the fine thing to do, or because it is a disgrace not to endure them. And the more completely a man possesses virtue, and the happier he is, the more he will be distressed at the thought of death. For to such a man life is supremely worth living; and he is losing the greatest blessings, and he knows it; and this is a grievous thing. But that does not make him any less brave; he is probably even braver for it, because in preference to these blessings he chooses a gallant end in war. It is not true, then, of every virtue that the exercise of it is pleasurable, except in so far as one attains the end. Presumably it is quite possible that the best professional soldiers are made not out of men like this but of others who are less brave but have nothing apart from their lives to lose; because the latter are ready to meet dangers, and sell their lives for petty gains.

So much for our account of courage. In the light of what has been said it should not be difficult to grasp (in outline at any rate) what courage is.

Temperance or self-control, and the pleasures with which it is concerned

x. Next after courage let us say something about temperance,[1] because these two virtues are considered to belong to the irrational parts[2] of the soul. We have already said[3] that temperance is a mean state with regard to pleasures (for it is less concerned with pains, and in a different way[4]). Licentiousness[5] is shown in the same field. So let us now determine with what kind of pleasures they are concerned.

1. *sōphrosunē*; see Glossary.
2. Plato's view; A.'s psychological theory was slightly different (cf. 1102a26ff.).
3. 1107b4ff.   4. Cf. below, 1118b28ff.   5. *akolasia*; see Glossary.

Pleasures are either psychical or physical

We must first distinguish pleasures of the soul from pleasures of the body. Examples of the former are love of civic distinction[1] and love of learning. In either case when the subject enjoys what he loves it is not his body that is affected but rather his mind; and those who are concerned with pleasures of this sort are called neither temperate nor licentious. Similarly with all others who are concerned with pleasures that are not physical. Those who like to hear marvellous tales or to relate anecdotes or to spend their days in aimless gossip we call idle and talkative, but not *licentious; nor should we so describe those who are grieved at the loss of money or friends.

It is the pleasures of the body, then, that are the concern of temperance; but not even all of them. Those who enjoy the objects of sight, like colours and shapes and pictures, are called neither temperate nor licentious. It may be supposed, however, that even in the case of these pleasure can be felt in the right degree, or too much, or too little. Similarly with the objects of hearing. Nobody calls people licentious for taking an inordinate pleasure in listening to music or an actor's voice, nor temperate if their enjoyment was duly restrained. Nor do we speak in this way about those who enjoy smells, except those who do so by association.[2] We do not call those who enjoy the smell of apples or roses or incense licentious; we apply this description rather to those who enjoy the smell of perfume and savoury dishes, for these are what licentious people enjoy, because through them they are reminded of the objects of their desires. One can see that others too enjoy the smell of food when they are hungry; but the enjoyment of such things is characteristic of the licentious person, because to him they are objects of

1. Or, more simply, ambition (*philotīmia*).

2. Strictly *per accidens*, 'accidentally', in virtue of some non-essential attribute, as distinct from *per se*, 'in virtue of itself'.

desire.[1] Animals do not experience pleasure through their
senses either, except by association; it is not the smell of
hares that hounds enjoy, but the eating of them; and the
smell calls attention to their presence. Nor is it the lowing of
an ox that a lion enjoys, but the feeding on it. The reason
why he seems to enjoy the lowing is that it was through it
that he became aware that the ox was near. Similarly he
does not take pleasure in the sight of 'a deer or a wild goat',[2]
but in the fact that he is going to have a meal.

The grossest pleasures are those of taste and, above all, touch

Thus temperance and licentiousness are concerned with
such pleasures as are shared by animals too (which makes
them regarded as low and brutish). These are touch and
taste. But even taste seems to play a small part, if any.[3] The
function of taste is to distinguish flavours, as wine-tasters do,
or cooks who are seasoning dishes. But it is not exactly the
flavours that gratify, at least not the licentious person; it is
rather the enjoyment, which depends entirely upon touch,
whether in the case of food or of drink or of what is called
sex. This is why one gourmet[4] prayed that his throat might
become longer than a crane's; which shows that he took
pleasure in the actual *contact.

Thus the sense that gives scope to licentiousness is the one
that is most widely shared; and it would seem to be justly
liable to reproach, because it attaches to us not as men but as
animals. So to enjoy such sensations and find the greatest
satisfaction in them is brutish. The most refined pleasures of
touch are excepted – I mean those that are experienced at

1. Normal people only enjoy them when they are hungry; he always
enjoys them, because he is greedy.
2. Homer, *Iliad* iii.24.
3. In affecting temperance and licentiousness.
4. Philoxenus, cf. Athenaeus XII.viii.

sports centres through the means of heat and massage – because for the licentious person touch is concerned only with certain parts of the body, not with the whole.

Desires or appetites; self-indulgence and insensibility

xi. Desires[1] seem to be either general or particular and adventitious. For example, the desire for food is natural, since everyone who needs food desires it either in solid or in liquid form, and sometimes in both; and similarly with sexual intercourse when, in Homer's phrase, he is young and lusty.[2] But not everyone desires this or that particular kind of food or sex, or the same kind always; so that appetite seems to be a matter of personal taste. Nevertheless there is a natural element in it, because different things please different kinds of people,[3] and some kinds are more than averagely pleasing to everyone.

Now in the case of natural desires few people go wrong, and only in one way, in the direction of too much; because to eat or drink indiscriminately until one is full to bursting is to exceed in quantity one's natural limit, since the natural desire is merely a replenishment of the deficiency. (Hence such people are called 'belly-mad', because they fill their bellies more than they ought. Those who behave in this way are extremely crude types of humanity.) But with regard to particular pleasures many people go wrong in many ways. Some of those who are called 'lovers' of this or that go wrong in enjoying the wrong objects, others in enjoying things with abnormal intensity, or in the wrong way; and the licentious display excess in every form. They enjoy some things that it is wrong to enjoy, because they are odious; and where it is right to enjoy something, they enjoy it more than is right, or more than is normal.

Clearly, then, excess in respect of pleasures is licentious-

1. The word is *epithūmia*; see Glossary.   2. *Iliad* xxiv.130.

3. Age-groups, social classes, even nations; so it is not just a matter of personal taste.

ness, and a culpable thing. As for pains, the situation is not as it was in the case of courage: a person is not called temperate for enduring them and licentious for not doing so; the licentious man is so called for being unduly distressed at missing what is pleasant (thus even his pain is caused by pleasure), whereas the temperate man is so called for not being distressed by the absence of what is pleasant, or by abstinence from it. *Thus the licentious man desires all pleasant things, or the most pleasant; and he is so carried away by his desire that he chooses them before anything else. Hence he feels pain both when he fails to get them and when he desires them (because desire involves pain); and it seems preposterous to feel pain on account of pleasure.

Cases of deficiency in respect of pleasures, that is of enjoying them less than one ought, hardly occur; because such insensibility is sub-human. Even the lower animals discriminate between different foods, and enjoy some but not others. If there is any creature to whom nothing is pleasant and everything indifferent, he must be very far from being human; and because such a type hardly occurs, it has not secured itself a name.[1]

The temperate man holds a mean position with regard to pleasures. He enjoys neither the things that the licentious man enjoys most (he positively objects to them) nor wrong pleasures in general, nor does he enjoy any pleasure violently; he is not distressed by the absence of pleasures, nor does he desire them – or if he does, he desires them moderately, and not more than is right, or at the wrong time, or in general with any other such qualification. But such pleasures as conduce to health and bodily fitness he will try to secure in moderation and in the right way; and also all other pleasures that are not incompatible with these, or dishonourable,[2] or beyond his means. For the man who disregards these limitations sets too high a value on such pleasures; but the temperate man is not like that: he appreciates them as the right principle directs.

---

1. But cf. 1107b8.   2. 'Contrary to what is *kalos*'.

Licentiousness is more voluntary than cowardice

xii.   Licentiousness is more like a voluntary thing than cowardice. The former is caused by pleasure and the latter by pain, of which the one is to be chosen[1] and the other avoided; and pain distracts the sufferer and impairs his natural state, but pleasure has no such effect; therefore licentiousness is more voluntary. Hence it is also more reprehensible, since it is easier to train oneself to resist pleasures, because there are plenty of such opportunities in life, and the methods of habituation involve no danger; but with terrors the reverse is the case. It might seem that cowardice[2] is not voluntary in the same way that particular instances of cowardice are, because *it* involves no pain, but *they* so distract a person with pain that he even throws away his weapons and disgraces himself in every other way; and for this reason they are considered to be compulsive. But for the licentious man, on the contrary, particular acts are voluntary, since he does them from desire and appetite; but the condition as a whole is less so, because nobody *desires* to be licentious.

Licentious people are like spoilt children

We apply the name of licentiousness[3] to the faults of children too, because *they bear a certain resemblance to it. Which is called after the other makes no difference for our present purpose, but obviously the later use must come from the earlier.[4] The metaphor seems not to be a bad one, because restraint is necessary for anything that has low[5] appetites

1. In general; not, of course, invariably.
2. As a fully developed state.   3. See Glossary s.v. *akolasia*.
4. Or perhaps rather 'the (logically) posterior . . . from the prior'. Presumably he means that the word was first used in its literal sense 'lack of restraint' to describe children.
5. *aischros*.

and a marked capacity for growth; and these qualities are possessed in the highest degree by desire and a child. For children too live as their desires impel them, and it is in them that the appetite for pleasant things is strongest; so unless this is rendered docile and submissive to authority it will pass all bounds. For in an irrational being the appetite for what gives it pleasure is insatiable and indiscriminate, and the exercise of the desire increases its innate tendency; and if these appetites are strong and violent, they actually drive out reason. So they must be moderate and few, and in no way opposed to the dictates of principle – this is what we mean by 'docile' and 'restrained' – and just as the child ought to live in accordance with the directions of his tutor,[1] so the desiderative element in us ought to be controlled by rational principle. Thus the desiderative element of the temperate man ought to be in harmony with the rational principle; because both have the same object: the attainment of what is admirable.[2] Also the temperate man desires the right things in the right way and at the right time, and this also is prescribed by rational principle.

So much for our account of temperance.

1. The *paidagōgos*, a slave with special responsibility for the child's general education.

2. The word is *kalos*, used here in its widest sense.

IV

OTHER MORAL VIRTUES

Liberality: the right attitude towards money

i.   Let us next speak about liberality.[1] It seems to be the
intermediate disposition with regard to money; because it
is not in military affairs nor in the same sphere as temperance nor again in legal decisions that a person is praised as
liberal, but with regard to the giving and receiving of
money – more particularly in the giving of it (by 'money' we
mean everything of which the value is measured in terms of
some currency). Prodigality and illiberality,[2] too, are cases
of excess and deficiency in respect of money. We always
ascribe illiberality to persons who take money too seriously:
but we sometimes apply the term prodigality with a wider
connotation, because we call prodigal those who are incontinent and squander their money on self-indulgence
(hence they are considered to be the worst of all characters,
because they possess several vices at the same time). But
they are not properly so described. 'Prodigal' means a
person who has one definite vice, *that of wasting his substance; because a prodigal man is one who is ruined by
himself,[3] and the wasting of a man's property is considered
to be a sort of self-destruction, on the ground that his
possessions are the source of his livelihood. This, then, is the
sense in which we here understand the term prodigality.

Things that have a use can be used both well and badly;
and wealth is a thing that can be used. The person who
makes the best use of any given thing is the person who
possesses the relevant virtue; therefore that person will also
make the best use of wealth who possesses the virtue relevant
to wealth; and this is the liberal man. The use of money is
considered to consist in spending and giving; receiving and

1. *eleutheriotēs*.   2. *asotia* and *aneleutheria*.
3. The word *asōtos* means literally 'not saved' or 'beyond saving'.

142

keeping it are more a matter of acquisition. Hence it is more the mark of the liberal man to give to the right people than to receive from the right people, or not to receive from the wrong people; because virtue consists more in doing good than in receiving it, and more in doing fine actions than in refraining from disgraceful ones. It is not hard to see that doing good and performing fine actions go along with giving, while receiving good or not acting disgracefully goes with receiving. Also gratitude is directed towards the person who gives, not towards the person who refuses to take: and this is even more true of praise. Also it is easier not to take than to give; for people are less inclined to give up what is their own than not to take what belongs to somebody else. Again, those who give are called liberal, but those who do not take[1] are praised not for liberality but quite as much for justice; and those who do take are not praised at all. Of all those who are called virtuous the liberal are probably the best liked, because they are helpful; and their help consists in giving.

Virtuous actions are fine, and are done for a fine end; so the liberal man too will give with a fine end in view, and in the right way; because he will give to the right people, and the right amounts, and at the right time, and will observe all the other conditions that accompany right giving. And he will have pleasure, or at least no pain, in doing this; because a virtuous act is pleasant or painless, but certainly not painful. The man who gives to the wrong people, or not for a fine end but for some other reason, must be called not liberal but some other name; and so must the man whom it hurts to give, because he would rather keep his money than do a fine deed, and that is not the way of the liberal man.

Nor will he accept money from a wrong source; because such acceptance is inconsistent with indifference to money. Nor again can he be inclined to ask for it; because it is not in the character of one who confers benefits to receive them readily. But he will accept money from the right source, e.g. from his *own property; not because it is a fine thing to do

1. What is not due to them.

so, but because it is necessary so that he may have something to give. Nor will he neglect his own property, because he wants to help people by its means. He will avoid giving to any and everybody, so that he may have something to give to the right people at the right time and in circumstances in which it is a fine thing to do. But it is especially characteristic of the liberal man to carry giving too far, so as to leave himself less than his due; because it is the nature of the liberal man not to regard his own interest.

Liberality is recognized as such in relation to the giver's resources, because the liberality of an act depends not upon the number of the things given but upon the disposition of the giver; and this makes him give according to his means. There is no reason why a man who gives less than another should not be more liberal, if his resources are smaller. People who have inherited their estate instead of acquiring it themselves are supposed to be more liberal, because they have not experienced shortage of money, and all people are fonder of what they have produced themselves – just like parents and poets.[1]

It is not easy for a liberal man to be rich, since he is neither acquisitive nor retentive of money, but is ready to part with it, and does not value it for itself, but only with a view to giving. (This is why Fortune is criticized on the ground that it is the people who deserve wealth most that have it least. But it is not unreasonable that this should be so, since it is not possible to have money without taking trouble to have it – just as with anything else.) On the other hand the liberal man will not give to the wrong persons, nor at the wrong time, nor in any other wrong circumstances, since if he did he would no longer be acting in accordance with his liberality; and if he spent money upon the wrong objects, he would have none left to spend on the right ones. For (as we have said[2]) the liberal man is the one who spends in proportion to his means, and on the right objects; and the

1. As the Greek word for 'poet' really means 'maker' (cf. Scots), the sense may be 'creative artist'; cf. 1168a1.
2. All these points are made earlier in the chapter.

man who spends excessively is prodigal. This is why we do not call despots prodigal; because it does not seem that the multitude of their possessions could be easily surpassed by their gifts and expenditure.[1]

Since liberality is an intermediate disposition with regard to the giving and receiving of money, the liberal man will not only give and spend the right amount on the right objects, in great and small matters alike, and do it with pleasure; he will also accept the right amounts from the right sources. For since his virtue is an intermediate condition in respect of both giving and receiving, he will do both in the right way, because right giving implies right receiving, whereas wrong receiving is incompatible with it. Activities that imply one another can take place in the same subject, but those that are incompatible *obviously cannot.

If the liberal man finds himself spending inconsistently with what is right and proper, he will be distressed (but moderately, i.e. in the right degree); because it is the nature of virtue to be pleased and pained at the right objects and in the right manner. Again, the liberal man is easy to do business with, because he can be treated unfairly, being indifferent to money, and more vexed if he has not paid what he ought than annoyed if he has paid something that there was no need to pay; he does not approve of Simonides' saying.[2] But the prodigal man goes wrong in these circumstances too; he feels neither pleasure nor pain at the right degree – but this will become clearer as we proceed.

Prodigality has certain merits and is far better than illiberality

We have already stated[3] that prodigality and illiberality are cases of excess and deficiency, and this in two respects, in

1. Cf. 1121a17f.
2. Perhaps an allusion to the anecdote quoted at *Rhetoric* 1391a8ff. Asked whether it was better to be rich or wise, Simonides replied 'Rich; because I see the wise hanging around rich men's doors.'
3. 1119b27ff.

giving and in receiving (spending we include under giving). Prodigality goes too far in giving and not receiving, and falls short in receiving; and illiberality falls short in giving and goes too far in receiving, but only in the case of small sums.[1] Thus the faults of prodigality are hardly ever found together (since it is not easy to give to everybody if one receives from nobody, because the means of a private person – as the prodigal man is assumed to be[2] – are soon exhausted). However, such a person would seem to be not a little better than the illiberal man: he is easily cured both by age and by poverty, and is capable of attaining to the mean, because he has the attribute of the liberal man, since he gives without receiving; but he does neither in the right degree or manner. If he could be trained or otherwise changed in this respect, he would be liberal, because he will give to the right people, and will not receive from the wrong sources. For this reason too he is not considered to be bad in character, because to carry giving and not receiving too far is the mark not of a worthless or low person but of a foolish one. The man who is prodigal in this way is considered to be a much better person than the illiberal man; both for the reasons given above and because he benefits a number of people, whereas the other benefits nobody; not even himself.

The dangers of prodigality

However, as we have said,[3] most prodigal people also take from the wrong sources, and on this account they are illiberal; they become acquisitive because they want to spend money and cannot do so readily, since their resources quickly run out; so they are forced to get a supply *from elsewhere. What is more, since they care nothing for honourable conduct, they take money irresponsibly from

1. On a larger scale illiberality (meanness) becomes positive injustice (dishonesty).
2. Cf. 1120b25.   3. Only by implication; cf. 1121a25.

any source; because they are eager to give, and it makes no difference to them how or from where they get it. For this very reason their gifts are not liberal either, because they are not fine, nor given from a fine motive, nor in the right degree. Sometimes they enrich those who ought to be poor; and while they would not give anything to people of respectable character, they heap gifts on flatterers or purveyors of some other pleasure. Hence most of them are licentious as well; because, spending freely as they do, they squander their money on forms of self-indulgence, and as they do not direct their lives towards an honourable end, they fall into sensuality. Such is the state into which the prodigal person declines if left without supervision; although if he gets proper care he may attain to the mean, i.e. the right disposition.

Illiberality or meanness is a much more serious state

As for illiberality, it is both incurable (because it seems to be caused by old age and disability of any kind) and more deeply rooted in human nature than prodigality is, because most people are avaricious rather than open-handed. Also it is wide-spread, and takes many shapes, because there seem to be various forms of illiberality. For since it consists in two faults, deficiency in giving and excess in receiving, it does not come in its entirety to everyone, but sometimes it divides itself; and one set of people goes too far in receiving, and the other falls short in giving. The people who come under such descriptions as 'stingy', 'grasping' and 'niggardly' are all deficient in giving, but do not covet other people's property, and have no desire to get it; some through a certain sense of fairness and avoidance of anything dishonourable (because some people are supposed, or at any rate profess, to take care of their money for fear of being forced some day to do something dishonourable – to this class belong the skinflint and everyone else of this kind; he is so called from his extreme reluctance to part with anything to anybody); others again hold off from other people's property from fear, on the ground that it is not easy for anyone to take other people's property without their taking his; so they content themselves with neither taking nor giving.

The other class[1] go to excess in receiving by taking anything from anybody; for instance, those who follow illiberal occupations, like ponces and all people of that kind; and moneylenders who make small loans at a high rate of interest; *for all these receive more than is right, and not from the right sources. Their common characteristic is obviously their sordid avarice, because they all put up with a bad reputation for the sake of gain – and a small gain at that. I say this because we do not call illiberal those who wrongly take large sums from wrong sources, e.g. despots who sack cities and plunder temples – they are more properly called wicked and impious and unjust. But the card-sharper[2] and the clothes-stealer[3] belong to the illiberal class, because they are sordidly avaricious: it is for gain that both types follow their profession and submit to a bad reputation, the one[4] accepting the severest risks for the sake of their pilferings, the other profiting at the expense of their friends, to whom they ought to give; so both are sordidly avaricious, because they want to make gain from a wrong source. All such ways of obtaining money are illiberal.

Illiberality is naturally spoken of as the contrary of liberality, for not only is it a worse evil than prodigality, but more people err in its direction than in that of prodigality as we have described it.[5] So much for our account of liberality and the vices that are opposed to it.

1. See above, b20f.   2. Literally 'dicer'.
3. Or 'pickpocket'; any petty thief.   4. The clothes-stealer.
5. 1119b34–1120a3, 1121a8–b12.

Magnificence or munificence is a special kind of liberality

ii.   Our next task, it would seem, is to discuss magnificence,[1] because this too is regarded as a virtue that has to do with money. But unlike liberality it does not extend to all financial transactions, but only to such as involve expenditure. In these it surpasses liberality in scale, because (as its very name implies) it is befitting expenditure on a large scale. But the largeness is relative; for the outlay is not the same for the man who maintains a warship as it is for one who leads a delegation to a festival.[2] So the suitability is relative to the agent himself, and to the circumstances and the object of his expenditure. The man who spends duly in small or moderate transactions, as the poet says

Oft to the wanderer I would give,[3]

is not called magnificent – only the one who does so on a grand scale; because although the magnificent man is liberal, the liberal man is not necessarily magnificent.

The deficiency of this sort of disposition is called pettiness and the excess vulgarity, lack of taste, and any other such description. They show excess not in the amount that they spend on right objects but in ostentatious outlay in wrong circumstances and in a wrong manner. But we will speak of them later.[4]

Magnificence is a sort of artistry

The magnificent man is a sort of connoisseur; he has an eye for fitness, and can spend large sums with good taste (for as *we said at the beginning,[5] a disposition is determined by

1. *megaloprepeia*; see Glossary.
2. Two examples of 'liturgies' or public services at Athens; see Appendix I.
3. Homer, *Odyssey* xvii.420 (said by Odysseus disguised as a beggar who was once rich).
4. 1123a19ff.   5. Cf. 1103a26ff., 1104a27ff.

its activities and objects); so his outlay will be large, and appropriate. Then the results must be similar, for only so will there be an outlay that is large and appropriate to the results. So the result must be worthy of the expense, and the expense worthy of the result, or even in excess of it. The motive of the magnificent man in making such outlays will be fine, because this is a feature common to all the virtues. Moreover he will spend gladly and generously, because precise reckoning of the cost is petty. He will consider how he can achieve the finest and most appropriate result rather than how much it will cost and how it can be done most cheaply. It follows that the magnificent man must also be liberal. For the liberal man too will spend the right amounts and in the right manner; but it is in fulfilling these conditions (which are also the concern of liberality) that the magnificent man shows his magnitude or greatness;[1] he will produce a more magnificent result[2] with the same outlay. For the excellence of an achievement is not the same as that of a possession: the possession that we prize most is that which is most valuable, e.g. gold; but the achievement is the one that is great and splendid (because the contemplation of such a thing excites one's admiration, and magnificence is an object of admiration), and magnificence in an achievement is excellence on a grand scale.

Magnificence requires some wealth, although the appropriate outlay depends upon circumstances

Now there are some kinds of expenditure that we describe as honourable[3], e.g. services paid to the gods – votive offerings, buildings and sacrifices – and similarly with anything of a religious nature; and all objects of public-spirited

1. A. is thinking partly of the grand scale on which he gives, and partly also of the part of the word *megaloprepeia* which means 'great' (cf. 1122a22f.).
2. Than the merely liberal man.   3. i.e. deserving of recognition.

ambition, e.g. in any case where it is thought to be a duty to make a fine show by the provision of a chorus,[1] or the maintenance of a warship, or even by entertaining the whole city at a banquet. But in every case (as we have said[2]) the expenditure is related to the position and resources of the agent; because it must be worthy of these, and appropriate not only to the result produced but also to the man who produces it. Hence a poor man cannot be magnificent, because he has not the means to meet heavy expenses suitably; and anyone who attempts to do so is foolish, because he is spending more than is due and right, and to be virtuous an act must be done in the correct way. But such expenditure befits those who have appropriate resources, acquired either by themselves or from ancestors or connections, and persons of noble birth or great reputation or other such qualities, because these all involve grandeur and distinction. These are the primary requirements for the magnificent man, and it is chiefly in outlays of this sort that magnificence is exercised (as we have said[3]), because they are the grandest and most highly esteemed. But it is shown also on private occasions *that are unique, such as a wedding or something of that sort, or any event that excites the interest of the whole community, or of people in high positions; or entertainments to mark the arrival or departure of foreign guests, or the exchange of complimentary presents; for the magnificent man spends not upon himself but upon public objects, and his gifts have some resemblance to votive offerings.[4] It is also characteristic of him to furnish his house in a way suitable to his wealth (because even this is a kind of ornament), and to spend his money for preference upon results that are long-lasting (because these are the finest), and in every set of circumstances to spend what is appropriate (because the same expenditure is not equally due to gods and men, nor is the same outlay proper in the case of a temple as in that of a tomb). And since the greatness of any expenditure depends

1. See Appendix I.   2. 1122a24.   3. 1122b19ff.
4. These usually took the form of public monuments.

upon the kind of object for which it was incurred; and while the most magnificent expenditure generally[1] is that which is great and applied to a great object, in each given case it is that which is great relatively to that case; and greatness in the effect produced is different from greatness in the expenditure (because a really fine ball or cup[2] is magnificent as a present for a child, although its value is slight and unworthy of a liberal person): it is therefore the mark of the magnificent man, whatever kind of result he is producing, to produce it magnificently (because such a result is not easily surpassed), and to make it worthy of what he spent on it.

Vulgarity and pettiness

Such, then, is the magnificent man. The man who goes to excess and is vulgar exceeds (as we have said)[3] by spending more than he ought. He uses trivial occasions to spend large sums of money and make a jarring display: e.g. by entertaining the members of his club[4] as if they were wedding-guests, and (if he is financing a comedy) by bringing on the chorus in purple robes at their first entrance, as they do at Megara.[5] And all this he will do not from a fine motive but to show off his wealth, expecting to be admired for this sort of conduct; spending little where he ought to spend much, and much where he ought to spend little.

On the other hand the petty man will fall short in all respects. After spending vast sums he will spoil the beauty of the effect by some trifling detail; he hesitates over everything that he does, considering how he can spend the least money, and lamenting over that, and assuming that he is doing everything on a larger scale than the occasion demands.

1. This must be the sense, whatever reading is adopted.
2. Really 'oil-flask', a toilet accessory. 3. 1122a31.
4. A group of friends who either brought their own food to a shared meal or took turns to act as host.
5. See Appendix I.

These dispositions are vices, but they do not actually bring disrepute, because they are neither harmful to one's neighbours nor particularly offensive.

Magnanimity is the proper estimation of one's own worth in relation to the highest honours

iii.   Greatness of soul,[1] as the very name suggests, is concerned with things that are great, and we must first grasp of what sort these are. It *makes no difference whether we consider the disposition or the person who corresponds to it. Well, a person is considered to be magnanimous if he thinks that he is worthy of great things, provided that he *is* worthy of them; because anyone who esteems his own worth unduly is foolish, and nobody who acts virtuously is foolish or stupid. The magnanimous man, then, is as we have described him. The man who is worthy of little consideration and thinks that he is such is temperate,[2] but not magnanimous, because magnanimity implies greatness, just as beauty implies a well-developed body: i.e. small people can be neat and well-proportioned, but not beautiful.[3] The man who thinks that he is worthy of great things although he is not worthy of them is conceited; but not everybody is conceited who has too high an opinion of his own worth. On the other hand the man who has too low an opinion is pusillanimous: and it makes no difference whether his worth is great or moderate or little, if his opinion of it is too low. Indeed the man whose worth is great might be regarded as especially pusillanimous, because what would his behaviour be if his worth were not so great? So although the

1. *megalopsuchia*: magnanimity, proper pride, self-respect – there is no real English equivalent for this very upper-class Greek virtue. The description is based, as usual, upon common opinion, and A. accepts the ideal, on the whole, sympathetically (although with an occasional laugh up his sleeve); indeed it underlies his own doctrine of self-love in Book IX.

2. In the popular sense of 'moderate'.

3. He is thinking of the beauty of the male athlete.

magnanimous man is an extreme as regards the greatness of his claims, as regards its rectitude he is a mean, because he estimates himself at his true worth. The others show excess and deficiency.

If, then, the magnanimous man makes, and deservedly makes, great claims, and especially the greatest claims, he must have one special object in view. Now when one speaks of worth, it is in relation to external goods; and we should assume the greatest of these to be that which we render to the gods, and which is most desired by the eminent, and is the prize for the finest achievements; and that which answers this description is honour, because it is clearly the greatest external good. So the magnanimous man has the right attitude towards honours and dishonours. Indeed it is apparent even without argument that magnanimous people are concerned with honour, because it is honour above all that they claim as their due, and deservedly. The pusillanimous man, on the other hand, falls short in comparison both with his own merit and with the claim of the magnanimous man; and the conceited man goes too far in comparison with his own merit, but does not exceed the magnanimous man.[1]

Since the magnanimous man has the greatest deserts, he must be the best man of all; because the better a man is the greater his deserts are, and the best man's deserts are the greatest. So the truly magnanimous man must be good. It would seem that the magnanimous man is characterized by greatness in every virtue. It would not be at all fitting for him to run away at top speed,[2] or to do a wrong; for what motive could induce one so imperturbable[3] to behave disgracefully? If one considers all the various departments of conduct it will be obvious that the idea of a magnanimous man's not being good is utterly ridiculous. Besides, he could not be worthy of honour if he were bad, because honour is

1. i.e. his (undeserved) claim does not exceed the other's (deserved) claim.

2. 'With arms waving'.

3. 'One to whom nothing is great'; cf. 1125a3, 15.

the prize of virtue, and is rendered *to the good. So magnanimity seems to be a sort of crown of the virtues, because it enhances them and is never found apart from them. This makes it hard to be truly magnanimous, because it is impossible without all-round excellence.[1]

It is chiefly with honours and dishonours, then, that the magnanimous man is concerned. At great honours bestowed by responsible persons he will feel pleasure, but only a moderate one, because he will feel that he is getting no more than his due, or rather less, since no honour can be enough for perfect excellence. Nevertheless he will accept such honours, on the ground that there is nothing greater that they can give him. But honour conferred by ordinary people for trivial reasons he will utterly despise, because that sort of thing is beneath his dignity. And similarly with dishonour, because it cannot rightfully attach to him.

Magnanimity in relation to other external goods

It is chiefly with honours, then (as we have just said[2]), that the magnanimous man is concerned; but he will also be moderately disposed towards wealth, power, and every kind of good and bad fortune, however it befalls him: that is, he will neither be overjoyed at good nor over-distressed at bad fortune, since he does not regard even honour as a very great thing. For power and wealth are desirable for the honour that they bring – at any rate those who possess them wish for honour by their means. So the man who thinks little even of honour will think little of any other advantage. This is why magnanimous people are thought to be supercilious.

The advantages of fortune are also supposed to contribute something to this disposition; for people of high birth or great power or wealth are felt to deserve honour, because they are in a position of superiority, and anything that is

1. *kalokāgathia*, 'beauty and goodness', physical and moral excellence.
2. In the paragraph above.

superior in something good is held in greater honour. So
these advantages too make their owners more magnanimous,[1]
because they are held in honour by some people. In real
truth only the good man ought to be honoured; but the
possessor of both qualifications[2] is felt to deserve additional
honour. As for those who have the aforesaid advantages
without possessing virtue, they neither have a just claim to
great honours nor are rightly called magnanimous, because
these conditions are impossible without complete virtue.
And the possessors of the said advantages also become supercilious and overbearing, because without virtue it is not easy
to bear the gifts of fortune inoffensively; so being unable *to
cope with them, and supposing themselves to be superior to
everyone else, they despise other people, and behave as
the fancy takes them. For they imitate the magnanimous
man, although they are not like him, and they can only behave in this way where imitation is possible; so they do not
perform virtuous acts, but they do despise other people. The
magnanimous man's disdain is justifiable, because his estimate is true; but most people's disdain is capricious.

A portrait of the magnanimous man

The magnanimous man does not take petty risks, nor does he
court danger, because there are few things that he values
highly; but he takes great risks, and when he faces danger he
is unsparing of his life, because to him there are some circumstances in which it is not worth living. He is disposed to
confer benefits, but is ashamed to accept them, because the
one is the act of a superior and the other that of an inferior.
When he repays a service he does so with interest, because in
this way the original benefactor will become his debtor and
beneficiary. People of this kind are thought to remember the
benefits that they have conferred, but not those that they
have received (because the beneficiary is inferior to the

1. i.e. increase their self-esteem.
2. Both goodness and advantages.

benefactor, and the magnanimous man wants to be superior), and to enjoy being reminded of the former, but not of
the latter – which is why Thetis does not recount her services to Zeus,[1] and why the Spartans did not mention theirs
to the Athenians, but only the benefits that they had received.[2] Another mark of the magnanimous man is that he
never, or only reluctantly, makes a request, whereas he is
eager to help others. He is haughty towards those who are influential and successful, but moderate towards those who
have an intermediate position in society, because in the
former case to be superior is difficult and impressive, but in
the latter it is easy; and to create an impression at the expense of the former is not ill-bred, but to do so among the
humble is vulgar – like using one's strength against the weak.
He does not enter for popular contests, or ones in which
others distinguish themselves; he hangs back or does nothing
at all, except where the honour or the feat is a great one.
The tasks that he undertakes are few, but grand and celebrated. He is bound to be open in his likes and dislikes (because concealment, i.e. caring less for the truth than for
what people think, is a mark of timidity), and to speak and
act straightforwardly (his superior attitude makes him out-
spoken and candid – except for what he says in irony[3] to the
general public); and he cannot bear to live in dependence
upon somebody else, *except a friend, because such conduct
is servile; which is why all flatterers are of the lowest class,
and humble people are flatterers. He is not prone to express
admiration, because nothing is great in his eyes.[4] He does
not nurse resentment, because it is beneath a magnanimous
man to remember things against people, especially wrongs;

1. Not in detail, as Achilles advised her, but in general terms (Homer,
Iliad i.394ff., 503ff.).

2. A puzzling allusion. The Aldine scholiast refers it to Callisthenes'
account of an appeal for help against a Theban attack (presumably
that of 369 B.C.), but Xenophon's report (*Hellenica* VI.v.33f.) does not
square with Aristotle's.

3. Cf. 1108a19–22, and below, 1127a22f., b22ff. Here 'irony' seems
better than 'understatement' (*eirōneia*).

4. Cf. 1123b32, and a15 below.

it is more like him to overlook them. He does not care for personal conversation; he will talk neither about himself nor about anyone else, because he does not care to be complimented himself or to hear others criticized; nor again is he inclined to pay compliments. For this reason he is not abusive either, not even of his enemies, unless he intends to be insulting. In troubles that are unavoidable or of minor importance he is the last person to complain or ask for help, because such an attitude would imply that he took them seriously. He is the sort of person to prefer possessions that are beautiful but unprofitable to those that are profitable and useful, because this is more consistent with self-sufficiency. The accepted view of the magnanimous man is that his gait is measured, his voice deep, and his speech unhurried. For since he takes few things seriously, he is not excitable, and since he regards nothing as great, he is not highly strung; and those are the qualities that make for shrillness of voice and hastiness of movement.

Pusillanimity and vanity

Such, then, is the magnanimous man. The one who errs through deficiency is pusillanimous, and the one who does so through excess is conceited. These too[1] are generally thought of not as bad (since they do no harm) but as mistaken. The pusillanimous man is one who, though deserving, deprives himself of the advantages that he deserves, and through not claiming his deserts conveys the impression of having some defect, and even of not knowing his own quality – because otherwise he would have tried to secure his deserts, being to his advantage. Such people are regarded not as foolish but rather as diffident; and having this sort of reputation seems to make them even worse; for people of every kind try to secure what they are entitled to, and these hold back from fine actions and pursuits, and similarly from external goods, because they feel unworthy of them. Con-

1. Cf. 1123a31ff.

ceited people, on the other hand, are foolish, being ignorant of their own limitations, and that quite obviously; because they attempt honourable undertakings for which they are not qualified, and then are exposed as incompetent. Also they are affected in their dress and manner, and so on. And they want their successes to be noticed, and make them the subject of their talk, hoping in this way to win respect. Pusillanimity is more opposed to magnanimity than vanity, because it is both a more common fault and a worse one.[1] Magnanimity is concerned with honour on the grand scale, as we have said.[2]

Attitudes towards honour on a small scale: ambition, unambitiousness, and the nameless mean

iv. *It seems, however, that in the sphere of honour too there is a kind of virtue, as we said at the beginning,[3] which may be regarded as related to magnanimity in much the same way as liberality is to magnificence. For both these states are unconcerned with greatness, but dispose us in the right way towards matters of moderate or little importance. Just as in the receiving and giving of money there is a mean and an excess and a deficiency, so also in the desire for honour there are degrees of too much and too little, and a right source and a right manner. We blame the man who loves honour[4] for seeking it too much or from the wrong source; and the man who is indifferent to it for not choosing to be honoured even for fine actions. But there are occasions when we praise the man who loves honour as being manly and noble-minded, and the man who is indifferent to it as being moderate and temperate (as we said in our first dis-

1. No doubt he is thinking of the inhibiting effect of diffidence in public life.
2. 1107b26; cf. 1123a34f., b13–24, 1124a4–13.
3. 1107b24ff.
4. i.e. the ambitious man, *philotimos*; but in this passage the more literal rendering suits the argument better.

cussion[1]). Since people are called lovers of so-and-so in more than one sense, obviously we do not always apply the description 'lover of honour' to the same quality; sometimes we apply it in a good sense to one who loves honour more than most people do, and sometimes in a bad sense to one who loves it more than is right. As the mean state of character has no name, the extremes dispute possession, so to speak, of the vacant territory. But where there are excess and deficiency there is also a mean; and people desire honour both more and less than is right, so there is also a *right* degree of desire. Accordingly it is this disposition, which is an intermediate attitude towards honour, that is commended – although it has no name. Compared with love of honour it appears to be indifference to honour, and vice versa; and compared with both it appears to be in a sense both. This seems to happen in the case of the other virtues too; but here the fact that the man has no name makes the extremes seem to be opposed to each other.[2]

The right disposition towards anger is something like patience; the excess is irascibility, the deficiency has no real name

v.   Patience[3] is an intermediate state with regard to anger. The mean is really nameless, and the extremes nearly so; but we apply the name patience to the mean, although it tends towards describing the deficiency, which also lacks a name. The excess might be called a sort of irascibility, because the feeling is anger; and this is produced in us by a variety of causes.

The man who gets angry at the right things and with the right people, and also in the right way and at the right time and for the right length of time, is commended; so this person will be patient, inasmuch as patience is commendable, because a patient person tends to be unperturbed and

1. 1107b24ff.   2. With nothing intermediate between them.
3. *prāotēs*: see Glossary.

not carried away by his feelings, but indignant only in the
way and on the grounds and for the *length of time that his
principle[1] prescribes. He is considered to err, if at all, on the
side of deficiency, because the patient man is not revengeful;
he is more inclined to be forgiving. The deficiency – whether
it is a sort of imperturbability or whatever else it may be – is
blamed, because those who do not get angry at things that
ought to make them angry are considered to be foolish, and
so are those who do not get angry in the right way or at the
right time or with the right people. Such a person seems to
be deficient in perceptivity and sensitivity, and (because he
does not get angry) incapable of defending himself; and to
put up with insults to oneself, and overlook those done to
one's friends, is regarded as servile. The excess occurs in
respect of all the circumstances: with the wrong people,
for the wrong reasons, more than is right, too quickly, and
for too long a time; but of course these conditions do not all
attach to the same subject. This could not be, because evil
destroys even itself, and if it is unmitigated, becomes intoler-
able.

Grades of irascibility

Irascible people get angry quickly and with the wrong
people and at the wrong things and too violently, but they
stop quickly, and this is the best thing about them. The
reason for it is that they do not repress their anger but, being
quick-tempered, vent it openly and then drop it. The
hypercholeric are exceedingly quick-tempered, and get
angry at anything on any occasion; hence their name.
Bitter people are hard to reconcile, and keep up their
anger for a long time, because they suppress their animosity.[2]
Relief comes only with retaliation; for revenge provides
release from anger by substituting pleasure for pain. In
default of this they still labour under the weight of resentment; because owing to its concealment nobody helps to

1. *logos*.   2. Or 'temper': *thūmos*.

persuade the sufferer out of it, and it takes him time to digest his anger internally. People of this kind cause a great deal of trouble to themselves and their closest friends. We call people irritable if they get annoyed at the wrong things, and too much, and for too long a time, and if they are only pacified by inflicting vengeance or punishment.

The right disposition is hard to define precisely

It is the excess that we treat as more directly opposed to patience. For one thing, it occurs more commonly (because revenge is more natural to man ⟨than forgiveness⟩), and irritable people are worse to live with. But our present discussion shows the truth of what we said before:[1] that it is not easy to define how and with whom and for what reasons and how long one ought to be angry, or within what limits a person does this rightly or wrongly. One who transgresses a little (whether towards excess or deficiency) is not blamed for it; indeed we sometimes praise those *who fall short of the mean, and call them patient, or call those who show annoyance manly as being capable of leadership. So it is not easy to define by rule how, and how far, a person may go wrong before he incurs blame; because this depends upon particular circumstances, and the decision lies with our perception. However, this much is clear: that the mean state, which makes us angry with the right people for the right reasons in the right way (and all the rest) is commendable, while the excesses and deficiencies are to be censured – gently or more strongly or very strongly according to the degree of the error. Clearly, then, we must keep closely to the mean state.

So much for our account of the dispositions connected with anger.

1. 1109b14-26.

The social virtue of amiability, and the corresponding vices

vi.   In contacts with other people, that is, in daily life and
in discussions and dealings with others, some people are
considered to be obsequious:[1] to make themselves pleasant
they praise everything, and offer no resistance, thinking
that they must avoid causing annoyance to the people that
they meet. Those who take the opposite line to these,
offering resistance to everything and not worrying at all
about causing annoyance, are called surly or quarrelsome.[2]
It is not difficult to see that the said dispositions are culpable,
and that the one that is intermediate between them, which
will enable one to accept (and similarly to reject) the right
things in the right way, is praiseworthy. It has no definite
name assigned to it, but what it most closely resembles is
friendliness;[3] because the person who corresponds to the
intermediate state is of the sort that we mean when we speak
of a good friend; although that implies an element of
affection. But this quality differs from friendship in that it is
independent of feeling, that is, of affection for those with
whom its possessor associates; since it is not from friendship
or enmity that he accepts each kind of action in the right
way, but because he has this kind of disposition. For he will
act in the same way towards strangers and acquaintances,
towards those with whom he is and those with whom he is
not familiar – except that he will act in a way suitable to the
particular circumstances; because it is not proper to show
the same consideration, or lack of it, for intimate acquaintances as for total strangers.

We have stated generally, then, that this man will
associate with others in the right way; and by referring
constantly to the standards of what is fine and advantageous, will aim at either not causing[4] pain to others or adding

1. *areskos*.   2. *duskolos* or *duseris*.
3. It is called *philia* at 1108a26ff.; the English equivalent is really
'amiability' (Burnet).
4. Rackham's text omits the negative.

to their pleasure; because it seems that he is concerned with the pleasures and pains that arise in social intercourse. To any of these which it is not honourable or expedient for him to encourage, he will object, and will prefer to cause pain.[1] Also if a pleasure brings no small discredit or harm to the agent, while opposition to it causes little pain, he will refuse assent and object to it. He will behave differently with eminent and with ordinary people, *with those whom he knows well and with those whom he knows less well, and will similarly take into account all other differences, rendering the appropriate treatment to each class of person, preferring, for its own sake, to contribute to the pleasure of others, and taking care not to cause them pain, but being guided by the consequences – I mean by what is honourable and advantageous – if they are more important. He will also inflict little pains for the sake of a great pleasure in the future.

Such, then, is the man of the intermediate disposition; but he has no specific name. Of those who assist the pleasures of others, the one who aims at being agreeable for no ulterior motive is obsequious, but anyone who does so with a view to benefit in respect of money or the things that money buys is a flatterer. We have said already[2] that the man who disapproves of everything is surly and quarrelsome. The reason why the extremes seem to be opposed to each other[3] is that the mean has no name.

Social qualities concerned with truth and falsehood

vii.   The same field of action, roughly speaking, belongs to the disposition intermediate between boasting and understatement.[4] It too has no name; but we may as well examine these nameless qualities too, because we shall improve our knowledge of the aspects of character if we discuss them

1. By refusing to join in.   2. 1126b14ff.
3. With nothing in between; cf. 1125b24f. above.
4. *alazoneia* and *eirōneia*; see Glossary.

individually, and we shall convince ourselves that the virtues are mean states if we gain a comprehensive view that it is so in every case.

We have spoken above of those who cause pain and pleasure by their social relations with others. Let us now deal similarly with those who exhibit truth and falsehood in their speech and actions, i.e. in their pretensions. Well, the boaster is regarded as one who pretends to have distinguished qualities which he possesses either not at all or to a lesser degree than he pretends. The ironical man conversely is thought to disclaim qualities that he does possess, or to depreciate them; while the one who is intermediate between these two is a sort of individualist, sincere both in his daily life and in his speech, acknowledging the qualities that he possesses and neither exaggerating nor depreciating them. All these three types may perform their several actions either with or without an ulterior object; but in the latter case each of them speaks and acts and lives in accordance with his character.[1] Falsehood is in itself bad and reprehensible, while the truth is a fine and praiseworthy thing; accordingly the sincere man, who holds the mean position, is praiseworthy, while both the deceivers are to be censured, particularly the boaster.

The sincere or truthful man

Let us discuss each type, taking the sincere[2] man first. We are not here concerned with the person who speaks the truth in making an agreement, nor with conduct that involves justice or injustice (because *this would be the field of another virtue[3]), but with cases in which, since no such complication is present, a man is truthful both in speech and in the way he lives because he is like that in disposition. Such a person would seem to be a good type; for a lover of the truth, who speaks it when nothing depends

1. i.e., other things being equal, the boaster boasts, etc.
2. Or truthful: *alētheutikos*.   3. i.e. justice; see Book V.

upon it, will speak it all the more when something does depend upon it; because since he is guarded against falsehood as such, he will guard against it ⟨all the more⟩ as something dishonourable. Such a man is to be commended. His inclination, if any, is towards understatement, because this seems to be in better taste, since exaggeration is wearisome.

The boaster or exaggerator

As for the man who pretends that his qualifications are higher than they are, if he has no ulterior purpose, he gives a bad impression (because a good man would not enjoy telling a lie); but he seems to be more irresponsible than vicious. If he has a purpose, then if it is to win fame or honour, he is not to be censured too much, as a boaster; but the man whose object is money or what money will buy is more disreputable (it is not the capacity that makes one a boaster, but the deliberate choice: because he is a boaster in virtue of his disposition, i.e. because he is that sort of man[1]); just as a liar may be either one who enjoys lying for its own sake or one who is striving to gain glory or profit. Well, those who boast with a view to glory pretend to such qualities as earn praise or congratulation, while those whose object is gain claim such as both convey some advantage to their neighbours and can escape detection as being non-existent – e.g. prophetic powers, or philosophical insight, or medical skill. It is for this reason that most people pretend to have, and boast of, such qualifications; because they have the aforesaid characteristics.

Irony or self-depreciation

Ironical people who employ understatement appear more attractive in character, because their object is felt to be not

1. As with other vices, it is the choice of wrong means (here misrepresentation) that develops a vicious disposition.

profit but the avoidance of ostentation. They also especially
disclaim qualities that are held in general regard, just as
Socrates used to do.[1] Those who disclaim trifling or commonplace qualities are called pretentious humbugs, and
invite greater contempt. Sometimes their conduct has the
appearance of boasting; for instance Spartan dress;[2]
because exaggerated deficiency is as ostentatious as excess.
But those who make a moderate use of understatement,
treating ironically of subjects not too commonplace or
obvious, make a pleasant impression. The boaster is considered to be the opposite of the sincere man, because he is a
worse character.[3]

Conversational qualities: wit, buffoonery and boorishness

viii.   Since one part of life is relaxation, and one aspect of
this is entertaining conversation, it is considered that here
too there is a kind of social conduct *that is in good taste:
that there are things that it is right to say, and a right way of
saying them; and similarly with listening. And it will be
an advantage if those in whose presence we talk and to
whom we listen accept such standards. Clearly in this field
too it is possible to exceed or fall short of the mean.

Those who go too far in being funny are regarded as
buffoons[4] and vulgar persons who exert themselves to be
funny at all costs and who are more set upon raising a laugh
than upon decency of expression and consideration for their
victim's feelings. Those who both refuse to say anything
funny themselves and take exception to the jokes of other
people are regarded as boorish and sour;[5] but those who
exercise their humour with good taste are called witty, as
one might say 'nimble-witted',[6] because witticisms are con-

1. Disclaiming wisdom; cf. Plato, *Apology* 20B–23D.
2. i.e. the affectation of it by some Athenians.
3. Than the ironical man.   4. *bōmolochos.*   5. *agroikos* and *sklēros.*
6. The two Greek words *eutrapelos* and *eutropos* express respectively
mental and physical agility.

sidered to be movements of the character, and characters, like bodies, are judged by their movements. As material for humour is ready to hand, and most people like fun and ridicule more than they should, even buffoons are called witty, as being good company; but that there is a difference between the two, and not a small one, is clear from what we have said.

The intermediate disposition also has the property of tact,[1] and the mark of tact is saying and listening to the sort of things that are suitable for a man of honourable and liberal character; because there are certain things that it is appropriate for such a person to say and allow to be said to him in fun, and the liberal man's sense of humour is different from a servile person's, just as an educated man's is from an uneducated man's. One can see this even from a comparison of the Old and New comedies; because to the earlier writers humour consisted in ribaldry, but the later ones preferred innuendo. There is no little difference between these two in respect of decency. Should we, then, distinguish the man who uses ridicule rightly by his ability to use language that is not unsuitable for a well-bred person,[2] or by the fact that he does not annoy the person about whom he is speaking, but actually gives him pleasure? (Probably the latter qualification, at any rate, is still vague; because different people have different likes and dislikes.) The humour to which he listens will be of the same kind, because he is regarded as actually making the jokes that he tolerates hearing. Now he will not go to all lengths; because ridicule is a sort of defamation, and some forms of defamation are forbidden by law, and presumably some kinds of ridicule should be forbidden too. The cultured and well-bred person, then, will exhibit this disposition, acting as a law to himself.[3] This is the sort of man who observes the mean, whether he is called witty or tactful. The buffoon cannot resist a joke, sparing neither himself nor anybody else provided that he can raise a laugh, and saying things *that a man of taste

1. *epidexiotēs*.   2. 'A liberal man'.
3. i.e. refraining from offensive humour.

would never dream of saying, and some that he would not listen to either. As for the boor, he is useless for any kind of social intercourse, because he contributes nothing and takes offence at everything, whereas relaxation and amusement seem to be necessary in our life.

So in our social life there are three intermediate dispositions, as we have described them; and they are all concerned with participation in some sort of conversation or action, but they differ inasmuch as one is concerned with truth and the other two with pleasure. Of the latter, one is exercised in the sphere of recreation and the other in the associations that belong to the rest of life.

Modesty is not a virtue; it is good only as a curb of youthful indiscretion

x.   It is not correct to speak of modesty[1] as a kind of virtue, because it is more like a feeling than a state. It is defined, at any rate, as a sort of fear of disrepute, and it has an effect very like that produced by the fear of danger;[2] modesty makes people blush, and the fear of death turns them pale. So both appear to be in some sense corporeal, and this is thought to be more the mark of a feeling than of a state. The feeling is not appropriate to every age: only to youth. We consider that adolescents ought to be modest because, living as they do under sway of their feelings, they often make mistakes, but are restrained by modesty. Also we commend a modest youth, but nobody would commend an older man for being shamefaced, because we think that he ought not to do anything to be ashamed of. In fact shame is not the emotion of a good man, if it is felt for doing bad actions, because such actions ought not to be done (and it makes no difference whether the things done are really shameful or are only thought to be so; they should not be done in either case); so the emotion ought not to be felt. It is the bad man

1. *aidōs*.
2. Both cause a change of colour, although the colours are different.

who ought to feel shame, because he is the sort of man to do a shameful deed; but it is absurd to think that being so constituted as to feel shame at doing something shameful makes you a good man, because modesty is felt about voluntary actions, and the good man will never voluntarily do bad ones.

Modesty can only be good in a conditional sense: that if the agent were to do so-and-so he would be ashamed; but this is not true of the virtues. Although shamelessness, that is, not being ashamed to do what is disgraceful, is a bad thing, it does not follow any the more from this that to be ashamed if one behaves disgracefully is a good thing. In the same way continence[1] is not to be regarded as altogether a virtue either; it is a sort of combination of virtue with something else. This will be explained later.[2] We must now discuss Justice.

1. *enkrateia.*   2. In Book VII.

V

JUSTICE

What do we mean by justice and injustice?

i.   *In treating of justice and injustice we have to consider with what sort of actions they are actually concerned, what sort of a mean justice is, and what the extremes are between which justice lies. Let us conduct our inquiry on the same lines as our foregoing account.[1]

Well, when people speak of justice we see that they all mean that kind of state of character that disposes them to perform just acts, and behave in a just manner, and wish for what is just; and in the same way they mean by injustice the state that makes them act unjustly and wish for unjust things. So we too may begin by making these assumptions as a basis for our discussion. For in fact the case is not the same with states as it is with sciences and faculties; because whereas both members of a pair of contraries are held to be the concern of the same science or faculty,[2] a *state* that has a contrary does not cause results that are contrary to itself: e.g. health causes only healthy actions and not the contrary kind, for we say that a person walks healthily when he walks as a healthy man would.[3]

The nature of a contrary state is often recognized from its contrary, and states are often recognized from the subjects to which they belong; for if we know what is meant by a sound condition of the body, we get to know also what is meant by an unsound condition; and we recognize sound bodily condition from our knowledge of bodies in that condition, and vice versa. For instance, if bodily soundness

1. By considering views actually held about them.

2. Medicine studies both health and disease, and a faculty (art or skill) can operate in opposite ways: a good mechanic can service or sabotage a machine.

3. i.e. we rule out the possibility that his health might make him walk unhealthily.

is firmness of flesh, then bodily unsoundness must be flabbiness of flesh, and what conduces to soundness must be that which is productive of firmness in flesh. Also if one contrary is ambiguous, it follows for the most part[1] that the other is also; e.g. that if 'just' is ambiguous, 'unjust' will be too.

Unjust means either lawless or unfair; therefore just means either lawful or fair (equitable)

Now it appears that the words justice and injustice *are* ambiguous; but as the different senses covered by the same name are very close to each other, the equivocation passes unnoticed and is not comparatively obvious as it is where they are far apart (because then the difference in outward appearance is considerable); e.g. the word 'key' is used equivocally both of the bone below the neck in animals[2] and of the key with which doors are locked.

Let us begin, then, by taking the various senses in which a man is said to be unjust. Well, the word is considered to describe both one who breaks the law and one who takes advantage of another, i.e. acts unfairly.[3] Then evidently also both the law-abiding man and the fair man will be just. So just means lawful and fair; *and unjust means both unlawful and unfair. And since the unjust man takes more than his share, he will be concerned with goods – not all goods, but with those that make up the field of good and bad fortune: things that are always good in themselves, but not always good for the individual.[4] These latter goods are what human beings pray for and try to obtain, but this is wrong: they should *pray* that what is good in itself may be good for them, but *choose* what is good for them.

1. Not invariably, because individual words acquire specialized meanings; cf. *Topics* 106a9ff., especially a36–b12.

2. The collar bone, called 'key' in Greek; cf. Latin *clavicula*.

3. Cf. b6–10 below.

4. External goods, which for defective characters are sometimes disastrous (e.g. wealth for a spendthrift).

The unjust man does not always choose the larger share; of things that are bad in themselves he actually chooses the lesser share, but he is none the less regarded as trying to get too much, because 'getting too much' refers to what is *good*, and the lesser evil is considered to be in a sense good. Let us call him unfair, for that is a comprehensive word that covers both meanings. Since the lawless man is, as we saw,[1] unjust, and the law-abiding man just, it is clear that all lawful things are in some sense just; because what is pre-scribed by legislation is lawful, and we hold that every such ordinance is just. The laws prescribe for all the departments of life, aiming at the common advantage either of all the citizens or of the best of them, or of the ruling class, or on some other such basis. So in one sense we call just anything that tends to produce or conserve the happiness (and the constituents of the happiness) of a political association. Besides this the law enjoins brave conduct – e.g. not to leave one's post, or take to flight, or throw away one's weapons – and temperate conduct – e.g. not to commit adultery or assault – and patient conduct – e.g. to refrain from blows or abuse – and similarly with all the other forms of goodness and wickedness, the law commands some kinds of behaviour and forbids others; rightly if the law is rightly enacted, but not so well if it is an improvised measure.

Justice in the former sense is complete virtue : this is universal justice

Justice in this sense, then, is complete virtue; virtue, how-ever, not unqualified but in relation to somebody else. Hence it is often regarded as the sovereign virtue, and 'neither evening nor morning star is such a wonder'.[2] We express it in a proverb:

In justice is summed up the whole of virtue.[3]

1. Above, a32–b1.   2. Cf. Euripides fr. 490.
3. The saying is attributed to both Theognis and Phocylides.

It is complete virtue in the fullest sense, because it is the active exercise[1] of complete virtue; and it is complete because its possessor can exercise it in relation to another person, and not only by himself. I say this because there are plenty of people who can behave uprightly in their own affairs, but are incapable of doing so in relation to somebody else. *That is why Bias's saying 'Office will reveal the man'[2] is felt to be valid; because an official is *eo ipso* in a relation to, and associated with, somebody else. And for this same reason – that it implies a relation to somebody else – justice is the only virtue that is regarded as someone else's good, because it secures advantage for another person, either an official or a partner.[3] So the worst person is the one who exercises his wickedness towards both himself and his friends, and the best is not the one who exercises his virtue towards himself but the one who exercises it towards another; because this is a difficult task. Justice in this sense, then, is not a part of virtue but the whole of it, and the injustice contrary to it is not a part but the whole of vice.

It is clear, from what we have said, what the difference is between virtue and justice in this sense: they are the same, except that their essence is not the same; that which, considered in relation to somebody else, is justice, when considered simply as a certain kind of moral state is virtue.

We are now concerned with particular justice and injustice

ii.   But what we are looking for is justice as a *part* of virtue (and similarly with particular injustice); because there is such a form of justice, as we maintain. There is an indication that this is so: in all other cases the person who does wrong gains no advantage from his misconduct: e.g. the man who through cowardice throws away his shield,[4] or through bad

1. Not merely the possession of it.
2. Cf. Sophocles, *Antigone* 175ff. Bias of Priene was one of the Seven Sages.
3. Cf. Plato, *Republic* 343c.   4. In order to run away faster.

temper uses abusive language, or through illiberality refuses
financial help.[1] But when a man takes more than his share,
although he is often actuated by none (much less by all) of
these vices, yet what actuates him is certainly some kind of
wickedness (because we blame it): viz., injustice. Therefore
there is another kind of injustice which is a part of universal
injustice, and there is a kind of 'unjust' which is a part of
the unjust in general which means 'contrary to the law'.
Further, if one man commits adultery for gain, making
money by it, and another pays out money and is penalized
for gratifying his desire, the second would be regarded as
licentious[2] rather than grasping, but the former would be
regarded as unjust, though not licentious. This makes it
clear that the act is unjust because it is done for gain.
Besides, all other unjust acts are always attributed to some
particular wickedness: e.g. adultery to licentiousness,
abandoning a comrade in battle to cowardice, bodily
assault to anger; but if the offender has profited from his
offence, it is attributed to injustice and to no other wickedness.

It is evident, then, that besides universal justice there is
another kind which is particular, and has the same name,
because its definition is in *the same genus,[3] since both are
effective in relation to somebody other than the agent. But
whereas particular injustice is concerned with honour or
money or security or any single name that we can use to
cover all three, and is actuated by the pleasure that the
advantage offers, universal justice has the same field of
action as the good man.[4]

Clearly, then, there is more than one kind of justice: i.e.
there is a form of it distinguishable from virtue as a whole.
We must try to comprehend what this is and what its
qualities are.[5]

1. An unfortunate example, because saving money at another person's
expense is little better than taking an unfair advantage.

2. *akolastos*: see Glossary.

3. Naturally, because particular is a species of universal justice.

4. i.e. that of virtuous conduct.   5. i.e. its genus and differentia.

175

Well, we have distinguished two senses of unjust, viz., unlawful and unfair, and two of just, viz., lawful and fair. Now injustice in the sense described above corresponds to unlawful; and since the unfair and the unlawful are not the same, but differ as part and whole do (because everything that is unfair is unlawful, but not everything that is unlawful is unfair); so also the unjust and injustice in this sense[1] are not the same as, but different from, those in the former sense, being related to them as parts to wholes; and the two kinds of justice are similarly related. So we must also discuss both particular justice and particular injustice, and likewise the just and unjust in the particular sense.

Let us, then, dismiss the justice and injustice that correspond to virtue in general – the one consisting in the exercise towards another of general virtue, and the other in the similar exercise of general vice. It is also evident how we must distinguish the terms just and unjust in the corresponding senses. For, broadly speaking, most of the acts laid down by law are enjoined from the point of view of virtue as a whole, because the law directs us to live in accordance with every virtue, and refrain from every kind of wickedness. Also the things that promote virtue in general are the regulations laid down by law with a view to education in citizenship. As for the education of the individual, that which makes him simply a good man, we must determine later[2] whether it falls under political science or some other; because presumably it is not always[3] the same thing to be a good man and a good citizen.

Particular justice is either distributive or rectificatory

One kind of particular justice, and of that which is just in the corresponding sense, is that which is shown in the distribution of honour or money or such other assets as are

1. In the sense of unfair.
2. The point is discussed below, 1179b20–1181b12, and in *Politics* III.
3. e.g. under a corrupt régime.

divisible among the members of the community (for in
these cases it is possible for one person to have either an
equal or an unequal share with another); and another kind
*which rectifies the conditions of a transaction. This latter
kind has two parts, because some transactions are voluntary
and others involuntary.[1] Voluntary transactions are, e.g.,
selling, buying, lending at interest, pledging, lending
without interest, depositing, and letting (these are called
voluntary because the initial stage of the transaction is
voluntary). Involuntary transactions are either secret, such
as theft, adultery, poisoning, procuring, enticement of
slaves, killing by stealth, and testifying falsely; or violent,
e.g. assault, forcible confinement, murder, robbery, maim-
ing, defamation, and public insult.

Distributive justice employs geometrical proportion

iii.   Both the unjust man and the unjust act are unfair or
unequal, and clearly in each case of inequality there is
something intermediate, viz., that which is equal; because
in any action that admits degrees of more and less there is
also an equal. Then if what is unjust is unequal, what is just
is equal; as is univerally accepted even without the support
of argument. And since what is equal is a mean, what is just
will be a sort of mean. But an instance of equality involves
two terms at least. Therefore what is just must be a mean,
and equal, and relative (i.e. just for certain persons[2]); and
qua mean, it must be between extremes (i.e. a greater and a
less); and *qua* equal, it must involve two things; and *qua* just,
it affects certain persons. So a just act necessarily involves at
least four terms: two persons for whom it is in fact just, and
two shares in which its justice is exhibited. And there will be
the same equality between the shares as between the persons,
because the shares will be in the same ratio to one another
as the persons; for if the persons are not equal, they will not

1. A transaction is involuntary when it lacks the consent of one party.
2. Some editors reject the bracketed words.

have equal shares; and it is when equals have or are assigned
unequal shares, or people who are not equal, equal shares,
that quarrels and complaints break out.

This is also clear from the principle of assignment according to merit. Everyone agrees that justice in distribution
must be in accordance with merit in some sense, but they do
not all mean the same kind of merit: the democratic view is
that the criterion is free birth; the oligarchic that it is
wealth or good family; the aristocratic that it is excellence.

So justice is a sort of proportion; for proportion is a property not only of number as composed of abstract units, but
of number in general; for proportion is an equality of ratios,
and involves four terms at least (that a discrete proportion[1]
involves four terms is obvious, but so does a continuous proportion, because it treats one term as two, i.e. states it twice:
*e.g. $A:B = B:C$. Thus B has been stated twice. So if B is
taken twice there will be four proportionals). Justice too involves at least four terms, and the ratio is the same ⟨between
the first two and the last two⟩; for the persons and the shares
have been divided in the same ratio,[2] so the third term will
be to the fourth as the first is to the second, and so by alter-
nation the second will be to the fourth as the first to the
third. And so also the sum ⟨of the first and third⟩ is to the
sum ⟨of the second and fourth⟩. This is the combination produced by the allocation of shares; and if it is made up in this
way it is a just combination. Therefore justice in distribution
consists in conjunction of the first with the third term, and
of the second with the fourth; and what is just in this sense is
a mean, whereas what is unjust violates the proportion, because the proportional is a mean, and what is just is proportional. (This kind of proportion is called geometrical by
mathematicians, because in geometrical proportion the
effect is that the ratio of whole to whole is the same as that of

1. A proportion of four terms; a continuous one has three terms of
which the middle one is used twice.

2. The letters evidently represent the lines in a diagram, but below the
'terms' seem to be represented merely by letters.

each part to each corresponding part.) But this proportion[1] is not continuous, because in it we do not get one and the same term representing both a person and a share.

What is just in this sense, then, is what is proportional, and what is unjust is what violates the proportion. So one share becomes too large and the other too small. This is exactly what happens in practice: the man who acts unjustly gets too much and the victim of injustice too little of what is good. In the case of an evil the position is reversed, for in comparison with the greater the lesser evil is reckoned as a good, because the lesser evil is more to be chosen than the greater, and what is to be chosen is a good, and what is more to be chosen is a greater good.

This, then, is one kind of justice.

Rectificatory justice remedies an inequitable division
between two parties by means of a sort of
arithmetical progression

iv.   The remaining kind of justice is rectificatory:[2] it occurs in transactions, both voluntary and involuntary.[3] This kind of justice takes a form different from that of the preceding one. For justice that is distributive of common property is always in accordance with the proportion that we have described above (because if the distribution is made from common funds it will be in the same ratio as the corresponding contributions bear to one another), and the injustice that is its opposite is that which violates this proportion. But what is just in transactions is a kind of equal (and what is un*just a kind of unequal) – in accordance, however, not with the aforesaid proportion but with arith-

1. The one that represents just distribution.
2. The traditional 'corrective' is unfortunate, because it suggests moral correction, whereas the object of this kind of justice is merely adjustment.
3. Cf. 1131a1ff. above.

metical proportion.[1] For it makes no difference whether a good man has defrauded a bad one or vice versa, nor whether a good man or a bad one has committed adultery; all that the law considers is the difference caused by the injury; and it treats the parties as equals, only asking whether one has committed and the other suffered an injustice, or whether one has inflicted and the other suffered a hurt. Accordingly the judge[2] tries to equalize the inequality of this injustice. Even when one party has received and the other given a blow, or one has killed and the other been killed, the active and passive aspects of the affair exhibit an unequal division;[3] but the judge tries to equalize them with the help of the penalty, by reducing the gain. The term 'gain' is used generally in such cases, even though it is not the appropriate word for some offences, e.g. in the case of assault; and similarly with 'loss' for the victim; at any rate when the damage has been estimated the effects are called loss and gain respectively. Thus what is equal is a mean between greater and less, and the gain and loss are greater and less in contrary senses: that which contains more good and less bad being gain, and its contrary loss. The mean between them is, as we have said,[4] the equal, which we assert to be the just. It follows that what is just in the rectificatory sense will be the mean between loss and gain.[5]

These expressions 'gain' and 'loss' are derived from the process of voluntary exchange. In that process to have more than one's own share is called gaining, and to have less than one had at the start, losing; for example, in buying and

1. An expression of the type B–A = D–C; not a proportion in our sense, but if C–B also = B–A, an arithmetical progression.

2. Probably he means 'arbitrator', since at Athens nearly all private suits were submitted first to arbitration.

3. Evidently another diagram is shown. The point (made clearer below) is that even assault is viewed as gain to the one party and loss to the other.

4. 1131b33.

5. The next paragraph was transferred here by Gauthier from 1132b11–20.

selling and all other transactions in which the law gives im-
munity;[1] but when neither party has too much or too little
but both have exactly what they gave, they are said to 'have
their own', and there is no question of gaining or losing. It
follows that in involuntary transactions justice is a mean
between a sort of gain and loss: it is to have an equal
amount both before and after the transaction.

That is why, when disputes occur, people have recourse to
a judge; and to do this is to have recourse to justice, because
the object of the judge is to be a sort of personified Justice.
Also they look for a judge as an intermediary between them
(indeed in some places judges are called 'mediators'[2]) in
the belief that if they secure a mean they will secure what is
just. So justice is a sort of mean, inasmuch as the judge is
one.

What the judge does is to restore equality. It is as if a line
were divided into two unequal parts; the judge takes away
that by which the greater segment exceeds the half of the
line, and adds it to the lesser segment. When the whole has
been divided into two halves, then each is said to have his
own – when they have received equal shares. This is why
what is equal is called *dikaion* (just); because it is *dicha* (in
half), as if one were to call it *dichaion*: and a *dikastēs* (judge)
is a *dichastēs* (divider).[3] In arithmetical proportion the equal
is a mean between the greater and the less. For when a portion is taken away from one of the equal parts and added to
the other, the second exceeds the first by twice that portion;
for if it had been taken away but not added, *the second
would exceed the first by only once that portion. So the
second part exceeds the mean by one portion, and the mean
exceeds by one portion the part from which the portion was
taken away. This, then, is the method by which we shall
discover what must be taken away from the party who has

1. i.e. in which the law provides no redress.

2. e.g. at Larisa or Abydos (*Politics* 1306a26ff.).

3. The derivation is false; but one can see now why the word for
judge was used above instead of that for an arbitrator. In the MS this
sentence follows the next.

too much and added to the party who has too little That is, we must add to the party who has too little the amount by which the mean exceeds what he has, and take away from the greatest[1] the amount by which the mean is exceeded by what he has.

The lines AA', BB', CC' are equal to one another. Let the segment AE be taken from AA' and the segment CD be added to CC', so that the whole line DCC' exceeds the line EA' by CD+CF. Then DCC' will exceed the line BB' by the segment CD.[2]

Although justice cannot be equated with simple reciprocity, proportional reciprocation is the basis of all fair exchange

v.   There are some who even think that what is just is simple reciprocity, as the Pythagoreans maintained, because they defined justice simply as having done to one what one has done to another.[3] But ⟨simple⟩ reciprocity does not square with either distributive or rectificatory justice (although people try to make out that this is the meaning of Rhadamanthus's justice:

> If a man suffer even as he wrought,
> Then justice will be rendered as it ought;)[4]

1. The greatest single segment, which stands for the party who has too much.

2. (Here in the MS there is a short interpolation from 1133a13–16.) Aristotle's diagram is like this:

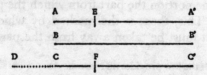

3. A view that represented justice as a sort of equation would have suited their mathematical bent very well; see Appendix A.

4. Cf. Hesiod fr. 286 (Merkelbach and West).

because in many cases they disagree. For example, if an official strikes some one, it is wrong for him to be struck in return; and if some one strikes an official it is right for him not only to be struck in return but to be punished as well. Again, it makes a great difference whether the act was voluntary or involuntary.[1] It is true that in associations for exchange justice in this form – i.e. reciprocity – is the bond;[2] but it is reciprocity based on proportion, not on equality. It is proportional requital that holds the state together; because people expect either to return evil for evil – and *if they cannot, feel that they have lost their liberty – or good for good, and if this is impossible no exchange can take place; and it is exchange that holds them together.[3] That is why they set up a temple of the Graces in a public place to encourage the repayment of benefits; this is the distinguishing mark of gratitude,[4] because it is right both to repay a service to a benefactor and at another time to take the initiative in benefaction.

Proportional requital implies some standard for the valuation of unequal services

Proportional requital is effected by 'diagonal conjunction'. A is a builder, B a shoemaker, C a house, D a shoe. It is required that the builder shall receive from the shoemaker some part of what the latter produces, giving him at the same time some part of what he produces himself. Then if proportional equality[5] is first established, and then reciprocation takes place, the stated requirement will be achieved; but otherwise the transaction is not equal, and breaks down. For there is no reason why the product of the one should not be more valuable than that of the other, so

1. From the standpoint of the injured party; cf. 1131a2ff.
2. That maintains the association.
3. The basis of any society is exchange of produce, goods or services.
4. The same Greek word (*charis*) stands for grace and gratitude.
5. The relative value of houses and shoes.

they must be equated.[1] This applies also to all the other arts and crafts. They would have ceased to exist if the patient did not receive just the same, both in quantity and in quality, as the agent produced.[2] An association for exchange is formed not from two doctors but from a doctor and a farmer, and in general from parties that are different and not equal; but these must be equated. Hence all products that are exchanged must be in some way comparable. It is this that has led to the introduction of money, which serves as a sort of mean,[3] since it is a measure of everything, and so a measure of the excess and deficiency of value, informing us, for example, how many shoes are equivalent to a house or so much food. Then as a builder is to a shoemaker, so must x shoes be to a house or so much food.[4] Apart from this formula there can be no exchange and no association; and the formula cannot be applied unless the products are somehow equated.[5]

This standard is really demand, which is conveniently represented by money

There must, therefore, be (as was said above[6]) one standard by which all commodities are measured. This standard is in fact demand, which holds everything together[7] (for if people had no needs, or needs on a different scale, there could be no exchange, or else it must be on different lines); but by a convention demand has come to be represented by money. This is why money is so called, because it exists not by nature but by custom,[8] and it is in our power to change its value or render it useless.

1. A fair basis of exchange must be found.
2. The text is doubtful and the language odd, but the sense is that each party must give and receive an equal product or service.
3. i.e. a medium of exchange.
4. The ratio is presumably that of the parties' needs for each other's commodities (cf. below); but it is not clear how this is calculated.
5. In value.   6. a19ff.   7. Cf. 1132b31ff. and notes thereon.
8. The word *nomisma* 'money' has the same root as *nomos* 'law' or 'custom'.

There will be reciprocity, then, when the products have been equated, so that as the farmer is to the shoemaker, so is the product of the shoemaker to the product of the farmer. *But the terms must not be reduced to the form of a proportion *after* they have exchanged their products (otherwise one extreme will have both excesses[1]), but when they still have their own; under these conditions they are equal, and can enter into an association with each other, because their case admits of such equality. (A = farmer, C = food, B = shoemaker, D = his product when equated.[2]) If reciprocal proportion could not be arrived at in this way, there could be no association between them. That it is demand, forming as it does a single standard, that holds such associations together is clear from the fact that when neither party, or only one party, needs the services of the other, they make no exchange (as, for example, when someone wants something that the consumer has not got: e.g. offering an export licence for corn in exchange for wine[3]). This inequality of demand, therefore, has to be equalized.

What money does for us is to act as a guarantee of exchange in the future: that if it is not needed now, it will take place if the need arises; because the bearer of money must be able to obtain what he wants. Of course money is affected in the same way as other commodities, because its purchasing power varies; nevertheless it tends to be more constant. This is why everything must have its money value fixed, because then there will always be exchange, and if exchange, association. So money acts as a measure which, by making things commensurable, enables us to equate them. Without exchange there would be no association, without equality there would be no exchange, without commensurability there would be no equality. Strictly speaking,

1. One of the parties will get too much and give too little; cf. 1132a32ff.

2. The value of C expressed in terms of shoes.

3. The text is uncertain (some editors reject both this and the next sentence), but the point is that a (presumably Athenian) trader cannot avail himself of the licence offered by a Black Sea corn-growing state because he cannot pay for it in wine.

things so widely different cannot become commensurable; but in relation to demand a sufficient degree of accuracy is possible. So there must be some one standard, and that on an agreed basis (which is why money is so called[1]), because this makes all products commensurable, since they can all be measured in terms of money. A stands for a house, B for ten minae,[2] C for a bed. Then supposing the value of the house to be five minae or its equivalent, A is half of B, and C, the bed, is one tenth of B, so it is easy to see how many beds are equal to a house, viz. five. Obviously before money existed exchange was effected in this way; for it makes no difference whether you pay five beds for a house or the value of five beds.

Such are particular justice and injustice, the latter being a single vice exhibiting both excess and deficiency

We have now described what justice and injustice are. Now that these distinctions have been drawn we can see that just behaviour is intermediate between doing injustice and suffering it; for the one is to have more and the other to have less than one's share. And justice is a sort of mean state, only not in the same way as the other virtues are, but because it aims at a mean, *whereas injustice aims at the extremes.[3] Also justice is that state in virtue of which a just man is said to be capable of doing just acts from choice, and of assigning property – both to himself in relation to another, and to another in relation to a third party – not in such a way as to give more of the desirable thing to himself and less to his neighbour (and conversely with what is harmful), but assigning to each that which is proportionately equal;

1. See note 8, p. 184.

2. One mina = 100 ancient drachmae. It is hardly possible to estimate a contemporary equivalent in English money; and anyhow A.'s relative values are only taken *exempli gratia*.

3. Maximum advantage for oneself, minimum advantage for the other party.

and similarly in distributing between two other parties. Injustice, on the contrary, is a state that chooses what is unjust, i.e. excess and deficiency, in defiance of proportion, of what is beneficial and harmful respectively. Thus injustice consists in excess and deficiency in the sense that it is productive of these: in the case of oneself, excess of what is generally beneficial and deficiency of what is harmful, while in the case of others, although the result as a whole is the same, in which way the proportion is violated is a matter of chance.[1] In an unjust act to have the smaller share is to be treated, and to have the larger is to act, unjustly.

So much for our account of the nature of justice and injustice, and similarly of what is just and unjust generally.[2]

A note on injustice in the wider sense of wrongdoing

vi.   Since it is possible to act unjustly without yet being an unjust man,[3] what are the offences the commission of which makes a man unjust in each kind of wrongdoing – e.g. a thief, an adulterer, a brigand? Probably the quality of the act will make no difference: for example, a man may lie with a woman in full knowledge of who she is,[4] yet not from the efficient cause of deliberate choice,[5] but under the influence of passion. Then although his conduct is unjust, he is not an unjust man; I mean that the act of stealing does not make a man a thief, nor the act of adultery make him an adulterer; and similarly in all other cases.

1. If the distributor has no personal interest in the recipients it is a matter of chance which his unjust distribution favours.

2. Contrasted with the discussion of justice and injustice in special aspects and relationships, which occupies the following chapters.

3. The point raised in this paragraph is out of place here; it is further considered in ch. viii.

4. i.e. that she is another man's wife.   5. Cf. 1113a6.

Political justice: its conditions

The relation of reciprocity to justice has been discussed already.[1] But we must not overlook the fact that the subject of our inquiry is not only justice in general but *political* justice. Political justice obtains between those who share a life for the satisfaction of their needs as persons free and equal, either artithmetically or proportionately.[2] Hence in associations where these conditions are not present there is no political justice between the members, but only a sort of approximation to justice. For justice is only found among those whose mutual relations are controlled by law, and law is only found among those who are liable to injustice; for legal justice consists in distinguishing between what is just and what is unjust. But injustice implies unjust conduct (although unjust conduct does not always imply injustice[3]); and this consists in assigning to oneself too much of what is generally good and too little of what is generally bad. That is why we do not allow a man to rule, but the principle ⟨of law⟩;[4] because a man does so *for his own advantage, and becomes a despot, whereas the ruler is the upholder of justice, and if of justice, of equality. And since it is agreed that if he is a just man he derives no advantage (because he does not assign himself a larger share of what is generally good, unless the share is proportionate to his merits, so that his labours are altruistic: hence the saying, already mentioned,[5] that justice is the good of others): it follows that he ought to be given some reward, viz. honour and dignity. It is those who are not satisfied with these rewards that develop into despots.

1. 1132b21ff.
2. Citizens whose rights are equal either absolutely or relatively to their value as citizens.
3. Cf. a17 above.
4. *logos* is the reading of nearly all the mss, whereas *nomos* (law) is what one would expect from the context; the translation attempts a compromise.
5. 1130a3f.

Domestic justice is similar, but distinct

Justice on the part of a master or father[1] is not the same as, although it is analogous to, the forms already discussed. There cannot be injustice in an unqualified sense towards that which is one's own; and a chattel, or a child until it is of a certain age and has attained independence, is as it were a part of oneself;[2] and nobody chooses to injure himself (hence there can be no injustice towards oneself); and so neither can there be any conduct towards them that is politically just or unjust. For political justice is, as we saw,[3] defined by law, and is found in communities where law is naturally accepted: those whose members share equally in ruling and being ruled. Hence justice is more fully realized between husband and wife than between father and children or master and slaves; it[4] is in fact domestic justice; but this too is distinct from political justice.

Political justice may be based upon natural or upon civil law

vii.   There are two sorts of political justice, one natural and the other legal. The natural is that which has the same validity everywhere and does not depend upon acceptance; the legal is that which in the first place can take one form or another indifferently, but which, once laid down, is decisive: e.g. that the ransom for a prisoner of war shall be one mina,[5] or that a goat shall be sacrificed and not two sheep; and also any enactments for particular circumstances, such as the sacrifices in honour of Brasidas,[6] and decisions made

1. Towards a slave or child respectively.
2. i.e. of the master or father.   3. Above, 1134a3off.
4. Viz. justice in the household – whether between husband and wife, father and child, or master and slave; cf. *Politics* 1253b8ff.
5. See note on 1133b23.
6. See Index of Names.

by special resolution. Some hold the view that all regulations are of this kind, on the ground that whereas natural laws are immutable and have the same validity everywhere (as fire burns both here and in Persia), they can see that notions of justice are variable. But this contention[1] is not true as stated, although it is true in a sense. Among the gods, indeed, justice presumably never changes at all; but in our world, although there is such a thing as natural law, everything is subject to change;[2] but still some things are so by nature and some are not, and it is easy to see what sort of thing, among those that admit of being otherwise, is so by nature and what is not, but is legal and conventional, assuming that both alike are changeable. And the same distinction will apply in all other cases; for the right hand is by nature the stronger, and yet it is possible for everyone to become ambidextrous.

Rules of justice established by convention and on the ground of expediency may be *compared to standard measures; because the measures used in the wine and corn trades are not everywhere equal: they are larger[3] in the wholesale and smaller in the retail trade. Similarly laws that are not natural but man-made are not the same everywhere, because forms of government are not the same either; but everywhere there is only one natural form of government, namely that which is best.

The several rules of law and justice are related to the actions performed in conformity with them as the universal is to the particular, because the latter are many, but each of the former is only one, being universal.

1. That natural laws are immutable.

2. For the rest of the paragraph the translation follows Bywater's text.

3. M. Ostwald (p. 132 of his translation of the *Ethics*, Indianapolis, 1962) rightly rejects the prevalent view that A. is contrasting official wholesale with official retail measures (the language here and at 1134b24–27 above clearly refers to local variations); but what truth, if any, underlies the generalization is still obscure.

Distinctions between certain cognate terms

'That which is unjust' is not the same as an unjust act, nor is
'that which is just' the same as a just act. A thing is unjust by
nature or ordinance; the same thing, when done, is an unjust act; but until it is done, it is not – merely unjust.
Similarly with a just act, *dikaiōma*, though a better word for
the general term is *dikaiopragēma*, since the former strictly
means the reparation of an injustice.

The number and nature of the several rules of justice, and
the kinds of action that they actually cover, must be considered later.[1]

Voluntary and involuntary acts: the importance of intention

viii.   Since just and unjust acts are as we have described
them, it is only when a person acts voluntarily that he does a
just or unjust act. When he acts involuntarily his action is
neither just nor unjust, except incidentally; because people
do perform actions to which justice and injustice are incidental.[2] Thus just and unjust conduct are distinguished by
being voluntary or involuntary, because it is when an act is
voluntary that it is blamed, and then also that it becomes an
unjust act. So there can be something that is unjust, but
stops short of being an unjust act, unless voluntariness is
present too. By a voluntary act I mean (as has been said
above[3]) any act lying in the agent's power that he does
knowingly, i.e. not being ignorant either of the person affected or of the instrument used or of the result (e.g. *whom* he
is striking, or *with what*, or *to what effect*), no particular being
due to accident or compulsion. Thus if a man were to seize
the hand of another and with it strike a third party, the

---

1. No such discussion has come down to us.
2. When the agent is not aware of all the circumstances, as is explained
below.
3. 1111a20ff.

second man would not be a voluntary agent, because he could not help himself. It is possible for the person struck to be the agent's father, although the agent is only aware that he is a human being, or one of the company, and not that he is his father. The same sort of distinction may be similarly assumed with regard to the result and the action as a whole. An involuntary act, then, is an act done in ignorance, or if not in ignorance, outside the agent's control, or under compulsion (for there are actually a number of the natural processes that we carry out *or experience, none of which are either voluntary or involuntary, although we are fully conscious of them: e.g. growing old or dying). In the case of just and unjust acts alike there is also an accidental factor. For example, a man may return a deposit unwillingly and through fear; then we must not say that he is acting justly, or doing a right action, except incidentally. Similarly we must admit that a man who fails to return a deposit only under compulsion and against his will is only incidentally acting unjustly or doing a wrong action. Some of our voluntary acts we do from choice, and some we do not; those which are the result of deliberation are chosen, and those which are not the result of deliberation are not chosen.

Grades of misconduct

Thus in associations there are three kinds of injury. Those that are done in ignorance are Mistakes – when the patient or the act or the instrument or the effect was different from what the agent supposed, because he either did not mean to hit anyone, or not with that missile, or not that person, or not with that effect; but the result was different from what he expected (e.g. he only meant to give the other a prick, not a wound), or the person or the missile was different. When the injury occurs contrary to reasonable expectation it is a Misadventure; but when it occurs not contrary to reasonable expectation but without malicious intent it is a mistake (for the agent makes a mistake when the origin of the responsibility lies in himself; when it lies outside him his act is a misadventure). When the agent acts knowingly but without premeditation it is an Injury; such are all acts due to temper or any other of the unavoidable and natural feelings to which human beings are liable. For those who commit these injuries and mistakes are doing wrong, and their acts are injuries; but this does not of itself make them unjust or wicked men, because the harm that they did was not due to malice; it is when a man does a wrong on purpose that he is unjust and wicked.

Acts done under provocation; and a note on ignorance

Hence acts prompted by temper are rightly judged to be unpremeditated, because the aggressor is not the man who acts in a temper but the person who made him angry. Further, the point at issue is not whether the act was done or not, but whether there was justification; because the ground of the anger is an apparent injustice. For it is not the *fact* that is in question, as it is in disputes about a contract, where one of the parties to the dispute must be a rogue, unless the dispute is due[1] to a lapse of memory. Here they agree about the fact, but dispute about the side on which justice lies (whereas a man who has deliberately attacked another is not ignorant of the fact); so that one thinks that he is *wronged, and the other disagrees. But if a man deliberately causes injury, he is guilty of injustice; and the doer of this sort of injury, when it violates proportion or equality,[2] is *eo ipso* an unjust man. Similarly a man is just when he acts justly from choice; but if he only acts voluntarily, he is merely acting justly.

Involuntary acts are either pardonable or unpardonable.

1. Or perhaps 'the wrong was due . . .', one of the parties having forgotten his obligation.
2. i.e. distributive or rectificatory justice.

Mistakes committed not only *in* ignorance but *as the result* of ignorance are pardonable; those that are committed in ignorance but are due not to ignorance but to an unnatural and sub-human reaction are unpardonable.

Is it possible to suffer injustice willingly?

ix.   It might be questioned whether the distinctions that we have drawn with reference to the doing and suffering of injustice are adequate; first, whether there is anything in Euripides' extraordinary suggestion in the lines:[1]

> 'I have slain my mother – that's my tale in brief.'
> 'By will of both, or both unwillingly?'

Is it really possible for a person to suffer an injustice[2] willingly? Or is this impossible, and is every such experience involuntary, just as every unjust act is voluntary? And is all suffering of injustice either one or the other, or is some voluntary and some involuntary? – and similarly in the case of being treated justly; because all just *conduct* is voluntary[3]), so that it is reasonable to suppose that there is a similar opposition in either case: that both being unjustly and being justly treated are either ⟨always⟩ voluntary or ⟨always⟩ involuntary. Yet it would seem absurd even in the case of being justly treated that it should always be voluntary, because some people are justly treated against their will.[4] The further question might also be raised: whether everyone who has had an unjust thing done to him is unjustly treated, or whether it is the same with suffering as it is with doing something unjust – because in both cases it is possible to participate incidentally in just acts, and clearly the case is similar

1. Cf. note on 1110a27. The speaker of the first line is Alcmaeon. In fact, although the poet probably could not resist the antithesis, the question is not absurd: Eriphyle might have felt such keen remorse that she accepted her fate as a *just* punishment.

2. Probably in the wider sense of 'wrong'.

3. Cf. 1135a15ff.

4. e.g. the recipient of a just punishment.

with unjust acts; because doing unjust acts is not the same as acting unjustly, nor is suffering unjust acts the same as being treated unjustly; and the same is true of acting justly and being justly treated, for it is impossible to be unjustly treated unless somebody acts unjustly, or to be treated justly unless somebody acts justly.

But if to act unjustly is simply to harm someone voluntarily, and the fact that the agent acts voluntarily implies that he knows the patient, the instrument and the manner of the injury; and if the incontinent[1] man voluntarily injures himself: then not only will he voluntarily be unjustly treated, but it will be possible for him to treat himself unjustly (this also is one of the problems that are *raised:[2] whether it is possible to treat oneself unjustly). Again, a person might, through incontinence, voluntarily submit to being harmed by another acting voluntarily; so that it would be possible to be voluntarily treated unjustly. But probably our definition is incorrect, and to the formula 'doing an injury with knowledge of the patient, the instrument and the manner' we should add 'against the patient's will'; then one does voluntarily suffer *harm* and unjust treatment, but nobody is voluntarily treated unjustly, not even the incontinent man; he acts against his will, for nobody *wills* what he does not think to be good, but the incontinent man does things that he does not think ought to be done.[3] The man who gives away what is his own property, as Homer says[4] Glaucus gave to Diomede

> Gold arms for bronze, a hundred oxen's worth
> For the worth of nine,

is not unjustly treated, because it lies with himself to make gifts, but it does not lie with himself to be unjustly treated – there must be somebody else to treat him unjustly. Thus it is clear that being treated unjustly is involuntary.

1. *akratēs*, the man who lacks strength of will.
2. No programme such as seems to be implied has been suggested; the subject is considered in ch. xi below.
3. He sees what is good for him, but lacks the strength of will to do it.
4. *Iliad* vi.236. Glaucus's conduct is represented as an aberration.

*Is it the distributor or the recipient that is guilty of
injustice in unfair distribution?*

There remain two of the problems that we set ourselves to
consider:[1] is it the person who has unfairly *assigned* too large a
share, or the *possessor* of it, that acts unjustly? and is it possible to treat oneself unjustly? ⟨These questions are connected;⟩ because if the first alternative is possible, i.e. if it is
the distributor, not the possessor, of the unduly large share
that acts unjustly, then if somebody knowingly and voluntarily assigns a larger share to another than to himself, he
is treating himself unjustly. (This is what unselfish people are
generally supposed to do, because an equitable[2] man tends
to take less than his due.) Or perhaps even this is an over-
simplification; for the person who took the smaller share
may conceivably have gained more of another good, such as
reputation or sheer nobility of character. Besides, the problem can also be solved on the lines of our definition of unjust behaviour; for the agent suffers nothing against his own
will, so that he is not unjustly treated on this score; or if he
suffers at all, it is only a loss.

It is evident also that the distributor of the larger share
acts unjustly, but the possessor of it does not always do so;
because the person who acts unjustly is not the one to whom
the unjust result attaches, but the one to whom it attaches to
produce it intentionally, that is the person with whom the
action originates; and the origin of the action lies in the distributor, not in the recipient.

Also, since producing an effect is spoken of in more than
one way, and there is a sense in which an inanimate object,
or a hand, or a slave at his master's command, commits a
murder, although the recipient 'does' what is unjust, he is
not acting unjustly.[3] Again, if the distributor made his

1. Cf. note on a34 above. The third problem has not been mentioned
before; the fourth has been partly answered already.
2. *epieikēs*; cf. 1138a1f.
3. Assuming that his acceptance is involuntary.

decision in ignorance, he is not acting unjustly in respect of legal justice, nor is his decision unjust (although it is unjust in a sense, because legal is different from primary justice). But if he knowingly made his *decision unjustly, then he too is taking more than his share of either favour or revenge.[1] So the man who has decided unjustly from such motives[2] 'has more than his share' just as much as if he were to participate in the proceeds of the unjust act; because for awarding possession of the land on that condition, although he did not receive land, he received a money payment.[3]

To be just is not easy, because just conduct presupposes a virtuous moral state

People suppose that it is in their power to act unjustly, and that therefore it is easy to be just; but this is not so. To go to bed with your neighbour's wife, to strike the man next to you, to slip money into somebody's hand – this is easy and lies in their power; but it is not easy, nor in their power, to do these things as the outcome of a certain state of character. Similarly they assume that it takes no special wisdom to recognize what is just and unjust, because it is not difficult to understand the instructions that the law gives us (although the acts that it prescribes are just only incidentally[4]); but how actions are to be performed and distributions made in order to be just – to know that is a harder task than to know what one's health requires; because in medicine too, although it is easy to know what honey and wine and hellebore[5] and cautery and surgery are, to know *how* and *to whom* and *when* they should be applied to produce health is no less a task than to be a qualified doctor. It is for this very

1. According to the motive that influenced his decision.

2. To secure favour or revenge.

3. Which shows that the unfair gain can be different in kind from what is distributed.

4. They are *essentially* just only when performed from a just state of character.

5. The standard sedative in Greek medicine.

reason[1] that people actually suppose that a just man is as capable of unjust as of just behaviour, on the ground that he could do any unjust act not less well but even better than a just one:[2] commit adultery or assault; and the brave man could throw away his shield, turn and run in either direction.[3] But to be a coward, or to act unjustly, is not merely to do these acts (except incidentally[4]), but to do them from a certain ⟨moral⟩ state; just as being a doctor or curing a patient is a matter not merely of using or not using surgery or medication, but of using them in a particular way.

Particular justice is exercised between parties of normal human probity

Just acts take place between persons who have a share of things generally good,[5] and for whom that share may be too large or too small. For some beings – e.g. presumably for the gods – no share can be too great, and for others – the incurably vicious – no particle is beneficial; all are injurious. But there are others who do benefit from them up to a point; and therefore justice is a human concern.

A digression on equity, which corrects the deficiencies of legal justice

x.   Our next task is to say something about equity and the equitable: what is the relation of equity to justice, and of what is equitable to what is just? When we look into the matter we find that justice and equity are neither absolutely identical nor generically different.[6] Sometimes we commend

1. Because they think that justice consists in keeping certain rules of conduct.
2. Cf. Plato, *Republic* 334A.
3. To either flank – not to the rear, which would be too obvious (?).
4. Cf. note on a12 above.
5. i.e. external goods, which are normally beneficial.
6. They are species of the same genus.

what is equitable and the equitable man, to the extent of transferring *the word to other contexts as a term of approbation instead of 'good', thus showing that what is more equitable is better. At other times, however, when we follow out the line of argument it seems odd that what is equitable should be commendable if it does not coincide with what is just; because if it is something different, then either what is just or what is equitable is not good; or alternatively if both are good, they are identical.

These, broadly speaking, are the arguments that raise the difficulty about what is equitable: yet there is a sense in which they are all correct, and there is no inconsistency between them. For equity, though superior to one kind of justice,[1] is still just, it is not superior to justice as being a different genus. Thus justice and equity coincide, and although both are good, equity is superior. What causes the difficulty is the fact that equity is just, but not what is legally just: it is a rectification of legal justice. The explanation of this is that all law is universal,[2] and there are some things about which it is not possible to pronounce rightly in general terms; therefore in cases where it is necessary to make a general pronouncement, but impossible to do so rightly, the law takes account of the majority of cases, though not unaware that in this way errors are made. And the law is none the less right; because the error lies not in the law nor in the legislator, but in the nature of the case; for the raw material of human behaviour is essentially of this kind.[3] So when the law states a general rule, and a case arises under this that is exceptional, then it is right, where the legislator owing to the generality of his language has erred in not covering that case, to correct the omission by a ruling such as the legislator himself would have given if he had been present there, and as he would have enacted if he had been aware of the circumstances.

1. Viz. legal justice; see below.
2. i.e. lays down general principles.
3. The circumstances of our actions are often too particular and complicated to be covered satisfactorily by any generalization.

This is why equity, although just, and better than a kind of justice, is not better than absolute justice – only than the error due to generalization. This is the essential nature of equity; it is a rectification of law in so far as law is defective on account of its generality. This in fact is also the reason why everything is not regulated by law: it is because there are some cases that no law can be framed to cover, so that they require a special ordinance. An irregular object has a rule of irregular shape, like the leaden rule of Lesbian architecture:[1] just as this rule is not rigid but is adapted to the shape of the stone, so the ordinance is framed to fit the circumstances.

It is now clear what equity is, and that it is just, and superior to one kind of justice. This also makes plain what the equitable man is. He is one who chooses and does equitable acts, and *is not unduly insistent upon his rights, but accepts less than his share, although he has the law on his side. Such a disposition is equity: it is a kind of justice, and not a distinct state of character.

Return to the question: can a man treat himself unjustly?

xi.   Whether a man can treat himself unjustly or not is evident from what has been said above.[2] For there are some just acts enjoined by law as consistent with virtue in general; e.g. the law does not allow a man to kill himself.[3] Again, when a man voluntarily – that is, knowing who the victim and what the instrument is – injures another (not by way of retaliation) contrary to the law, he is acting unjustly. But a man who cuts his throat in a fit of anger is voluntarily doing, contrary to the right principle, what the law does not allow; therefore he is acting unjustly. But towards whom? Surely

1. Lesbian moulding was ogival, i.e. took the form of a double curve; its regularity was checked by a leaden rule bent to the required shape.

2. Cf. 1129a32–b1 and 1136a10–1137a4.

3. The standard text, however interpreted, is hardly convincing; the reading adopted is that which Joachim attributes to Cook Wilson.

not himself, but the state; because he suffers voluntarily, and nobody is voluntarily treated unjustly. It is for this reason that the state imposes a penalty, and a kind of dishonour[1] is attached to a man who has taken his own life, on the ground that he is guilty of an offence against the state.

Further, in so far as the offender is merely unjust and not totally bad, it is impossible for him to treat himself unjustly (this case is different from the other, for there is a sense in which the unjust man is bad in the same way as the coward: as exhibiting a badness that is not total, so that his injustice does not exhibit total badness either);[2] otherwise it would be possible for the same thing to have been subtracted from and added to the same person at the same time; and this is impossible: justice and injustice must always involve more than one person. Again, an unjust act is voluntary, and deliberate, and aggressive (because a person who does no more than repay the same wrong that he suffered is not considered to act unjustly); but when a man injures himself he both does and suffers the same thing at the same time.[3] Again, it would be possible to be treated unjustly voluntarily. Furthermore, nobody acts unjustly apart from particular acts of injustice; and nobody can commit adultery with his own wife, or burgle his own house, or steal his own property. But in general the question of whether one can treat oneself unjustly is answerable by reference to the distinction made with regard to the voluntary suffering of injustice.[4]

It is worse to commit than to suffer injustice

It is also evident that being treated unjustly and acting unjustly are both evils, because the former is to have less and the latter to have more than the mean, whereas acting justly

---

1. His right hand was cut off and buried separately; also his descendants were perhaps disfranchised.

2. Because particular injustice is only a species of vice.

3. He seems to imply that the active is prior to the passive aspect of the injury, but this is surely a mistake.

4. 1136b2–14.

corresponds to what is conducive to health in the case of medical science and what is conducive to fitness in the case of physical training; but nevertheless acting unjustly is the worse,[1] because it implies vice and is censurable (the vice being either complete and absolute or nearly so – for not every voluntary act of injustice implies vice), whereas being unjustly treated does not imply vice or injustice.[2] So being unjustly treated is in itself the lesser evil, *although there is no reason why it should not be incidentally the greater misfortune. But this is no concern of scientific theory; medical science pronounces pleurisy to be a more serious ailment than a sprain, although the latter might incidentally prove to be the worse, if it so happened that the victim of a sprain should, through falling, be taken by the enemy and put to death.

How justice and injustice towards oneself are possible

In a metaphorical and analogical sense there is such a thing as justice not towards oneself but between certain parts of the self; only justice not in the full sense but as it subsists between master and slave, or in the management of a household. I say this because in discussions of this subject[3] the rational is contrasted with the irrational part of the soul, and those who take this contrast seriously actually believe that there is such a thing as injustice towards oneself, because it is possible for each of these parts to have its impulses thwarted to some extent ⟨by the other⟩; so that there is a sort of justice between them similar to that which there is between ruler and subject.

This may be taken as completing our analysis of justice and the other – that is, the other moral – virtues.

1. Cf. Plato, *Gorgias* 469A-c and 508c-609c.
2. In the patient.
3. By Plato in particular; cf. especially *Republic* 351E–352A, 430E–431E, 441D–442D, 443C–444A, and *Laws* 626D–E.

VI

INTELLECTUAL VIRTUES

What is the right principle that should regulate conduct?

i. We have already said[1] that one should choose the mean – not the excess, nor the deficiency – and that the mean is as the right principle dictates. Let us now analyse this latter statement.

In all the states that we have described (as in all other cases too) there is a sort of target; and it is with his eyes on this that the man who has the principle stretches or relaxes his string.[2] There is also a sort of limit determining the mean states which, as we hold, lie between excess and deficiency, and which accord with the right principle. But although to say this is true, it is not at all explicit, because as a matter of fact in all the other occupations about which there is a science it is true to say that one should exert oneself and relax neither too much nor too little, but to a mean extent and as the right principle dictates; but if you grasped only this, you would know nothing more – e.g. you would not know *what* remedies to apply to your body if someone told you to take what medical science prescribes and as a medical man prescribes it. Hence in the case of the states of the soul also it is not enough to have this precept truly enunciated; we need also to have it determined what the right principle is, and what the standard is by which it is established.

1. 1106a26ff.
2. i.e. raises or lowers his aim; in the context the string must surely be that of a bow.

Contemplative and calculative intellect

Now when we classified the virtues of the soul we said[1] that
*some of them were virtues of the character and others of the
intellect. We have already discussed the moral virtues; let
us now proceed to speak of the remainder as follows, first
making some observations about the soul.

It has been said above[2] that there are two parts of the soul,
one rational and one irrational. We must now make a similar
distinction in the case of the rational part: let us assume that
it consists of two parts, one with which we contemplate those
things whose first principles are invariable, and one with
which we contemplate things that are variable.[3] For assuming that the knowledge of them depends upon some
similarity and affinity between subject and object,[4] the two
parts of the soul that are naturally adapted to the cognition
of the two different kinds of object are themselves different
in kind. Let us call one of them the scientific and the other
the calculative part; because deliberation and calculation
are the same, and nobody deliberates about things that are
invariable; so the calculative is one distinct part of the
rational soul. We must therefore grasp what is the best state
of each of these two parts, because that will be the virtue of
each.

1. 1103a3ff.
2. 1102a26ff.
3. The sublunary world of practical science, as contrasted with the
intellectual world of theoretical science.
4. Empedocles' doctrine that like is cognized by like (e.g. that it is
brightness in the eye that responds to brightness in the visible object),
adopted and developed by Plato; cf. *Timaeus* 45Bff., *Republic* 490B.

Both kinds of intellect aim at truth, but the calculative
faculty aims at truth as rightly desired by the
exercise of choice

ii.   The virtue of a thing is related to its proper function.
Now there are in the soul three things that control action[1]
and ⟨the attainment of⟩ truth, viz. sensation, intellect and
appetition. Of these sensation is not the origin of any action,
as is clear from the fact that the brutes have sensation, but
no share in action.

Pursuit and avoidance in the sphere of appetition correspond exactly to affirmation and negation in the sphere
of intellect; so that, since moral virtue is a state involving
choice,[2] and choice is deliberate appetition,[3] it follows that
if the choice is to be a good one, both the reasoning must be
true and the desire right; and the desire must pursue the
same things that the reasoning asserts.[4] We are here speaking of intellect and truth in a practical sense: in the case of
contemplative (as distinct from practical and productive) intellect, right and wrong are truth and falsehood. To arrive at
the truth is indeed the function of intellect in any aspect, but
the function of practical intellect is to arrive at the truth
that corresponds to right appetition.

Now the origin of action (the efficient, not the final cause)
is choice,[5] and the origin of choice is appetition and purposive reasoning. Hence choice necessarily involves not only
intellect and thought, but a certain moral state; for good
conduct and its contrary necessarily involve thought and
character. But no process is set going by mere thought –
only by purposive and practical thought, *for it is this that
also originates productive thought. Everyone who makes
anything makes it for some purpose, and the product is not

   1. Here as elsewhere 'action' represents *praxis*, which for Aristotle
means *purposive* action.
   2. 1106b36.   3. 1113a9ff.
   4. That is, asserts to be good and therefore desirable.
   5. Cf. 1111b4ff.

an end in itself but only a relative or particular end.[1] But an action is an end in itself,[2] because good action is an end, and the object of appetition. Hence choice is either appetitive intellect or intellectual appetition; and man is a principle of this kind.[3]

(No past event is an object of choice – e.g. nobody chooses to have been the sacker of Ilium – because nobody deliberates about the past either, but only about a possibility in the future; and it is impossible for what has happened not to have happened. Hence Agathon was right:[4]

> For one thing is denied even to God:
> To make what has been done undone again.)

Thus the attainment of truth is the task of both the intellectual parts of the soul; so their respective virtues are the states that will best enable them to arrive at the truth.

Five modes of thought or states of mind by which truth is reached

iii.   Let us, then, discuss these states again, making a start further back;[5] let us assume that there are five ways in which the soul arrives at truth by affirmation or denial, viz. art,[6] science, prudence, wisdom, and intuition. Judgement and opinion are liable to be quite mistaken.[7]

---

1. e.g. a pair of shoes is made (a) generally as an aid to the good life, (b) because X needs shoes.

2. Not *qua* action, but in so far as, being well done, it contributes to the good life.

3. i.e. a causative union of reason with appetition.

4. Fragment 5.   5. i.e. taking less for granted.

6. See below, 1141a1ff.

7. They are therefore excluded from consideration.

Science or scientific knowledge (epistēmē)

What science is – if we are to give a precise account and not
follow the guidance of similes[1] – will be clear from the following argument. We all assume that what we *know* cannot be
otherwise than it is, whereas in the case of things that may
be otherwise, when they have passed out of our view we can
no longer tell whether they exist or not. Therefore the object
of scientific knowledge is of necessity. Therefore it is eternal,
because everything that *is of necessity* in the unqualified sense
is eternal; and what is eternal cannot come into being or
cease to be. Again, all scientific knowledge is supposed to be
teachable, and its object to be capable of being learnt. But
all teaching starts from what is already known, as we state
in the *Analytics*;[2] because it proceeds either by induction or
by deduction. Induction introduces us to first principles and
universals, while deduction starts from universals. Therefore there are principles from which deduction starts which
are not deducible; therefore they are reached by induction.
Thus scientific knowledge is a demonstrative state,[3] with all
the further qualifications set out in the *Analytics*;[4] i.e. a person has scientific knowledge when his belief is conditioned
in a certain way, and the first principles are known to him;
because if they are not better known to him than the conclusion drawn from them he will have knowledge only incidentally.[5]

This may serve as a description of scientific knowledge.

1. A hit at Plato's images in *Theaetetus* 191cff., 197cff.
2. *An. Post.* 71a1.
3. i.e. a state of mind capable of demonstrating what it knows.
4. *An. Post.* 71b20.
5. His knowledge will not be scientific because he cannot demonstrate
its truth.

Art or technical skill (technē)

*iv. The class of variables[1] includes both products and acts; but production is different from action (we base our views about them partly on extraneous discourses[2]); and so the reasoned state that is capable of action is also different from that which is capable of production. Hence neither is included in the other; because action is not production, nor production action. And since (e.g.) building is an art, and is essentially a reasoned productive state, and since there is no art that is not a state of this kind, and no state of this kind that is not an art, it follows that art is the same as a productive state that is truly reasoned. Every art is concerned with bringing something into being, and the practice of an art is the study of how to bring into being something that is capable either of being or of not being, and the cause[3] of which is in the producer and not in the product. For it is not with things that are or come to be *of necessity* that art is concerned, nor with natural objects (because these have their origin in themselves). And since production is not the same as action, art must be concerned with production, not with action. There is a sense in which art and chance operate in the same sphere, as Agathon says:[4]

Art has a love for chance, and chance for art.

Art, then, as we have said, is a productive state that is truly reasoned, while its contrary non-art[5] is a productive state that is falsely reasoned; both operate in the sphere of the variable.

1. 'What can be otherwise': strictly anything not determined by natural law, but here apparently confined to human activities.
2. Probably Academic; cf. 1102a26f.
3. The efficient cause.
4. Fragment 4; he means that they are inseparable.   5. *atechnia*.

Prudence or practical wisdom (phronēsis)

v. We may grasp the nature of prudence if we consider
what sort of people we call prudent.[1] Well, it is thought to be
the mark of a prudent man to be able to deliberate rightly
about what is good and advantageous for himself; not in
particular respects, e.g. what is good for health or physical
strength, but what is conducive to the good life generally.
A sign of this is the fact that we call people prudent in particular respects when they have calculated successfully with
a view to some serious[2] end (outside the sphere of art[3]); so
that in general also the man who is capable of deliberation
will be prudent. But nobody deliberates about things that
are invariable, or about things that he cannot do himself.
So since scientific knowledge implies the ability to demonstrate, and there is no demonstration of things whose
originative causes are variable (because all such things may
actually be otherwise), and it is impossible *to deliberate
about things that are *necessarily* so, prudence cannot be
science or art; not science because what can be done is a
variable,[4] and not art because action and production are
generically different. For production aims at an end other
than itself; but this is impossible in the case of action,
because the end is merely doing *well*. What remains, then,
is that it is a true state,[5] reasoned, and capable of action
with regard to things that are good or bad for man. Hence
we think that Pericles and others like him are prudent,
because they can envisage what is good for themselves and
for people in general; we consider that this quality belongs
to those who understand the management of households or
states. This is why we call temperance (*sōphrosunē*[6]) by this

  1. *phronēsis* (see Glossary) means 'practical common-sense'; but for
convenience the traditional 'prudence' has been retained.
  2. *spoudaios*; see Glossary.   3. i.e. in the practical sphere.
  4. It may be done in different ways, or not done at all.
  5. It is developed in accordance with a true theory or principle.
  6. See Glossary.

name, on the ground that it preserves wisdom. It does preserve this sort of judgement. ⟨I say 'this sort'⟩ because it is
not every sort of judgement that is destroyed or perverted by
pleasant and painful experiences; not, e.g., judgements
such as that the sum of the angles of a triangle is or is not
equal to two right angles, but judgements about what is to
be done. For the originative cause of an action is the
purpose for which it is done;[1] but a person who is corrupted
by pleasure or pain ceases at once to see that this is a cause
at all: that is, he does not realize that he ought to make
every choice as a means to that end, and perform every act
on account of it; for vice tends to destroy the ⟨authority of
the⟩ originative cause.[2]

Thus prudence must be a true state, reasoned and capable
of action in the sphere of human goods. Moreover, whereas
there is an excellence in art, there is no such thing in prudence; and in art the man who makes a mistake is rated
higher if he makes it voluntarily, but in the case of prudence he is rated lower, just as in the case of the ⟨moral⟩
virtues. Clearly, then, prudence is a virtue, not an art. And
as there are two parts of the soul that are susceptible of
reason, it must be the virtue of one of these, viz. the one
that forms opinions;[3] because both opinion and prudence
are concerned with the variable. Yet it is not merely a
rational state, as is indicated by the fact that such a state
can be forgotten, but prudence cannot.[4]

Intelligence or intuition (nous)

vi. Scientific knowledge consists in forming judgements
about things that are universal and necessary; and demonstrable truths, and every kind of scientific knowledge

1. i.e. some good, ideally the supreme good.
2. *archē* (see Glossary) means not only 'origin', etc., but also 'rule' or
'authority'; and A. seems to have this in mind: vice is a sort of anarchy,
as Plato said (*Republic* 444B).
3. Cf. 1139a12, where it is called calculative.
4. Because, being practical, it is constantly exercised; cf. 1100b17.

(because this involves reasoning), depend upon first principles. It follows that the first principles of scientific truths cannot be grasped either by science or by art or by prudence. For the scientific truth is demonstrable,[1] whereas art and prudence are *only concerned with the variable. Nor again are first principles the concern[2] of wisdom, because the wise man possesses the ability to *demonstrate* some things. So if the states of mind by means of which we reach the truth, and are never led into error, with regard to things both variable and invariable are science, prudence, wisdom and intuition; and if it cannot be any one of three of them, viz. prudence, science and wisdom: what remains is that the state of mind that apprehends first principles is intuition.[3]

Wisdom (sophia)

vii.   We apply the term 'wisdom' in the arts to the most finished experts in the arts; e.g. we call Phidias a wise sculptor and Polyclitus a wise statuary. Here all that we mean by the word is excellence in the art. But we regard some people as wise without qualification, not in a particular sense nor 'wise at something else', as Homer says in the *Margites*:[4]

> Nor digger him the Gods had made, nor ploughman,
> Nor wise in aught beside.

So evidently wisdom must be the most finished form of knowledge. The wise man, then, must not only know all that follows from the first principles, but must also have a true understanding of those principles. Therefore wisdom must be intuition *and* scientific knowledge: knowledge

---

1. And so invariable.   2. That is, not the sole concern.

3. The immediate perception of truth. But A. sometimes uses *nous* in the popular sense of 'intelligence' which has passed into English.

4. A famous satirical poem (not by Homer) of which only a few lines remain.

'complete with head'[1] (as it were) of the most precious truths.

(〈Most precious:〉 for it is extraordinary that anyone should regard political science or prudence as most important,[2] unless man is the highest being in the world. But if what is wholesome or good is different for human beings and for fish, whereas what is white or straight is always the same, so too everyone would mean the same by wise, but something different by prudent; for every kind of creature accepts as prudent, and will commit itself to, that which studies its good.[3] That is why some even of the brutes are said to be prudent, viz. those that can be seen to have the ability to provide for their own survival.[4] It is evident also that wisdom cannot be the same as political science. For if people are to give the name of wisdom to the knowledge of what is beneficial to themselves, there will be more than one wisdom; because there is no one wisdom that is concerned with the good of all animals, but a different kind for each species – unless there is also a single science of medicine for all creatures. To object that man is the highest animal makes no difference; because there are other beings far more *divine in nature than man, the most evident examples being those bodies[5] of which the heaven is composed.)

It is clear, then, from what has been said that wisdom is scientific and intuitive knowledge of what is by nature most precious. That is why people call Anaxagoras and Thales and men like them wise but not prudent when they observe them to be ignorant of their own advantage; and say that their knowledge is exceptional and marvellous and profound and supernatural, but useless, because the objects of

1. i.e. not truncated (like *epistēmē*) by severance from the first principles (the metaphor appears also at *Rhetoric* 1415b8 and in several passages in Plato).

2. *spoudaios*.

3. The text is uncertain but the general sense plain: that prudence studies particular goods, but wisdom universal truths.

4. e.g. by storing food.

5. The heavenly bodies, most obvious and most visible, whereas God, the First Mover, is invisible; see Appendix F.

their search are not human goods. But prudence is concerned with human goods, i.e. things about which deliberation is possible; for we hold that it is the function of the prudent man to deliberate well; and nobody deliberates about things that cannot be otherwise, or that are not means to an end, and that end a practical good.[1] And the man who is good at deliberation generally is the one who can aim, by the help of his calculation, at the best of the goods attainable by man.

Again, prudence is not concerned with universals only; it must also take cognizance of particulars, because it is concerned with conduct, and conduct has its sphere in particular circumstances. That is why some people who do not possess ⟨theoretical⟩ knowledge are more effective in action (especially if they are experienced) than others who do possess it. For example, suppose that someone knows that light flesh foods are digestible and wholesome, but does not know what kinds are light; he will be less likely to produce health than one who knows that chicken is wholesome. But prudence is practical, and therefore it must have both kinds of knowledge, or especially the latter. Here too, however, there must be some coordinating science.[2]

The political sciences are species of prudence

viii.   Political science and prudence are the same state of mind, but their essence is not the same.[3] Prudence concerning the state has two aspects: one, which is controlling and directive, is legislative science; the other, which deals with particular circumstances, bears the name that properly belongs to both, viz. political science.[4] This latter is practical

---

1. i.e. one that can be attained in action.   2. Viz. politics.

3. Politics is the fullest realization of prudence, which is also found at the lower levels of the household and individual.

4. In popular use the name 'politics' is confined to the daily administration of public affairs.

and deliberative; for an enactment is a thing that can be done, and the last step ⟨in a deliberative process⟩.[1] That is why only these persons[2] are said to take part in politics, because they are the only ones that perform actions, like the artisans ⟨in industry⟩. Prudence is also especially identified with that form of it which is concerned with the self and the individual, and bears the name, prudence, that rightly belongs to all the forms, the others being called domestic, legislative and political science, and the last-named being divided into deliberative and juridical science. Now knowing one's own interests will be one species of knowledge, but it is widely different from the other species; *and the man who knows and confines himself to his own interests is regarded as prudent, while politicians are considered to be busybodies. Hence the lines of Euripides:

> Should *I* be prudent? – I that might have lived
> A careless unit, one of the multitude,
> Sharing an equal fortune ⟨with the wisest⟩ . . .
> For the ambitious over-busy sort . . .
> ⟨We set on high as heroes of the state.⟩[3]

People do in fact seek their own good, and think that they are right to act in this way. It is from this belief that the notion has arisen that such people are prudent. Presumably, however, it is impossible to secure one's own good independently of domestic and political science. Besides, how the individual should manage his own interests is an obscure question which must be investigated.[4]

There is also confirmation of what we have said in the

1. Cf. 1112b23; the last step in the analysis becomes the first in the ensuing course of action.

2. Who deal with particular affairs.

3. Two incomplete quotations from the lost play *Philoctetes*, frr. 785–6; the words in angle brackets are intended to complete the sense, which is inferred from other sources.

4. It is not investigated in A.'s extant works.

fact that although the young develop ability in geometry and mathematics and become wise in such matters, they are not thought to develop prudence. The reason for this is that prudence also involves knowledge of particular facts,[1] which become known from experience; and a young man is not experienced, because experience takes some time to acquire. One might further ask why it is that a lad may become a mathematician, but not a philosopher or a natural scientist.[2] Probably it is because the former subject deals with abstractions, whereas the first principles of the two latter are grasped only as the result of experience; and the young repeat the doctrines of these without actually believing them, but in mathematics the reason why is not hard to see.

Again, error in deliberation is with reference either to the general principle or to the particular fact; e.g. thinking (mistakenly) that all heavy water[3] is bad, or that a given sample of water is heavy.

Prudence contrasted with science and intuition

It is obvious that prudence is not scientific knowledge, because it apprehends the last step, as we have said,[4] since the thing to be done is of this nature. Thus it is opposite to intuition; for intuition apprehends the definitions, which cannot be logically demonstrated; and prudence apprehends the ultimate particular, which cannot be apprehended by scientific knowledge, but only by perception – not that of objects peculiar to one sense, but the sort[5] by which we perceive that the ultimate figure in mathematics

1. As well as knowledge of universals.
2. A student of reality as exhibited in the world of nature.
3. Not, of course, deuterium oxide, D_2O, but (apparently) stagnant or muddy water; cf. Athenaeus 42c (quoting Theophrastus).
4. 1141b27f.; cf. 1112b20ff.
5. Not *sense*-perception at all, but intuition.

is a triangle;[1] because there too there will be a halt.[2] But
this is perception rather than prudence, although it is
another kind of perception.[3]

Resourcefulness or good deliberation (euboulia) distinguished from other intellectual qualities

ix. We[4] must also discover what resourcefulness is –
whether it is a kind of scientific knowledge, or opinion, or
ability to conjecture,[5] or some other kind of thing.

Well, it is not knowledge; for people do not inquire
*about things that they know, and resourcefulness is a kind of
deliberation, and a person who is deliberating inquires and
calculates. But to inquire is not the same as to deliberate;
because deliberation is a sort of inquiry. What is more, it is
not ability to conjecture either; because this is a rapid
thing and independent of reasoning, whereas deliberation
goes on for some time; and they say that one should carry
out quickly the *result* of one's deliberations, but deliberate
slowly. Readiness of mind,[6] again, is different from resourcefulness; it is a kind of ability to conjecture. Nor is resourcefulness any kind of opinion.

Since a person who deliberates badly makes a mistake,
while one who deliberates well does so correctly, clearly
resourcefulness is a species of correctness – but neither of
knowledge nor of opinion. For there is no such thing as
correctness of knowledge, since there is no such thing as
error of knowledge either; and correctness of opinion is
truth. Besides, everything that is an object of opinion is
already determined.[7] There is the further point that

1. The last stage in the analysis or division of a more complex figure.

2. The process of demonstration ceases on reaching particulars, just
as it does at the upper end of the scale on reaching first principles.

3. Intellectual, not sensory.

4. The sentence which in the MSS opens this chapter is translated
below after 'inquires and calculates'.

5. *eustochia.*   6. *anchinoia.*

7. Whereas deliberation is about a course of action that is not yet
decided.

resourcefulness involves reason. The remaining alternative, then, is that it is a correctness of thinking;[1] for thinking is a process towards assertion. Opinion[2] is not inquiry: it has reached the stage of assertion; and a person who deliberates, whether he does so well or badly, is inquiring into something and calculating. But resourcefulness is a species of correctness of deliberation; and therefore we must first inquire what deliberation is and what is its sphere.

Since the word 'correctness' is used in more than one sense, obviously it is not every kind of correctness that is in question. An incontinent or wicked person will achieve by means of his calculations the end that he sets before him, and will therefore be in the position of having deliberated correctly – and secured something very detrimental.[3] But the outcome of successful deliberation is generally assumed to be something good; because the sort of correctness in deliberation that constitutes resourcefulness is that which tends to secure something good. But it is possible to achieve even this by false inference: that is, to achieve the right end, but not by the right means, the middle term being false.[4] So this sort of correctness, through which we attain to the right end, but not by the right means, still does not constitute resourcefulness. Again, one person may succeed after long deliberation, and another quickly; then this[5] too still falls short of resourcefulness, which is correctness in estimating advantage with respect to the right object, the right means, and the right time. Again, it is possible to have deliberated well either in an absolute sense or in relation to a particular end. Then good deliberation in the absolute sense is that which succeeds in relation to the absolute end;[6] while particular good deliberation is that which succeeds in relation to a particular end. So if it is the

1. *dianoia.*   2. *doxa.*

3. Because neither really knows what is good for him.

4. Or rather, wrongly chosen, thus making one or more of the premisses of the practical syllogism false, although the conclusion correctly states the particular act needed to secure the required end; see Appendix G.

5. Or perhaps 'the former case', unless haste is as bad as slowness.

6. i.e. happiness.

mark of a prudent person to have deliberated well, excellence in deliberation will be correctness with regard to that which is advantageous in respect of the end, which[1] is truly apprehended by prudence.

Understanding (sunesis)

x. There is also understanding, and good understanding,[2] the qualities in virtue of which *people are said to be understanding and of good understanding. They are not entirely the same as ⟨scientific⟩ knowledge or opinion (for then everyone would be understanding),[3] nor is it[4] one of the particular sciences, such as medicine, which deals with health, or geometry, which deals with spatial magnitudes. For understanding is concerned not with things that are eternal and immutable, nor with any and everything that comes into being, but with matters that may cause perplexity and call for deliberation. Hence its sphere is the same as that of prudence; but understanding and prudence are not the same, because prudence is imperative (since its end is what one should or should not do), and understanding only makes judgements. (There is no essential difference between understanding and good understanding, or between people of understanding and people of good understanding.)

Understanding, then, is neither the possession nor the acquisition of prudence; but just as the act of learning is called understanding when one exercises the faculty of scientific knowledge, so too in exercising the faculty of opinion for the purpose of judging about another person's account of matters within the scope of prudence (and judging about it rightly, because 'well' is equivalent to 'rightly'), the act of judging is called understanding. Indeed

1. The means, not the end – prudence being practical.
2. *eusunesia*; this and the corresponding adjective are rare words and seem hardly worth mentioning.
3. Because opinion (if not knowledge) is common to all.
4. The change of number is unnoticeable in Greek.

this sense of the word, in virtue of which people are called good at understanding, is derived from the use in the case of learning; because we often say understand instead of learn.[1]

Judgement (gnōmē) and consideration

xi. What is called judgement,[2] in virtue of which we say that people are considerate and have ⟨sympathetic⟩ judgement, is the faculty of judging correctly what is equitable. An indication of this is the common view that the equitable man is especially sympathetic in his judgements, and that it is equitable to judge sympathetically in certain circumstances. And sympathetic judgement is a correct judgement that decides what is equitable; a correct judgement being one that arrives at the truth.

General comments on the various states of mind

All these states of mind naturally tend to coalesce, because we attribute judgement, understanding, prudence and intelligence[3] to the same persons, saying ⟨indifferently⟩ that they now have a mature judgement and intelligence, and that they are prudent and understanding. For all these faculties[4] are concerned with ultimate or particular things, and to be an understanding and considerate or sympathetic person consists in being able to judge about those things with which the prudent·man is concerned; for equitable acts are common to all good men in their behaviour towards

1. This is true of Greek but not of English.
2. The normal meaning of the word *gnōmē*, but A. is thinking also of the compounds, especially *sungnōmē* 'sympathy', in which the sense of feeling is prominent. He is also probably 'correcting' Plato, who had used *gnōmē* sometimes in the sense of 'knowledge'.
3. *nous* in the popular sense.
4. They are faculties (*dunameis*) as being natural tendencies that may or may not become established states (*hexeis*).

others. Now all acts belong to the class of ultimates or particulars, since the prudent man has to take cognizance of them; and understanding and judgement are also concerned with acts, and these are ultimates. And intuition[1] is concerned with ultimates in both directions; because it is intuition and not reason[2] that grasps both the first *and the ultimate terms:[3] the intuition concerned with demonstration having as its objects the primary immutable terms, and the intuition that operates in practical inferences being concerned with the ultimate and contingent, i.e. the minor premiss.[4] For these are the starting-points for arriving at the end, because it is from particular instances that general rules are established. So these particulars need to be perceived; and this perception is intuition.

That is why these states are considered to be natural gifts, whereas nobody is thought to be endowed by nature with wisdom, although he may have judgement and understanding and intuition. This is shown by our belief that these qualities depend upon age, i.e. that a given age possesses sense[5] and judgement, which implies that they are bestowed by nature. [Hence intuition is both a beginning and an end; because these particulars are both the starting-points and the subject-matter of demonstrations.][6] We should therefore pay no less attention to the unproved assertions and opinions of experienced and older people [or of prudent people][7] than to demonstrations of fact; because they have an insight from their experience which enables them to see correctly.

We have now explained what prudence and wisdom are, and what the sphere of each is; and that each is a virtue of a different part of the soul.

---

1. *nous* in the technical sense.

2. *logos* must surely mean 'reason' here.   3. Cf. 1142a25ff.

4. Intuition identifies the particular thing which (as the minor premiss of the practical syllogism informs us) must be done to realize the means to the required end (see Appendix G).

5. *nous* in the popular sense again.

6. This sentence is out of place; it should probably come at the end of the preceding paragraph.

7. Probably an addition; prudence is irrelevant here.

The value of the intellectual virtues

xii. A problem might be posed about the intellectual
virtues: what is the use of them? For wisdom studies none of
the things that go to make a man happy (because it is not
concerned with any kind of process); prudence has this
quality,[1] but for what purpose is it needed? It is concerned
with acts that are just and admirable and good for man;
but these are the acts that are characteristic of the good man,
and *knowing* about them does not make us any more capable of *doing* them, if the virtues are states of character. The
case is just the same as it is with knowledge about facts
relating to health and physical fitness (not as conducive to
them but as resultant from them); because the mere
possession of knowledge about medicine or physical training
does not make us any more capable of putting our knowledge into practice. On the other hand if we are to say that
prudence is useful not for this purpose but with a view to
becoming good, then it will be of no use to those who are
good already, and what is more, no use to those who are not
good, either; because it will make no difference whether
they possess prudence themselves or take the advice of
others who possess it, and it would be enough for us to
act as we do with regard to health; for although we wish
to be healthy, we do not learn the science of medicine.
Moreover, it might seem paradoxical that prudence,
though inferior to wisdom,[2] should prove to be more
authoritative; because a productive faculty controls what it
produces and issues instructions about it.[3] We must therefore discuss these problems, because so far we have merely
stated them.

*First, then, let us say that wisdom and prudence, both
being virtues – one of one part of the soul and the other of
the other[4] – must necessarily both be desirable in themselves,
even if neither of them produces any result. Next, they do

1. Of being relevant to happiness.   2. 1141a20ff.
3. Cf. below, 1145a6ff.   4. Cf. 1139a6–12.

produce results: wisdom produces happiness, not as medical science produces health, but as health does.[1] For wisdom is a part of virtue as a whole, and makes a person happy by his possession and exercise of it. Again, the full performance of man's function depends upon a combination of prudence and moral virtue; virtue ensures the correctness of the end at which we aim, and prudence that of the means towards it. (The fourth[2] or nutritive part of the soul has no virtue of this kind, because there is nothing that it has power to do or not to do.)

But we must reconsider the statement that prudence does not make us any more capable of doing fine and just acts; we must begin a little further back,[3] taking the following as our starting-point. Just as we say[4] that some people who perform just acts are still not just (for example, those who carry out the requirements of the law unwillingly, or through ignorance, or for some ulterior purpose and not for what they are, and yet are actually doing what is right, and all that a good man is bound to do); so, it seems, there is a state of mind in which a person can perform the various kinds of act in such a way as to be a good man: that is, when he does them from choice, and for the sake of the acts themselves. It is virtue that makes the choice correct; but the carrying out of all the natural stages of action with a view to that chosen end is a matter not for virtue but for a different faculty.

A new factor: the faculty of cleverness (deinotēs)

We must fix our attention on this matter and explain it more clearly. There is a faculty which is called cleverness. This is capable of carrying out the actions conducive to our

---

1. i.e. as formal cause, not (like the doctor's medical knowledge) as efficient cause.

2. Cf. 1102a32ff. Its activity is involuntary, so it has no choice between action and inaction.

3. i.e. taking less for granted (cf. 1139b14).   4. 1134a17ff.

proposed aim, and of achieving that aim. Then if that aim
is a noble one, the cleverness is praiseworthy; but if the aim
is ignoble, the cleverness is unscrupulousness (which is why
we call both prudent and unscrupulous people clever).[1]
Prudence is not identical with this faculty, but implies it.
On the other hand the insight of the soul that we have
mentioned[2] cannot attain to this state[3] without virtue, as has
been said above[4] and is obvious. For practical syllogisms
always have as their starting-point[5] 'Since the end or
supreme good is such-and-such' (whatever it may be; for
the sake of the argument it can be anything). Now only a
good man can discern this, because wickedness distorts the
vision and causes serious error about the principles of
conduct. Thus it is evident that one cannot be prudent
without being good.

How prudence is related to natural virtue and virtue proper

*xiii.   This means that we must reconsider the nature of
virtue, because in fact virtue exhibits a relation very like
that which prudence bears to cleverness: they are not
identical, but they are similar; and natural virtue is
related in the same way to virtue in the true sense. For while
it is universally believed that the various kinds of character
are in some sense the gifts of nature – because if we have a
disposition towards justice or temperance or courage or the
other virtues we have it from the moment of birth – at the
same time we expect to find that what is good in the strict
sense is something different, and that moral qualities are
acquired in another way; because the natural dispositions
are found in children and brutes, but without intelligence[6]
they are obviously apt to be harmful. This much, however,
seems to be an observed fact: that just as a powerfully built

1. The translation follows Allan's emendation.
2. 1143b13f. and cf. 1096b28f.   3. i.e. prudence.   4. a6ff.
5. i.e. the major premiss; see Appendix G.
6. *nous* in the popular sense.

man, if deprived of sight, is apt to fall heavily when he moves about, because he cannot see, so too in the moral sphere; but if the subject acquires intelligence he becomes outstanding in conduct, and his disposition, instead of *resembling* virtue, will now *be* virtue in the full sense. So just as in the case of the opinionative[1] faculty there are two kinds, cleverness and prudence, so also in the moral character there are two qualities, natural virtue and virtue in the full sense; and of these the latter implies prudence.

This is the reason why some people[2] maintain that all the virtues are forms of prudence; and why Socrates, though partly right, was also partly wrong in his inquiries, because he was mistaken in thinking that all the virtues are forms of prudence,[3] but he was quite right in asserting that they *imply* prudence. This is shown by the fact that even now all thinkers,[4] when defining virtue, after first saying what state it is and what its objects are, add the qualification 'in accordance with the right principle'; and the right principle is that which accords with prudence. So it appears that everybody as it were divines that virtue is a state of this kind, viz. in conformity with prudence. But we must go a little further than this, because virtue is not merely a state in conformity with the right principle, but one that implies the right principle;[5] and the right principle in moral conduct is prudence. So whereas Socrates thought that the virtues *are* principles (because he said that they are all forms of knowledge), we say thay they *imply* a principle. Thus we see from these arguments that it is not possible to be good in the true sense of the word without prudence, or to be prudent without moral goodness.

Indeed one might on these lines meet the dialectical argu-

1. i.e. calculative; cf. 1140b26.

2. Contemporary Academics or Socratics? The view recurs in Stoicism.

3. Plato generally makes him use the word *epistēmē*, not *phronēsis*; but the underlying idea is the same. For Socrates' views see Guthrie, *History of Greek Philosophy*, iii.450ff.

4. Probably Academics.

5. In other words, moral and intellectual goodness are complementary and in their highest form inseparable.

ment by which it could be contended that the virtues exist independently of each other, on the ground that the same man is not equally well endowed by nature in respect of them all, so that he will be already the possessor of one, but not yet the possessor of another. As far as the natural virtues are concerned, this is possible; but it is not possible *when the virtues are those that entitle a person to be called good without qualification; for the possession of the single virtue of prudence will carry with it the possession of them all.

It is clear, then, that even if prudence were not practical, it would still be necessary, because it is the virtue of its part;[1] and also that choice cannot be correct in default either of prudence or of goodness, since the one identifies the end and the other makes us perform the acts that are means towards it. At the same time, prudence does not exercise authority over wisdom or over the higher part of the soul, any more than the science of medicine exercises authority over health; for it does not use wisdom, but provides for its realization; and therefore issues orders not to it, but for its sake. Besides, it would be like saying that political science controls the gods because it gives instructions about everything in the state.[2]

1. The calculative part of the soul.
2. Including religious observances.

VII

CONTINENCE AND INCONTINENCE. THE NATURE OF PLEASURE

Moral virtues and their opposite vices: some commonly held views about them

i.   We must next observe – making a fresh start – that there are three kinds of states of character to be avoided, viz. vice, incontinence and brutishness.[1] The contraries of two of these are obvious: we call one of them virtue and the other continence. Corresponding to brutishness it might be most appropriate to suggest superhuman virtue: virtue on the heroic or godlike scale; as Homer makes Priam say of Hector that he was exceedingly brave,

> nor did he seem to be
> Son of a mortal sire, but of a god.[2]

So if, as they say, mortals become gods through superlative goodness,[3] the state opposed to brutishness would clearly be of this kind. For a god has no virtue or vice, any more than a brute has; the goodness of a god is more to be esteemed than virtue, and the badness of a brute is different in species from vice. And since it is rare for a man to be divine (as the Spartans are fond of calling anyone that they particularly admire: 'He iss a tifine man',[4] they say), in the same way a brutish person is also rare among human beings. The type is commonest among the non-Greek races, but some cases also occur[5] that are due to disease or arrested development. We also use the word brutish to express reprobation of extremely vicious persons.

However, of this kind of disposition we shall have to make

---

1. *kakia, akrasia* and *thēriotēs*.   2. *Iliad* xxiv.258f.
3. Not a common feature of Greek thought, but implicit in the mystery cults.
4. The Greek quotation is in Doric dialect.   5. Among Greeks.

some mention later,[1] and of vice we have spoken already.[2] We must now discuss incontinence and softness or effeminacy, and also continence and endurance,[3] for these *should neither be regarded as states identical with virtue and vice ⟨respectively⟩, nor as different from them in species. Here as in all our other discussions we must first set out the evidence, and then, after calling attention to the difficulties, proceed to establish, if possible, all the received opinions about these affections,[4] or failing that, as many as we can of those that are best supported. For if the discrepancies are resolved and received opinions left validated, the truth will be sufficiently demonstrated.

Well, people think (1) that continence and endurance are among good and commendable qualities, but incontinence and softness among those that are bad and censurable. (2) The continent man is identical with one who tends to abide by his own calculation,[5] and the incontinent with one who tends to depart from it. (3) The incontinent man does wrong because he feels like it, although he knows that it is wrong, whereas the continent man, when he knows that his desires are wrong, refuses assent to them because of his principle. (4) The temperate[6] man is continent and enduring; and some think that every man with these qualities is temperate, while others do not; and some call the licentious man incontinent and the incontinent licentious indiscriminately, while others hold that they are different. (5) It is sometimes maintained that it is impossible for the prudent man to be incontinent, and sometimes that some prudent and clever men *are* incontinent. (6) People are described as incontinent in respect of their temper, their ambition and their greed for gain. These are the views that are expressed.

1. Cf. 1149a1, 1150a1ff.
2. Generally, in discussing moral virtue; but it is equated with complete injustice at 1130a8ff.
3. i.e. *akrasia, malakia* and *truphē, enkrateia* and *karteria*.
4. They are really states, but the vaguer word *pathos* may have been used as being more appropriate to the morbid states.
5. i.e. his estimate of what it is right to do.   6. *sōphrōn*.

Inconsistencies involved in the foregoing views

ii.   The question may be raised: What sort of right conception can a man have, and yet be incontinent? Some say that it is impossible for a man who *knows*, because it is a shocking idea, as Socrates thought, that when a man actually has knowledge in him something else should overmaster it and 'drag it about like a slave'.[1] For Socrates was utterly opposed to this theory, on the ground that there is no such thing as incontinence; because he said that nobody acts consciously against what is best – only through ignorance. Now this reasoning is glaringly inconsistent with observed facts;[2] and it becomes necessary to inquire with regard to the condition in question: if it is due to ignorance, what is the manner of this ignorance? For it is clear that the person who acts incontinently does not think that it is right before he finds himself in the situation. But there are people who accept some parts of the doctrine and reject others. They agree that nothing is more potent than knowledge, but they do *not* agree that nobody acts against what he believed was the better course; and for this reason they maintain that when the incontinent man is unable to resist pleasures what he has is not knowledge but only opinion. And yet if it is really opinion and not knowledge – not a strong con*viction that puts up a resistance, but only a mild one such as you find in people who cannot make up their minds – one can forgive a man for not standing by his opinions in the face of powerful desires, but one cannot forgive wickedness or any other culpable attitude.

Is it, then, when prudence resists that yielding is culpable,[3] for prudence is a very potent force? But this involves a paradox, because the same person will be at the same time both prudent and incontinent, and there is nobody who would maintain that it is the mark of a prudent man vol-

---

1. Cf. Plato, *Protagoras* 352B.
2. Or perhaps 'is inconsistent with the plainest evidence'.
3. This is an examination of view (5) above.

untarily to perform the worst acts. Besides, it has already
been shown that the prudent man is *practical*[1] (because he is
concerned with ultimate particulars), and that he possesses
all the other virtues.[2]

Again,[3] if continence consists in having strong and evil desires, the temperate man will not be continent nor the continent man temperate, because neither excessive desires nor
evil ones are compatible with temperance. Yet the incontinent man must have both; for if his desires are good,
the state that prevents him from following them must be bad,
so that not all continence will be good; and if they are weak
and not bad, there is nothing to be proud of in resisting
them; nor is it much of an achievement if they are bad and
weak.

Again,[4] if continence makes a man disposed to persist in
every opinion, it is a bad thing: e.g. if it makes him persist
even in a false one. And if incontinence makes one inclined
to give up every opinion, there will be a good form of incontinence. An example of this is Neoptolemus in the
Philoctetes of Sophocles. He is to be commended for not per-
sisting in the course of action to which he was persuaded by
Odysseus, because it distressed him to sustain a false part.[5]

Again,[6] there is the difficulty contained in the argument
that the sophists employ. They want to trap people into
making paradoxical admissions, so as to appear clever when
they succeed; the inference that follows leads to a dilemma.
The victim's mind is completely tied up: unwilling to
remain where it is, because the conclusion is offensive, and
unable to proceed, because it cannot untie the knot of the
argument. Thus from one of their arguments it follows that
folly combined with incontinence is a virtue. For the subject,
because of his incontinence, behaves in a manner contrary
to his belief; now he believes that what is good is bad, and

1. i.e. acts on his decisions; cf. 1141b14ff., 1142a23ff.
2. 1144b30ff.   3. An examination of view (4).
4. Inconsistency between views (1) and (2).
5 See lines 895 916, and cf. 1151b17ff.
6. Inconsistency between (1) and (3).

that he ought not to do it; therefore he will do good deeds and not bad ones.

Again,[1] a man who does or pursues what is pleasurable from conviction and through choice might seem to be a better person than one who does the same not from calculation but from incontinence; because he is more likely to be cured, owing to the possibility of his being persuaded to change his ways. But the incontinent man lays himself open to the proverb 'If water chokes you, what's to wash it down?' – because if *he was convinced that he was doing what was right, a change of conviction might have caused him to stop;[2] but as it is he still persists in his conduct although his conviction is different.

Again,[3] if continence and incontinence can be exercised about *anything*, what sort of person is the absolutely incontinent man? – because nobody has *every* form of incontinence, and yet we call some people incontinent without any qualification.

Such, in general outline, are the difficulties that these views involve. Some of the points contained in them must be rejected and others established, because the solution of a difficulty consists in the discovery of the facts.[4]

Preliminary discussion of the conflicting views

iii. First, then, we must consider whether incontinent people act knowingly or unknowingly, and if knowingly, in what sense. Next, about what sort of things should we assume that people are continent and incontinent? – I mean, is it about every kind of pleasure and pain, or a certain limited range of them? Is the continent the same as the enduring man, or different? And similarly with all the other questions that are germane to the subject.

The first step in our inquiry is to ask whether the dif-

1. Inconsistency between (2) and (4).
2. If he had been a normally continent person.
3. View (6).   4. Cf. 1145b2–7.

ferentia[1] of the continent and incontinent consists in their
external circumstances or in their own attitudes; I mean
whether the incontinent man is such merely because he is in
certain circumstances, or because he has a certain attitude,
or for both reasons together. And next, whether continence
and incontinence are shown with regard to everything, or
not: because a man who is called incontinent without qualification is incontinent not in every respect but only in the
same respects as the licentious man; nor is he incontinent
simply by being concerned with them (for then incontinence
and licentiousness would be identical), but because he has a
certain attitude towards them. The licentious man is carried
away at his own choice, thinking that he ought always to
pursue the pleasure of the moment; the incontinent man
pursues it too, but has no such belief.

The view that it is true opinion, and not knowledge, that
people disregard when they behave incontinently has no
helpful bearing on our discussion. For some people hold
opinions without any hesitation, and believe that they have
precise knowledge. Consequently if it is owing to the weakness of their convictions that people who merely have
opinions are to be more liable to act against their conception ⟨of what is right⟩ than those who have knowledge, then
knowledge will be no different from opinion; because there
are some people who have no less confidence in their
opinions than others have in what they know. Heraclitus
shows that this is so.[2]

Suggested solutions

(1) *One may have knowledge without using it*

But since we use the word 'know' in two ways (because a
person who *has* knowledge but does not *use* it is said to know,
as well as the person who does use it), it will make a dif-

1. i.e. that which distinguishes them not from each other but from
other moral types or species.
2. A dig at Heraclitus's dogmatism.

ference whether a person does wrong while having but not reflecting upon his knowledge, or whether he does wrong while reflecting that he is doing wrong. The latter is felt to be shocking; but it does not shock us if he does wrong without reflecting upon it.

(2) *Errors may arise in the practical syllogism*

Since there are two *kinds of premiss,[1] it is quite possible for a person who has ⟨knowledge of⟩ them both to act inconsistently with his knowledge, given that he is exercising his knowledge of the universal but not his knowledge of the particular; because the things that we have to *do* are particulars. There is also a distinction in the case of the universal:[2] this refers partly to the agent himself and partly to the thing. E.g. 'Dry food is good for every man', and 'I am a man' or 'This sort of food is dry'; but whether this particular food is the right sort he either does not have the knowledge or is not using it. Thus there will be an immeasurable distance between these two ways of knowing; so that there is nothing strange in the man's[3] knowing in the way just described – it would be remarkable if he knew in the other way.

(3) *Circumstances may prevent the normal use of knowledge*

It is an attribute of man to have knowledge in another way besides those that we have described, because in the case of having knowledge without using it we can detect a different kind of *having*, so that a person can, in a sense, both have knowledge and not have it: e.g. if he is asleep or mentally disturbed or drunk. Now this is the condition of those who are in the grip of emotion; because quite obviously fits of temper and sexual craving and certain other such ex-

1. In the Practical Syllogism (Appendix G). The major premiss states a universal and the minor a particular connection; see next note, and cf. a25ff. below.

2. The major, which states a general connection between a human subject and a class of actions or objects.

3. The incontinent man's. If he fully realized the particular implications of the major premiss his conduct would be unaccountable.

citements actually produce physical changes, and in some cases even cause fits of madness. So evidently we should assert that incontinent people are in a similar state.[1] The fact of their using language that implies knowledge is no evidence, because people who are emotionally excited in the ways that we have described declaim proofs,[2] and passages from Empedocles;[3] and those who have just started learning a subject reel off a string of propositions which they do not yet understand; because knowledge has to be assimilated, and that takes time. So we must suppose that incontinent persons utter their sentiments as actors do.[4]

(4) *How desire can affect the practical syllogism*

One may also consider the cause of incontinence scientifically, as follows. The universal premiss[5] is an opinion, while the other is concerned with particulars, which fall within the scope of sensation. When the two are combined, in one kind of reasoning[6] the mind must *affirm* the conclusion, but in the practical syllogism it must immediately *act* on it. E.g. if all sweet things should be tasted, and x, one of the particulars ⟨forming a class⟩, is sweet, then the agent, if he has the power and is not prevented, must immediately act. So if there are two universal judgements present in the mind, one deterring the agent from tasting and the other asserting 'Everything sweet is pleasant' and 'x is sweet'[7] (and it is the latter that is realized) and at the same time desire is present, then although the former universal judgement is a deterrent, the desire carries his body forward (since desire can set the various parts of the body in motion). So it comes

1. i.e. not responsible for their actions.
2. Logical or geometrical; the point is that they seem to know what they are saying.
3. Probably from his *Purifications*, which contained moral maxims.
4. Not as expressing their own feelings at the time.
5. A considered solution is now offered to the difficulties raised about the practical syllogism; the universal premiss is of course the major (see Appendix G).
6. In a demonstrative syllogism.
7. This is a separate particular premiss.

about that *incontinent action is in a sense influenced by a rational principle and opinion, contrary not in itself but only incidentally (because it is the desire, not the opinion, that is contrary) to the right principle. So this is another reason why the brutes are not incontinent, viz. because they have no universal belief but only an impression and memory of particulars.

As for how the incontinent person's ignorance is dispelled and he recovers knowledge, the explanation is the same as in the case of intoxication and sleep: it is not peculiar to this experience. But on this point it is for the scientist to instruct us.

Since the final[1] premiss which controls action is an opinion about the percept, and the incontinent person, while under the influence of his emotion, either does not grasp it or grasps it only in such a way that the grasp, as we saw,[2] does not amount to knowing it but merely to repeating it, like the drunken man quoting Empedocles; and since the last term is not universal and is not regarded as an object of knowledge in the way that a universal judgement is, it does appear that the conclusion is that which Socrates tried to establish.[3] For the knowledge that is present when the emotion occurs is not what is regarded as knowledge in the strict sense; nor is it this that is 'dragged about' by the emotion, but only sensory knowledge.[4]

So much for our account of how it is possible to be incontinent knowingly and unknowingly; and if knowingly, in what sense.

The sphere of incontinence

iv. We must next discuss whether there is anyone who is incontinent without qualification, or whether all incontinent people are such in a particular respect; and if there is such a person, what he is incontinent about. In the first

1. i.e. that which immediately precedes the conclusion.
2. a11ff.   3. 1145b22–24.   4. A mere perceptive judgement.

place it is obvious that the experiences with regard to which
people are continent and enduring or incontinent and weak
are pleasures and pains. Of the things that give pleasure
there are two kinds, some being necessary and others desirable[1] in themselves but admitting of excess. The necessary
pleasures are the physical ones, by which I mean those connected with food and sexual needs, i.e. such physical pleasures as we took[2] to be the sphere of licentiousness and
temperance. The other pleasures are not necessary but desirable in themselves; I mean, e.g., victory, honour, wealth,
and any other things that are good and pleasant. Now those
who indulge to excess in this second class of pleasures, contrary to the right principle within them, we do not call incontinent without qualification; we qualify the bare word
'incontinent' by adding 'in respect of money' or 'gain' or
'honour' or 'temper', thus implying that they are distinct
from the absolutely incontinent, and are called incontinent
only by analogy – like Man the Olympic victor,[3] *because
in his case there was little difference between the general and
particular definitions, but nevertheless there *was* a difference.
(This is indicated by the fact that incontinence, whether
general or particular, is censured not only as a fault but as a
vice, whereas none of the types mentioned above is so
censured.) But in the case of bodily enjoyments, which we
hold[4] to be the sphere of the temperate and licentious, the
man who pursues excessive pleasures and avoids excessive[5]
pains like hunger and thirst, heat and cold, and all the dis-
comforts of touch and taste, not from choice but in opposition to it and to his reasoning, is described as incontinent
without any added determinant 'in respect of so-and-so',
e.g. anger, but simply without qualification. (This is supported by the fact that people are called 'soft' with respect

1. 'Choosable'.   2. 1118a1ff.

3. A person called Anthropos (Man) won the boxing event in 456 B.C.
The difference is the qualification 'the Olympic victor', which at once
stamps 'Man' as an individual. The illustration is partly humorous.

4. Cf. 1118a1ff.

5. No doubt an error for 'moderate'; cf. a19 below.

to these sensations, but not with respect to any of the former kind of pleasures.) That is why we class together the incontinent and the licentious man, the continent and the temperate man (but not any of the former kind[1]), because they are concerned, in a sense, with the same pleasures and pains; but although they are concerned with the same things, they are not concerned with them in the same way; the licentious act from choice and the incontinent do not. Hence we should more correctly call licentious the man who pursues excessive pleasures and avoids moderate pains under little, if any, impulse of desire, than the man who does so under a powerful impulse; for what would the former do under an excess of youthful passion and the torment of being denied his necessary pleasures?

Some desires and pleasures are concerned with things that are fine and good in kind – for some pleasant things are naturally desirable, others the contrary, and others intermediate between the two, in accordance with the classification that we made above[2] – e.g. money, gain, victory and honour; and with regard to all these things – whether of the former or of the intermediate kind – people are not blamed for being susceptible, i.e. liking or desiring them, but only for doing so in a particular way, viz. to excess. Hence those who, contrary to their principle, either cannot resist, or ⟨at any rate⟩ pursue, some naturally admirable and good thing: those, for example, who care too much for honour, or for their children or parents (for these too are good things, and those who care for them are commended; but nevertheless even here there is a possibility of going too far, supposing that like Niobe one tried to rival the gods,[3] or like Satyrus who was nicknamed *Father-lover for his attitude towards his father, because his infatuation seemed to be going too

1. Those whose incontinence is specific.
2. 1147b23ff.
3. Niobe had 12 (or 14) children, and claimed at least equality with Leto (Latona) who had only two; but these two, Apollo and Artemis, killed all Niobe's children with their arrows, and she was overcome with grief.

far[1]).[2] Well then, there is no actual wickedness involved in
these pleasures, for the reason stated above, that every one
of them is naturally choosable in itself; although over-
indulgence in them is a bad thing and to be avoided. Similarly there is no incontinence involved either; for incontinence is not only a thing to be avoided, but one of those that
are condemned. It is only by analogy with incontinence
proper that the word is used with reference to these particular pleasures, but always with the added qualification; just
as people describe as a bad doctor or bad actor a man whom
they would not call bad without any qualification. So just
as in this case we do not call people *bad*, because the particular failing is not a vice although like one by analogy, so in the
former one clearly we must regard as continence and incontinence only those states that are concerned with the
same pleasures as temperance and licentiousness, whereas
we use the word with reference to temper by analogy; which
is why we add the qualification and say 'incontinent in respect of temper', just as we say 'in respect of honour' or 'of
gain'.

Morbid or perverse pleasures

v.   (1) Some things are naturally pleasant, and of these (a)
some are pleasant absolutely and (b) others pleasant only to
certain kinds of men and animals. But (2) there are other
things that are not naturally pleasant but become so, either
(a) through injury[3] or (b) through habit or (c) through congenital depravity. Now corresponding to each of these types
of unnatural pleasures we can observe abnormal states of
character. I mean those that we call brutish,[4] such as the
female human[5] who, they say, cuts open pregnant women

---

1. What Satyrus did is not clear, and *Philopator* may have been a title.
2. The construction broken by this long parenthesis is never resumed.
3. Physical or mental disease or other damage.
4. Corresponding to 2(c) above.
5. The odd phrase may be meant to convey something like our
'fiend in human shape'.

and devours their babies, or certain savage tribes round the Black Sea, some of whom are said to have a taste for raw meat and others for human flesh, while others take turns in supplying children for the tribal feast; or the story told of Phalaris.[1] These states are brutish, but others[2] result from disease (and in some cases from madness, like the man who sacrificed and ate his mother, or the slave who ate the liver of his fellow-slave); and there are other morbid states that are the result of habit,[3] like pulling out hairs and nail-biting, or eating coal[4] and earth, and male homosexuality; because although these come naturally to some people, others acquire them from habit, e.g. those who have been victimized since childhood. Now where Nature is the cause nobody would charge the subjects with incontinence any more than one would apply the term to women on the ground that their role in coition is not active but passive; and the same holds good of those who are in a morbid condition as the result of habit. So the possession of these qualities falls in every case outside the *boundaries of vice; just as brutishness does. And the question of overcoming or being overcome by them is a matter not of incontinence unqualified, but of analogical incontinence; just as a person who has this sort of trouble with his fits of temper must be described as incontinent in respect of his feelings but not just as incontinent.

For all cases of excessive folly, cowardice, licentiousness and irritability are either brutish or morbid. A man so constituted by nature as to be frightened at anything, even the squeak of a mouse, is cowardly with a brutish[5] cowardice: and the man who was afraid of a weasel[6] was nervous as the result of an illness. In the case of folly, those who are congenitally incapable of reasoning and live only by sensation, like some tribes of remote barbarians, are brutish;

---

1. See Index of Names and cf. below, 1149a14.
2. Corresponding to 2(a). 3. Corresponding to 2(b).
4. Strictly 'charcoal'. 5. i.e. sub-human.
6. Or 'cat', because weasels were kept as mousers. The past tense suggests an actual event.

while those who are victims of disease (such as epilepsy) or madness are morbid. It is possible in certain cases for a man merely to have these proclivities without giving way to them; I mean, for example, supposing that Phalaris[1] restrained his desire to eat a baby or indulge in some abnormal sexual pleasure; but it is also possible not only to have them but also to be mastered by them. Then just as human wickedness is simply called wickedness, while other kinds are described by an added determinant, such as 'brutish' or 'morbid', obviously in the same way some incontinence is brutish and some is morbid, but only that which corresponds to human licentiousness is called simply incontinence.

It is clear, then, that continence and incontinence are concerned only with the same sort of things as licentiousness and temperance; and that the incontinence that is shown in other spheres is another kind, called incontinence by an extension of meaning, and not without qualification.

Incontinence of temper and desire

vi. Let us now consider the view that incontinence of temper is actually less shameful than incontinence in respect of one's desires. Temper seems to pay some attention to reason,[2] but to hear it imperfectly – just as eager servants go darting off before hearing the end of what is said to them, and then mistake their instructions, and dogs bark at a mere noise before investigating whether it is a friend: in the same way temper, owing to the heat and impetuosity of its nature, hears, but does not hear the order given,[3] and so hurries to take revenge. For when reason or imagination[4] informs somebody that he is being insulted or slighted, temper infers, as it were, that such a person is to be treated as an

1. Cf. 1148b24. For other writers he is a type of extreme cruelty, but not of perversion.
2. *logos*.
3. It hears the dissuasive voice, but does not take in what it says.
4. *phantasia*: a purely sensory impression.

enemy, and so instantly takes offence. But desire only needs
reason or the senses to tell it that a thing is pleasant, and sets
off to *enjoy it. Thus temper is amenable to reason up to a
point, but desire is not. So it is more disgraceful; because
the man who is incontinent of temper is up to a point
swayed by reason, but the other is swayed not by reason but
by desire.

Also it is more pardonable to be guided by the natural
appetites, inasmuch as it is more pardonable to be swayed
by such desires as are common to all, in so far as they are
common; and temper and resentment are more natural than
desires for excessive and unnecessary pleasures. It is like the
man defending himself for beating his father: 'Well,' he said,
'he beat his father and *he* beat the father before him; and
this fellow' he said, pointing to his little boy, 'will beat me
when he gets to be a man. It runs in the family.' Or the man
who, when his son was dragging him out of the house, used
to say 'Stop!' when they got to the front door; 'that's as far
as I dragged *my* father.'

Again, the craftier that people are, the more unjust they
are. Now the choleric man is not crafty any more than temper
is, but open; whereas desire *is* crafty, as Aphrodite is said to
be:

> Of the Cyprus-born, weaver of wiles;[1]

and Homer, speaking of her embroidered girdle, says that it
had on it

> Beguiling speech that steals the wisest wits.[2]

So if this kind[3] of incontinence is more unjust and disgraceful than incontinence of temper, it is both incontinence unqualified and (in a sense)[4] vice.

Again, nobody who behaves with wanton insolence does
so from a sense of grievance, but always with a feeling of

1. The phrase, ascribed to Sappho, is part of a description of Aphrodite's handmaid Persuasion.
2. An allegorical figure; *Iliad* xiv.217.
3. Incontinence of desire.
4. Not absolutely, because vice involves choice.

pleasure,[1] whereas everyone who acts in anger does so from a sense of grievance. So if actions are unjust in proportion to the justification of the anger that they arouse, incontinence of desire is more unjust than incontinence of temper, because there is no insolence in temper.

It is clear, then, that incontinence of desire is more disgraceful than incontinence of temper, and also that continence and incontinence are concerned with bodily desires and pleasures. But we must try to apprehend the differences between these desires and pleasures themselves; for, as we said at the beginning,[2] some are human and natural both in kind and in degree, some brutish, and some due to injuries or disease. Of these only the first kind make up the sphere of temperance and licentiousness. That is why we do not speak of the brutes as temperate or licentious (except metaphorically; that is of any species that is generally distinguishable from other animals for being lascivious or destructive or omnivorous[3]), because they possess neither choice nor calculation, but are aberrations from the natural, like the in*sane among human beings.[4] Brutishness is not as bad as vice, although it is more alarming, because it consists not in the corruption of the highest part,[5] as it does in man, but in the absence of it. Thus one might as well compare an animate with an inanimate object to see which is the worse; because the badness of that which has no active principle is always less destructive, and intelligence is an active principle. So it is very much like comparing injustice with an unjust man, because each is in a sense worse than the other;[6] for a bad man can do infinitely more harm than a brute.

1. The word *hubris* implies enjoyment of the victim's humiliation (cf. *Rhetoric* 1378b23ff. and 1380a34ff.).

2. 1145a15ff., 1148b15ff.   3. e.g. asses, wild boars, and pigs.

4. They are freaks, but not vicious.   5. Intelligence or reason.

6. Theoretically injustice is worse, because no man is absolutely unjust; but an unjust man is more dangerous, because he can initiate injustice.

Attitudes towards pleasure and pain

vii.   As for the pleasures and pains, desires and avoidances, that are excited by touch and taste – which we have already[1] determined as the sphere of temperance and licentiousness – it is possible on the one hand to be in such a state as to succumb even to those temptations to which most people are superior, and on the other to overcome even those to which most people succumb. Of these types those that are concerned with pleasures are the continent and the incontinent, and those that are concerned with pains the soft and the enduring man. The state of the great majority lies between these, although they incline rather towards the worse extremes.

We have already noted[2] that some pleasures are necessary and some are not, and that they are only necessary up to a point, while excessive or insufficient enjoyment of them is not necessary at all. The case is similar with desires and pains. The man who pursues excessive pleasures, or pursues necessary pleasures to excess and deliberately, for their own sake and not for any ulterior reason, is licentious,[3] because such a person must be unrepentant, and is therefore incurable, since anyone who is incapable of repentance is incurable. On the other hand the man who is deficient in the appreciation of pleasure is the opposite of the licentious man, while the temperate man is intermediate between them. Similarly[4] the man who avoids bodily pains not because he cannot bear them but from choice, is licentious. Those whose yielding is not due to choice are of two kinds: one is carried away by the pleasure, and the other by avoiding the pain, of his desire.[5] Thus there is a difference between those who yield from choice and those who do not. Anyone would think worse of a person if he did something

1. Cf. III.x.   2. Cf. 1147b21ff.
3. *akolastos*; cf. the discussion in III.x–xi., especially 1119a1ff.
4. The comparison is with the deliberate chooser of pleasure.
5. The pleasure of its satisfaction and the pain of its frustration.

disgraceful when he felt little or no desire to do it than if he acted under a powerful desire, and worse of one who thrashed someone else in cold blood than if he did it in anger; because what would he have done under the influence of passion? This is why the licentious is worse than the incontinent man.

Thus of the states mentioned above[1] one is more nearly a kind of softness;[2] the other is licentiousness. The opposite of the incontinent type is the continent, and of the soft type the enduring; for endurance consists in resisting one's desires, but continence in conquering them – two quite different things, just as avoiding defeat is different from winning. Hence continence is *preferable to endurance.

A man who fails to withstand pains which most people can and do support is soft and effeminate (indeed effeminacy is a kind of softness). He is the sort of man that lets his cloak trail to spare himself the trouble of lifting it, and while behaving like an invalid, does not regard himself as a pitiable person, although he resembles one. It is much the same with continence and incontinence. For a man to give way to violent or excessive pleasure or pain is not surprising – indeed it is forgivable if he does so only reluctantly, like Philoctetes after he was bitten by the viper in the play by Theodectes,[3] or Cercyon in the *Alopē* of Carcinus,[4] or like someone who tries to hold back a laugh and lets it out in a stentorian guffaw, as happened to Xenophantus[5] – but it *is* surprising if someone gives way without a struggle to pleasures and pains that most people can resist – unless his weakness is due to disease or congenital defect, like the hereditary effeminacy of the Scythian royal family, or the difference between male and female constitutions.

The lover of amusement is also regarded as licentious, but he is really soft; for amusement is relaxation, being a kind of

---

1. a19–25.   2. Not softness proper (a13–15 above).

3. See Index of Names.

4. Cercyon was heartbroken at his daughter Alope's seduction.

5. As Xenophantus was court musician to Alexander at Pella, this may be a personal reminiscence.

rest; and the love of amusement is excessive indulgence in relaxation.[1]

There are two forms of incontinence: impetuosity and weakness. Some people deliberate and then under the influence of their feelings fail to abide by their decision; others are carried away by their feelings because they have failed to deliberate.[2] For there are some people who can hold out against strong emotion, whether pleasurable or painful, if they feel or see it coming and have time to rouse themselves – that is, their calculative faculty – beforehand, just as a person cannot be tickled if he tickles his opponent first.[3] It is quick and excitable people that are most prone to the impetuous kind of incontinence, because the former are too hasty and the latter too vehement to wait for reason, since they are disposed to follow their own impressions.[4]

Further distinctions between licentiousness and incontinence

viii.   The licentious man, as we said,[5] is unrepentant, because he abides by his choice; but the incontinent one is always capable of repentance. Hence the facts are not as we suggested when we raised our questions;[6] it is the licentious man that is curable; the incontinent man is not. For vice is a disease like dropsy or tuberculosis, whereas incontinence is like epilepsy; because the one is a chronic and the other an intermittent malady. In general, too, incontinence and vice are generically different: vice is unconscious, incontinence is not. *Of the incontinent types themselves the impetuous are better than those who have a moral principle but do not abide by it, because the latter yield to a less compelling emotion, and are not caught unprepared, like the impetuous. Indeed the incontinent man is like those who quickly get in-

---

1. Cf. 1127b33ff.

2. The former are of course the weak and the latter the impetuous.

3. Cf. *Problems* 965a11ff. The point of the comparison is the incapacitating effect of surprise.

4. The data of sensation.   5. 1150a21.   6. 1146a31ff.

toxicated by a small quantity of wine which would not affect the average drinker.

Thus it is evident that incontinence is not vice (except perhaps in a qualified sense[1]), because it is contrary to the agent's choice, whereas vice is in accordance with choice. Nevertheless there is a similarity between the actions that result from them. It is just like Demodocus's epigram on the Milesians:

> Milesians are not stupid, I aver;
> But they behave the same as if they were.[2]

Similarly the incontinent are not wicked, but they do wicked things.

Again, the incontinent man, while pursuing bodily pleasures that are excessive and contrary to right principle, is so constituted that he pursues them without the conviction that he is right, whereas the licentious man has this conviction, because he is so constituted as to pursue them; consequently the former can easily be persuaded to change,[3] but the latter cannot. For virtue preserves, while vice destroys, the first principle,[4] and in conduct the first principle is the *end*, just as in mathematics the first principles are the assumptions.[5] Neither in moral nor in mathematical science is the knowledge of first principles reached by logical means: it is virtue, whether natural or acquired by habituation, that enables us to think rightly about the first principle. Such a person, then, is temperate, and his contrary licentious. But there is a type of man who is impelled by his feelings to deviate from the right principle, but who, although mastered by his feelings to the extent of not acting in accordance with the right principle, is not so completely mastered as to be

1. As tending to produce vicious results.

2. Fragment 1, Diehl.   3. His conduct.

4. Not the principle itself, but its influence upon us; cf. 1140b11ff.

5. The word is *hupothesis*, here used (apparently) to cover the meanings of *thesis* (assumption of existence) and *horismos* (definition), which are the *archai* of mathematical demonstrations. Grant's suggestion that the word here stands for the proposition to be proved (analytically), which, being an end, would provide a better parallel, is now out of favour.

capable of the conviction that he should pursue such pleasures unrestrainedly. This is the incontinent man. He is
superior to the licentious man, and is not to be called bad
without qualification, because in him the highest element,
the first principle, is preserved.[1] There is another type of
person, the contrary of this, who adheres to his choice and
cannot be diverted from it – not by his feelings, at any rate.
These considerations show that continence is a good and incontinence a bad state.

Inconsistency, obstinacy and insensibility. Continence contrasted with temperance

ix.   We now have to consider a problem that we raised before:[2] Is it in virtue of abiding by *any* principle and *any*
choice, or only in virtue of abiding by the *right* one, that a
person is continent? and is a person incontinent if he departs
from *any* choice and *any* principle, or only if he departs from
a principle that is not false, and a choice that is right?
Surely, although it may be incidentally by any choice, it is
essentially by the true principle and the right choice that the
one abides and the other does not. For if some one chooses
or tries to *secure A because of B, it is essentially B that is
his object, although incidentally it is A. By 'essentially' I
mean 'absolutely'. Thus there is a sense in which it can be
by any kind of opinion that the one abides and the other
does not, but absolutely it is by the true one.

There are some people who cling to their opinion whom
we call obstinate,[3] meaning that they are hard to convince
and to make change their minds. They are in one way
related to the continent man as the prodigal is to the liberal
or the rash to the courageous;[4] but in several ways they are
different. It is only under emotion or desire that the continent man refuses to change, since he will on occasion be

---

1. He is aware of and acknowledges (although he does not always
pursue) a moral end of human conduct.

2. 1146a16ff.   3. *ischŭrognōmōn*.   4. Cf. 1107a33ff.

open to conviction; but the obstinate are not influenced by argument, because they are susceptible to desires, and are often carried away by pleasure. Obstinate people can be divided into the opinionated, the ignorant, and the boorish. The opinionated are motivated by pleasure and pain, because they enjoy the sense of superiority if they are not prevailed upon to change their minds; while it vexes them if their own decisions are annulled, like decrees.[1] Thus they resemble the incontinent more than the continent.

There are some, however, who change their minds for some reason other than incontinence, like Neoptolemus in the *Philoctetes* of Sophocles.[2] It is true that it was pleasure that made him change, but it was a noble one, because to him it was a noble thing to tell the truth, and he had been persuaded by Odysseus to tell a lie. For the fact of doing something for pleasure does not always make a person licentious or bad or incontinent – only if the pleasure is a base one.

There is also a type of person[3] who finds too little enjoyment in bodily pleasures, and fails to abide by the right principle in this respect. The continent man represents the mean between this type and the incontinent, because the latter fails to abide by the principle through feeling too much enjoyment, and the former through feeling too little; but the continent man abides by the principle and does not depart from it in either way. Now if continence is a good thing, the two contrary states must both be bad – as they evidently are; but because one of them is observed only rarely and in few people, incontinence is regarded as the only contrary of continence – just as in the case of temperance and licentiousness.[4]

Many descriptions are based on analogy; and this is the reason why we have come to speak by analogy of the continence of the temperate man. For both the continent and the temperate man are so constituted that bodily pleasures never make them do *anything against principle; but the

---

1. The simile seems superfluous in English.   2. Cf. 1146a19.
3. The insensible (*anaisthētos*); see Subject Index.
4. Cf. 1108b35ff.

one[1] has bad desires and the other has not, and the one[2] is so constituted as to take no pleasure in anything contrary to his principle, while the other is liable to feel pleasure, but not to be carried away by it. There is also a resemblance between the incontinent and the licentious man, although they are quite different; both pursue bodily pleasures, but one[3] thinks it right to do so and the other does not.

Further notes on incontinence

x. It is impossible for the same person to be at the same time prudent and incontinent; for we have proved[4] that a prudent man is at the same time morally good. Besides, merely *knowing* what is right does not make a person prudent; he must be disposed to *do* it too: and the incontinent man is not so disposed. (On the other hand there is no reason why a clever[5] man should not be incontinent – which is why some people are sometimes actually supposed to be prudent but incontinent, because cleverness differs from prudence in the way described in our first discussions,[6] and although close to it in definition, differs from it in respect of choice.[7]) Nor does the incontinent man *know* what is right in the sense of actively contemplating it; only as a person asleep or drunk can be said to know a thing. Also he acts voluntarily (because in a sense he knows what he is doing and for what end), but he is not wicked, because his *choice* is morally sound, so that he is only half wicked. And he is not a criminal, because he is not deliberately malicious;[8] for of the two types one is not disposed to abide by the result of his deliberations, and the excitable one does not deliberate at all. In fact the incontinent man is like a state which

1. The continent. 2. The temperate. 3. The licentious.
4. 1144a11ff. 5. Cf. 1144a23ff.
6. A curious reference to Book VI *loc. cit.*
7. Choice is implicit in prudence, but not in cleverness.
8. Cf. 1135b19ff.

passes all the right decrees and has good laws, but makes no use of them – like the gibe of Anaxandrides,

> So willed our state, that nothing cares for law,[1]

whereas the bad man is like a state that implements its laws, only the laws that it implements are bad ones.

Both continence and incontinence are associated with abnormal dispositions, because the continent man shows more, and the incontinent man less, ability to stand his ground than the majority of people.

The kind of incontinence that is shown by excitable people is easier to cure than the kind shown by those who deliberate but do not abide by their decisions; and those whose incontinence is the result of habit are easier to cure than those to whom it is natural, because it is easier to alter one's habits than one's nature. In fact even habit is hard to change, because it is a sort of second nature, as Evenus says:[2]

> I tell you, friend, 'tis practice long pursued,
> And this at last becomes a man's own nature.

We have now described what continence and incontinence, endurance and softness are, and how these states are related to one another.

Three views critical of pleasure

*xi.   The study of pleasure and pain is the task of the political philosopher, because he is the master craftsman who decides the end which is the standard by which we call any given thing good or bad without qualification.[3] Besides, the examination of pleasure and pain is one of our necessary

---

1. Fr. incert. 16.   2. Fr. 9, Diehl.
3. Only in relation to the supreme end can a thing be called absolutely good or bad; things that are good or bad for minor ends must have their end specified.

tasks,[1] because we have established[2] that moral virtue and vice are concerned with pains and pleasures; and the great majority of people maintain that happiness involves pleasure (which is why the word for 'blessed' is derived from a word meaning 'to rejoice'[3]).

Some think that no pleasure is a good, either in itself or incidentally,[4] because goodness and pleasure are not the same. Others believe that some pleasures are good, but that most are bad. Besides these views there is a third: that even if all pleasures are good, nevertheless pleasure cannot be the supreme good.

(1) To prove that pleasure is not a good at all, it is argued as follows. (a) Every pleasure is a perceptible process towards a natural state; but no process belongs to the same genus as its ends – e.g. no process of building belongs to the same genus as a house. (b) The temperate man shuns pleasures. (c) The prudent man seeks not pleasure but freedom from pain. (d) Pleasures are a hindrance to thinking, and the more enjoyable they are, the greater the hindrance – for example, the pleasure of sex; for nobody could do any thinking against that background. (e) There is no *art* of pleasure, whereas every good thing is the product of an art. (f) Pleasures are pursued by children and brutes.

(2) To prove that not all pleasures are good, it is argued that (a) some pleasures are disgraceful and open to censure, and (b) some pleasures are harmful, because there are pleasant things that are bad for health.

(3) To prove that pleasure is not the supreme good, it is pointed out that pleasure is not an end but a process.

This is a rough summary of the views expressed on this subject.

1. The discussion which follows seems to belong properly to the *Eudemian Ethics*, and to have been superseded by the maturer treatment which occupies chs. i–v of Book X.

2. 1104b8–1105a13.

3. The words are *makarios* and *chairein*. Probably the adverb *mala*, greatly, should be understood before the latter, which would make the etymology look a little better; but it is quite fanciful.

4. The view of Plato's nephew Speusippus.

Objections to the foregoing criticisms

xii.   But that these arguments do not prove that pleasure is
not a good, nor even that it is not the supreme good, is clear
from the following considerations. (i) In the first place[1]
things are called good in two ways, sometimes as *absolutely*
good and sometimes as good *for somebody*;[2] and it will follow
that people's natures and states are also called good equivocally, and therefore the same will be true of movements and
processes. Also, of processes that are supposed to be bad,
some although bad absolutely are not bad relatively – indeed they may be desirable for a given person; and some
that are not even desirable for a given person generally, are
desirable for him occasionally and for a limited time, but not
absolutely. And some of these processes are not pleasures
either, although they appear to be – viz. all painful processes with a remedial purpose, such as the treatments that
invalids undergo.[3]

(ii)   A good may be either an activity or a state; and the
processes that restore us to our natural state are only incidentally pleasant, while the activity in cases of desire is
the activity of the normal state that remains unimpaired.[4]
For that matter there are pleasures that are quite independent of pain or *desire (e.g. the activity[5] of contemplation),
because in their case the natural state has no deficiency.
This is shown by the fact that people do not enjoy the same
things while their natural state is being replenished as they
do when the restoration is complete; in the restored state
they enjoy things that are absolutely pleasant, but while it is
being replenished they enjoy even things that are the reverse of pleasant; e.g. sour and bitter things, none of which
is naturally or absolutely pleasant. Hence the pleasures that

---

1. Answers to 1(a) and 3.   2. i.e. relatively to an individual.
3. For the theory underlying this and the following arguments see
Appendix H.
4. Cf. 1154b18f. below.
5. Following the reading of K[b] and Gauthier.

they give cannot be absolutely pleasant either; for the pleasures derived from different pleasant things differ just as the things do.

(iii) Again, the argument of some thinkers that there must be something better than pleasure, because the end is better than the process, is not conclusive; because pleasures are not processes, nor do they all involve a process; they are species of activity, and therefore an end.[1] They result not from the development of our powers, but from the use that we make of them. Nor have they all some end other than themselves; this is so only in the case of those that are involved in our advance to the completion of our nature. It is therefore incorrect to call pleasure a perceptible process; we ought rather to say 'an activity of our natural state', and 'unimpeded' instead of 'perceptible'. (Some think that pleasure is a process on the ground that it is good in the full sense of the word, because they suppose that an activity is a process. But it is nothing of the kind.)

The argument (2b) that pleasures are bad because some pleasant things are injurious to health, is the same as saying that healthful things are bad because some healthful things are bad for the pocket. Both are bad in this limited sense, but that does not prove them to be bad in themselves, since even contemplation is sometimes injurious to health.

(1d). Neither thought nor any other activity[2] is hindered by its proper pleasure, but only by pleasures of a different origin.[3] Indeed the pleasures that we derive from contemplation and learning will encourage us to contemplate and learn more.

(1e). That pleasure is not the product of any art is a natural consequence; for an art never produces an activity, but only a faculty. At the same time, the arts of the perfumer

1. They are (or rather accompany and perfect) unimpeded activities, which are ends in themselves, whereas processes are always relative to some end; cf. the discussion at 1173a29ff., and see Appendices E and H.

2. Here as elsewhere in discussing Academic views A. seems to use words with their Academic meanings. In his own terminology *phronēsis* would be 'prudence' and *hexis* 'state'.

3. Cf. 1175a29ff., where this view is more fully developed.

and chef are considered to be productive of pleasure. The
arguments (1b) that the temperate man shuns pleasure,
and (1c) that what the prudent man seeks is a life free from
pain, and (1f) that pleasure is pursued by children and
brutes, are all disposed of by the same reply. It has been
explained[1] how some pleasures are good without qualification, and how not all pleasures are good in this sense: it is the
latter kind that brutes and children pursue, and it is freedom
from the pain of being denied these pleasures that the
prudent man pursues – the pleasures, that is, that involve
desire and pain, viz. the bodily pleasures (for these are of
that nature), or their excessive forms, in which the licentious
man displays his licentiousness. That is why the temperate
man avoids them; because even he has his pleasures.

Some kind of pleasure may even be the supreme good

*xiii.   Further, it is admitted also that pain is an evil, and to
be avoided; because it is either absolutely an evil or in some
sense an impediment. But the contrary of that which is to be
avoided, *qua* to be avoided, and evil, is good. Therefore
pleasure must be a good. The argument by which Speusippus
tried to refute this reasoning – that good is contrary to both
pleasure and pain, just as greater is contrary to both less and
equal – breaks down, because he would not say that pleasure
is a species of evil.[2]

If (2a) some pleasures are bad, there is still no reason why
(3) some kind of pleasure should not be the supreme good; just
as some kind of knowledge may be supremely good although
some other kinds are bad. On the contrary, assuming that
there is an unimpeded exercise of every faculty, it is probable
that the exercise either of all the faculties or of one of them
(whether happiness consists in the exercise of all or of one),

1. 1147b23ff., 1148a22ff.
2. Speusippus seems to have regarded the good as a neutral or impas-
sive state; cf. 1173abff. But A.'s language is puzzling; for a discussion of
the passage see Appendix H.

if unimpeded, must be supremely desirable. But the unimpeded exercise of a faculty is a pleasure. Then the supreme good will be a kind of pleasure, even if the majority of pleasures are bad – perhaps absolutely bad. This is why everybody assumes that the happy life is a pleasant life, i.e. makes pleasure a constituent of happiness – with good reason. For no activity is perfect if it is impeded, and happiness is a perfect thing. That is why the happy man needs (besides his other qualifications) physical advantages as well as external goods and the gifts of fortune, so that he may not be hampered by lack of these things. (Those[1] who maintain that, provided he is good, a man is happy on the rack or surrounded by great disasters, are talking nonsense, whether intentionally or not.) It is because happiness needs fortune too that some people think that it is the same as good fortune; but it is not, because even good fortune itself, when excessive, is an impediment, and presumably loses its right to be called good fortune, since we estimate good fortune in relation to happiness.

Again, the fact that pleasure is pursued by all animals and human beings[2] is some indication that it is in some sense the supreme good:

> No saying altogether comes to naught
> That many voice...[3]

But since the natural and best state neither is, nor is thought to be, the same for all, they do not all pursue the same pleasure, although it is pleasure that they all pursue. In fact they probably *do* all pursue the same pleasure, and not that which they think, and would assert, that they pursue; because everything contains by nature something divine.[4] But since the pleasures that are most commonly encountered and are within everyone's experience are the pleasures of the body, these have appropriated the right to the name; and

1. Probably Cynics.   2. The argument of Eudoxus; see 1172b9ff.
3. Hesiod, *Works and Days* 763f. The quotation continues 'It is itself a god', i.e. divinely inspired.
4. Cf. previous note, and see 1173a4.

so people think that they are the only pleasures, *because they are the only familiar ones.

It is obvious also that if pleasure, or ⟨unimpeded⟩ activity, is not a good, then the life of the happy man will not be pleasant – for why should he need pleasure if it is not a good, and his life may equally well be a painful one? For pain is neither good nor bad if pleasure is neither too. Why, then, should he avoid it? And if the good man's activities are not more pleasant than other people's, his life is not more pleasant either.

Different kinds of pleasure distinguished

xiv.   Now with regard to bodily pleasures, those who hold that some pleasures, viz. the noble ones, are highly desirable, but bodily pleasures, which are the concern of the licentious man, are not, ought to consider why, in that case, the pains that are contrary to them are bad; because the contrary of a bad thing is a good one. Probably the necessary pleasures are good in the sense that even what is not bad is good; or perhaps they are good up to a point; because although you cannot have excessive pleasure from those states and processes that do not admit of excess above the limit of goodness,[1] you can have excessive pleasure from those that do admit of excess. Now you can have an excess of bodily goods; and it is the pursuit of this excess, not that of the necessary pleasures, that makes a man bad; because everyone enjoys tasty food and wine and sex in some degree, but not everyone to the right degree. With pain it is just the contrary. He[2] does not shun excessive pain; he shuns pain altogether. For the pain that is the contrary of excessive pleasure is not pain at all except to the person who pursues excessive pleasure.

1. Such excess – more than is good and right – is impossible in the case of a 'mean' moral state (e.g. justice) or of its activity and corresponding pleasure; but it is possible in the case of bodily pleasures.
2. The bad man.

We are bound, however, not merely to state the true explanation but to account for the false one; because this helps to carry conviction. For when a reasonable explanation is found of why something that is not true appears to be true, it gives us greater confidence in the true solution. We must therefore explain why bodily pleasures seem to be especially desirable.

(1) The first reason, then, is that pleasure drives out pain. That is, it is because they feel excessive pain that people pursue excessive pleasure, and bodily pleasure generally, as a cure for their suffering. These remedial pleasures are intense, and are consequently pursued, because they seem desirable by contrast with their contrary. (The view that pleasure is not a good is due, as we have said,[1] to two facts. (a) Some pleasures are activities that imply a debased nature, either congenitally bad, like that of a brute, or depraved by habit, like those of bad men. (b) Others are remedial of a defective state; and to be in a state[2] is better than *to be in process of reaching it. However, these pleasures occur in the course of a process towards perfection, so that they are only incidentally good.)

(2) Because they are intense, bodily pleasures are pursued by those who cannot enjoy other kinds (at any rate some people actually give themselves an artificial thirst). There is nothing culpable in this if the pleasures are harmless, but if they are not, it is bad. For such people have no other source of enjoyment; and also there are many to whom a neutral condition is painful because of their nature.[3] For every animal is always under some strain, as the scientists inform us; because they maintain that seeing and hearing are painful, but we have grown accustomed to the fact,[4] they say. Similarly in youth people are in a condition resembling intoxication, because they are growing, and youth is sweet; while people of an excitable nature are

1. The reference is not obvious, but cf. 1148b15ff. and 1152b26ff.
2. i.e. a normal one. The pleasure is therefore worse than the normal state but better than the defective one.
3. Or rather 'temperament'; see below.   4. And so do not realize it.

always in need of a remedial pleasure, because their temperament keeps their bodies in a condition of constant irritation, and they are always in a state of vehement desire. Now their pain is banished not only by the pleasure contrary to it, but by any pleasure, if it is strong enough. That is why people become licentious and vicious.

On the other hand, pleasures that are unaccompanied by pain do not admit of excess. These are the pleasures derived from things pleasant by nature[1] and not incidentally. By things that are pleasant incidentally I mean such as are remedial. The remedial effect is produced by an activity of that part of the subject that has remained healthy, and this makes the remedy itself seem pleasurable. But the things that are naturally pleasant are those that stimulate the activity of a given natural disposition.[2] It is not possible, however, for the same thing always to give pleasure, because our nature is not simple: it contains a separate element[3] which renders us mortal, so that when one of these elements is active it is counter to the nature of the other; and when they are exactly balanced, the effect is something that is not felt to be either painful or pleasurable. If any being had a simple nature, the same activity would always give him the greatest pleasure. That is why God enjoys one simple pleasure for ever. For there is an activity not only of movement but also one of immobility; and there is a truer pleasure in rest than in motion. Yet, as the poet[4] says, 'in all things change is sweet' – because of a fault in our nature. For just as a changeable man is faulty, so is a nature that needs change; for it is not simple or good.

We have now discussed the nature of continence and incontinence, pleasure and pain; and have shown in what sense they are respectively good and bad. Our next task will be to speak of Friendship.

1. i.e. aesthetic and intellectual pleasures; cf. 1152b33ff.
2. e.g. music or contemplation stimulates a musical or contemplative nature.
3. The physical; it is the old clash of body with soul.
4. Euripides, *Orestes* 234.

*VIII

THE KINDS OF FRIENDSHIP

Friendship is a necessity

i.   After this the next step will be to discuss friendship; for
it is a kind of virtue, or implies virtue, and it is also most
necessary for living. Nobody would choose to live without
friends even if he had all the other good things. Indeed
those who hold wealth and office and power are thought to
stand in special need of friends; for what is the use of such
prosperity to them if they are denied the opportunity for
beneficence, which is most commonly and most commend-
ably directed towards friends? Or how can their prosperity
be guarded and preserved without friends? because the
greater it is, the more precarious. In poverty too and all the
other misfortunes of life people regard their friends as their
only refuge. Friends are indeed a help both to the young,
in keeping them from mistakes; and to the old, in caring for
them and doing for them what through frailty they cannot
do for themselves; and to those in the prime of life, by
enabling them to carry out fine achievements:

When two together go[1]

they are better able both to see an opportunity and to take
it. And the affection of parent for child and of child for
parent seems to be a natural instinct not only in man but in
birds and most animals; and similarly the mutual friendliness between members of the same species, especially of
the human species; which is why we commend those who
love their fellow men. One can see also in one's travels
how near and dear a thing every man is to every other.
Friendship also seems to be the bond that holds communities together, and lawgivers seem to attach more
importance to it than to justice; because concord seems to

1. Homer, *Iliad* x.224.

be something like friendship, and concord is their primary object – that and eliminating faction, which is enmity. Between friends there is no need for justice, but people who are just still need the quality of friendship; and indeed friendliness is considered to be justice in the fullest sense. It is not only a necessary thing but a splendid one. We praise those who love their friends, and the possession of many friends is held to be one of the fine things of life. What is more, people think that good men and friends are the same.[1]

What constitutes friendship?

There are, however, not a few divergent views about friendship. Some hold that it is a matter of similarity: that our friends are those who are like ourselves. Hence the proverbial sayings 'Like to like',[2] 'Birds of a feather', etc. Others take the contrary view and say that people *who are closely alike are all potters[3] to each other. Some inquire into this same question more deeply on the lines of natural philosophy, Euripides saying:

> Earth like a lover longs for rain

when it is parched, and again:

> The holy heaven, too, being filled with rain,
> Yearns on the earth to fall.[4]

And Heraclitus says 'Opposition unites', and 'From the different comes the fairest harmony', and 'All things come from Strife'.[5] Others assert the contrary, and in particular Empedocles, who says 'Like is drawn to like'.[6]

1. Cf. Plato, *Lysis* 214C.
2. Cf. Homer, *Odyssey* xvii.218, and Plato, *Lysis* 214A.
3. An allusion to Hesiod, *Works and Days* 25: 'Potter is spiteful to potter'; cf. Plato, *Lysis* 215C.
4. Fr. 898; the play is unknown.
5. Fr. 8. The quotations are not exact, and it is unlikely that *harmonia* bears a musical sense.
6. There is no obvious reference, but the doctrine is essential to his system.

But such of these problems as belong to natural philosophy may be dismissed (since they are irrelevant to our present inquiry); let us turn our attention to those which have a human interest as bearing upon character and the emotions: e.g. whether friendship occurs between all kinds of person, or it is impossible for bad men to be friends; and whether there is one kind of friendship or more than one. Those who think that there is only one, on the ground that it admits of degrees, have based their belief on insufficient evidence, because things that differ in species also admit of differences of degree. We have discussed this point before.[1]

The objects and implications of affection

ii. Perhaps it will throw light on the subject if we get a clear conception of what an object of affection is. It is generally accepted that not everything is loved, but only what is lovable; and that this is either good, or pleasant, or useful. But it may be thought that 'useful' means nothing more than 'productive of some good or pleasure'; so that the only objects of love that are *ends* would be the good and the pleasant. Is it, then, the Good that people love, or only what is good *for them*? because sometimes these conflict; and similarly in the case of the pleasant. It seems that each individual loves what is good for himself; i.e. that while the Good is absolutely lovable, it is the good of the individual that is lovable for the individual. But the individual loves not what *is* good for him but what *appears* to be such. However, this will not affect the argument: the lovable will be what appears to be lovable.

Let us assume, then, that there are three reasons for loving. We do not speak of friendship in the case of our affection for inanimate objects, because there is no return of affection, and no wish for the good of the object (for presumably it would be absurd for a person to wish for the

1. Again there is no obvious reference. A difference in degree neither constitutes nor excludes a specific difference.

good of his wine; if he has any wish it is that the wine may
keep, so that he may have it himself). But in the case of a
friend they say that one ought to wish him good for his own
sake. Those who wish for the well-being of others in this
way are called well-disposed if the same feeling is not
evoked from the other party, because goodwill, they say,
is friendship only when it is reciprocated. Perhaps we should
add 'and recognized'; because people are often well-
disposed towards persons whom they have never seen, but
believe to be *good or helpful, and one of the latter might
feel the same towards the former: then clearly these people
are well-disposed towards each other, but how could we
call them friends when their feelings for one another are
not known? So friends must be well-disposed towards each
other, and recognized as wishing each other's good, for one
of the three reasons stated above.[1]

Three kinds of friendship

iii.   These reasons differ in kind, and therefore the affections and friendships that they arouse also differ in kind.
Consequently there are three kinds of friendship, equal in
number to the qualities that arouse love. For there is in each
case a kind of mutual affection, known to both parties; and
those who love each other wish for each other's good in
respect of the quality for which they love them. So those who
love each other on the ground of utility do not love each
other for their personal qualities, but only in so far as they
derive some benefit from each other. Similarly with those
who love one another on the ground of pleasure; because
it is not for being of a certain character that witty people
are liked, but because we find them pleasant. So when
people love each other on the ground of utility their affection
is motivated by their own good, and when they love on the
ground of pleasure it is motivated by their own pleasure;
that is, they love the other person not for what he is, but

1. 1155b19.

qua useful or pleasant. So these friendships are accidental,[1] because the person loved is not loved on the ground of his actual nature, but merely as providing some benefit or pleasure. Consequently such friendships are easily dissolved if the parties do not continue to show the same kind of qualities, because if they cease to be pleasant or useful the friendship comes to an end.

Friendship based on utility

Utility is an impermanent thing: it changes according to circumstances. So with the disappearance of the ground for friendship, the friendship also breaks up, because that was what kept it alive. Friendships of this kind seem to occur most frequently between the elderly (because at their age what they want is not pleasure but utility) and those in middle or early life who are pursuing their own advantage. Such persons do not spend much time together, because sometimes they do not even like one another, and therefore feel no need of such an association unless they are mutually useful. For they take pleasure in each other's company only in so far as they have hopes of advantage from it. Friendships with foreigners[2] are generally included in this class.

Friendship based on pleasure

Friendship between the young is thought to be grounded on pleasure, because the lives of the young are regulated by their feelings, and their chief interest is in their own pleasure and the opportunity of the moment. With advancing years, however, their tastes change too, so that they are quick to make and to break friendships; because their affection changes just as the things that please them *do, and this sort of pleasure changes rapidly. Also the young are

1. i.e. based on a non-essential ground.
2. Which would normally rest on a business relationship.

apt to fall in love, for erotic friendship is for the most part swayed by the feelings and based on pleasure. That is why they fall in and out of friendship quickly, changing their attitude often within the same day. But the young do like to spend the day and live together, because that is how they realize the object of their friendship.

Perfect friendship is based on goodness

Only the friendship of those who are good, and similar in their goodness, is perfect. For these people each alike wish good for the other *qua* good,[1] and they are good in themselves. And it is those who desire the good of their friends for the friends' sake that are most truly friends, because each loves the other for what he is, and not for any incidental quality. Accordingly the friendship of such men lasts so long as they remain good; and goodness is an enduring quality. Also each party is good both *absolutely* and *for his friend*, since the good are both good absolutely and useful to each other. Similarly they please one another too; for the good are pleasing both absolutely and to each other; because everyone is pleased with his own conduct and conduct that resembles it, and the conduct of good men is the same or similar. Friendship of this kind is permanent, reasonably enough; because in it are united all the attributes that friends ought to possess. For all friendship has as its object something good or pleasant – either absolutely or relatively to the person who feels the affection – and is based on some similarity between the parties. But in this friendship all the qualities that we have mentioned belong to the friends themselves; because in it there is similarity, etc.;[2] and what is absolutely good is also absolutely pleasant; and these are the most lovable qualities. Therefore it is

---

1. Cf. above, 1156a9ff.
2. They are alike, and both absolutely and relatively good and pleasant, in themselves and not incidentally.

between good men that both love and friendship are chiefly found and in the highest form.

That such friendships are rare is natural, because men of this kind are few. And in addition they[1] need time and intimacy; for as the saying goes, you cannot get to know each other until you have eaten the proverbial[2] quantity of salt together. Nor can one man accept another, or the two become friends, until each has proved to the other that he is worthy of love, and so won his trust. Those who are quick to make friendly advances to each other have the desire to be friends, but they are not unless they are worthy of love and know it. The wish for friendship develops rapidly, but friendship does not.

iv. This kind of friendship, then, is perfect both in point of duration and in all other respects; and in it each party receives from the other benefits that are in all respects the same or similar, as ought to be the case between friends.

The inferior kinds are less enduring, and are not confined to the good

Friendship *for the sake of pleasure has a resemblance to perfect friendship, because good men give each other pleasure; and so does friendship for the sake of utility, because good men are also useful to each other. In these associations too friendships last longest when each receives from the other the same benefit – e.g. pleasure – and not merely that, but from the same source, as in the case of two witty people, and not as in the relation of lover and be-loved. For the latter do not take pleasure in the same things: the one finds it in looking at his beloved, and the other in the attentions of his lover. And as beauty wanes, some-times the friendship wanes too, because the one loses pleasure

1. The friendships.

2. Apparently a *medimnos* (1½ bushels!); cf. *Eudemian Ethics* 1238a2. The sense clearly calls for a measure.

in the sight, and the other no longer receives the attentions; yet on the other hand many do remain friends if through their intimacy they have come to appreciate each other's characters as being like their own. But when it is not pleasure but gain that lovers exchange in their affairs, their love is less real and less enduring. Those who are friends for the sake of utility part as soon as the advantage ceases, because they were attracted not by each other but by the prospect of gain.

Thus where the object is pleasure or utility friendship is possible between two bad men, or between one good and one bad man, or between one who is neither good nor bad and one who is of any character; but obviously only good men can be friends for their own sakes. For bad people take no pleasure in each other unless there is a chance of some benefit.

Also it is only the friendship of the good that is proof against slander; because it is not easy for a person to take anyone else's word against a friend whom he himself has proved over a long period of time. Between friends like these there are the feelings 'I trust him'; 'He would never do me wrong'; and all the other conditions that one expects to find in true friendship. But in the other kinds of friendship such things[1] may easily occur. However, since people describe as friends those who are attracted to one another only for reasons of utility, as states are (because it is considered to be for advantage that they form alliances); or of pleasure, as children do; presumably we too should call such people friends, but add that there is more than one kind of friendship, and that friendship in the primary and proper sense is between good men in virtue of their goodness, whereas the rest are friendships only by analogy. For they are friends in so far as they are attracted by a kind of goodness, and by something similar to themselves; because to lovers of pleasure pleasure too is a good. However, these friendships are not very apt to coincide; that is, the same

1. The slanders, etc., mentioned in the context.

people do not become friends for pleasure as well as for utility, because incidental qualities are not often found in pairs.

*Now that we have divided friendship into these kinds we shall see that it is persons of low character that are friends on the ground of pleasure or utility, this being the similarity between them; while the good are friends for each other's sake, because their bond is goodness. These latter, then, are friends in the unqualified sense; the others are friends only incidentally and by analogy with them.

Friendship as a state, as an activity, and as a feeling

v. Just as in the case of the virtues some people are called good in respect of a state and others in respect of an activity, so too in the case of friendship. Those who spend their time together enjoy each other's company and confer mutual benefits, but those who are asleep or separated by distance, although they do not express their friendship in action, nevertheless retain the disposition to do so; because distance does not break off a friendship absolutely, but only in its active realization. However, if the absence lasts for a long time it does seem to cause forgetfulness even of the friendship. Hence the saying:

> How oft hath silence cut the bond of friendship![1]

Neither old people nor sour-tempered ones seem to make friends easily. For there is not much pleasure to be found in them, and nobody can live day after day with someone who annoys him, or even with one who is not agreeable; because nature seems above all things to avoid what is painful and to aim at what is pleasant. Those who approve of each other but do not spend all their time together seem to be well-disposed rather than friendly, because nothing is so characteristic of friends as spending time together. (Those who are in need are anxious for help, and even the supremely

1. The source is unknown.

happy are eager for company, for they above all are least
suited by a solitary existence.) But it is impossible for people
to live together if they are not agreeable to each other and
similar in their tastes, because this seems to be the essence of
comradeship.

Friendship in the truest sense, then, is friendship between
good men, as we have said several times already.[1] For it is
accepted that what is lovable and desirable is in general
that which is absolutely good or pleasant, while for the
individual it is that which is good or pleasant for the individual; and one good man is loved by another on both these
grounds.

Affection[2] resembles a feeling, but friendship is a state.
For affection can be felt equally well for inanimate objects,
but mutual affection involves choice, and choice proceeds
from a ⟨moral⟩ state. Also when people wish what is good
for those whom they love, for their sake, it is not from a
feeling but in accordance with a ⟨moral⟩ state. And in
loving a friend they are loving their own good. For when a
good man becomes a friend to another he becomes that
other's good; so each loves his own good, and repays what
he receives by wishing the good of the other and giving him
pleasure. There is a saying 'caring is sharing',[3] *and these
qualities belong especially to the friendship of good men.

Qualified and superficial friendships

vi.   Friendships are formed less readily in the case of sour
and elderly persons, inasmuch as they are less good-tempered
and sociable, and it is just these qualities that are felt to be
most amiable and conducive to friendship. This is why the
young make friends quickly but the old do not, because
people do not make friends with those whose company they
do not enjoy. Similarly neither do sour-tempered people.

1. Viz. 1156b7, 23, 33, 1157a30, b4.   2. *philēsis*.
3. Really 'friendship is equality'; but this loses the jingling effect of
the Greek *philotēs isotēs;* cf. 1168b8.

It is true that these types are well-disposed to one another, because they wish each other well and meet each other's needs; but they are not really friends, because they do not spend all their time together or enjoy each other's company: things that are considered to be the best evidence of friendly feeling.

On the other hand to have many friends in the way of perfect friendship is no more possible than to be in love with many persons at the same time (for love is a kind of excess, and such a feeling is naturally directed towards one person). It is not easy for a large number of people to be attractive at the same time to the same person or (presumably) to be men of good character. Besides, one has to get to know a man thoroughly and become intimate with him, which is extremely difficult. If the basis is utility or pleasure, however, it is possible to be attractive to a number of people, because there are plenty of this type, and such services take little time.

Of these secondary forms of friendship the nearer to true friendship is that which has pleasure for its object, when both parties make the same contribution and enjoy each other's company or the same occupations. The friendships of the young are of this kind, because one finds in them a more generous spirit, whereas utilitarian friendship belongs to the commercially-minded. The supremely happy, too, although not needing useful friends, do need agreeable ones; for they want companions of some kind, and although they can put up with unpleasantness for a short time, nobody could endure it continuously – not even the Good itself, if he found it unpleasant. So they look for agreeable friends. However, these ought presumably to be good as well, and good *for them*, because then they will have all the qualities that are necessary for a friend. People in high positions, on the other hand, seem to have friends of different types: some are useful to them and others agreeable, but it seldom happens that the same people are both, because what their superiors are looking for is not people who are pleasant and also good, nor people who are useful

for honourable ends, but witty talkers if they want to be
amused, and otherwise agents who are clever at carrying
out their instructions; and these qualities are rarely found
in the same person. We have said[1] that the good man is also
both useful and agreeable, but such a person does not
become the *friend* of a superior in rank unless the latter is his
superior in goodness too. Otherwise the inferior cannot
make a proportionately equal return.[2] But such goodness is
exceptional in the great.

*To resume. The friendships of which we have been
speaking are based on equality, since both parties receive the
same benefits and wish each other the same good, or else
exchange one thing for another, e.g. pleasure for help.
(We have remarked[3] that these are secondary friendships
and comparatively short-lived. Being both like and unlike
the same thing, they seem to be friendships in one way but
not in another. They appear to be friendships in virtue of
their similarity to friendship based on goodness, because one
involves pleasure and the other utility, and these are present
also in that friendship; but since it is proof against slander
and permanent, whereas they are quickly changeable and
differ in many other ways, their dissimilarity makes them
appear not to be friendship.)

Friendship between unequals

vii.   But there is another kind of friendship which involves
superiority: e.g. the affection of father for son (and generally
of the older for the younger) and of husband for wife and
of every person in authority for his subordinates. These
kinds of friendship differ also from one another. The affection of parents for their children is not the same as that of
rulers for subjects; indeed that of father for son is not the
same as that of son for father, nor that of husband for wife
the same as that of wife for husband. For each of these

1. 1156b13ff., 1157a1ff.   2. Cf. 1158b23ff., 1162a34ff.
3. 1156a16ff., 1157a20ff.

persons has a different excellence and function, and different reasons for feeling love; and therefore their loves and affections are different too. It follows, then, that the parties do not, and should not expect to, receive the same benefits each from the other; but when children render to parents what they owe to those who brought them into the world, and parents to their sons what they owe to their children, the friendship of such persons will be enduring and equitable. In all these friendships between persons of different standing the affection must be proportionate: i.e. the better person must be loved more than he loves, and so must the more useful, and each of the others similarly. For when the affection is proportionate to merit the result is a kind of equality, which of course is considered to be characteristic of friendship.

However, equality does not seem to be the same in friendship as it is in just actions; for in the case of just actions equality is primarily that which is in accordance with merit, quantitative equality being secondary; but in friendship quantitative equality is of primary and equality of merit only of secondary importance. This becomes evident if a wide gap develops between the parties in respect of virtue or vice, or of affluence or anything else; because they no longer remain friends, and do not even expect to do so. This is most evident in the case of the gods, because they are furthest above us in respect of all good things; but it is obvious *also in the case of royalty, because those who are far inferior do not expect to be their friends either, nor do people of no account expect to be friends of those who are outstandingly good or wise. In such cases there is no precise limit up to which they can remain friends, because friendship still lasts in spite of continual losses; but where there is a great gulf, as between God and man, friendship becomes impossible. This raises a problem: whether perhaps friends do not wish each other the *greatest* of goods, viz. to be gods; because then they will no longer have them as friends, and therefore they will *lose* certain goods, because friends are goods. So if we were right in saying[1] that a friend wishes his friend's good for his friend's sake, the latter must remain as he is, whatever that may be. So his friend will wish for him the greatest goods possible for a human being. And presumably not *all* of these; because it is for himself[2] that everyone most of all wishes what is good.

In friendship loving is more important than being loved

viii.　Most people seem to want to be loved rather than to love, the reason being their desire for honour.[3] This is why most people are fond of flattery, because a flatterer is a friend of inferior status, or professes to be such, and to love more than he is loved; and to be loved is felt to be the next thing to being honoured, which is the aim of most people, Yet they seem to choose honour not for its own sake, but indirectly. Most people enjoy being held in honour by those in authority because of their expectations; they think that they will get from them anything that they may want, so they enjoy their honour as a token of future favours. But those who are eager for honour from good men who know them have as their object the confirmation of their own opinion of themselves. Thus they enjoy the assurance that they are good men, relying on the judgement of those who tell them so. But people enjoy being loved for its own sake. Hence it may be supposed that being loved is better than being honoured, and that friendship is desirable for its own sake.

But friendship seems to consist more in giving than in receiving affection. An indication of this is the joy that mothers show in loving their children. Some women give their children to other women to bring up, and although they love them, knowing who they are, do not seek to be loved in return, if it is impossible to have this too; they are content if they see their children getting on well, and they

1. 1155b31.　　　　2. Cf. the doctrine of self-love, below 1168a28ff.
3. In the sense of esteem, *timē*.

bestow their love upon the children even though the children, through ignorance, make no response such as is due to a mother. So if friendship consists more in loving than in being loved, and if people are commended for loving their friends, it seems that loving is the distinctive virtue of friends. Thus it is when love is given in accordance with merit *that people remain friends and their friendship endures.

This condition offers the best prospect even for unequal parties to be friends, because their inequality can be compensated.[1] The basis of affection is equality[2] and similarity, especially similarity in goodness; because, being steadfast in themselves, they are steadfast also towards each other, and neither require nor render services of a low nature, but virtually preclude them; since it is characteristic of good men neither to go wrong themselves nor to allow their friends to do so. But people of bad character have no constancy, for they do not even remain self-consistent; but they do make temporary friendships, because they enjoy each other's wickedness. The friendships of those who are useful or agreeable are more durable, because they last so long as the friends afford each other pleasure or help. Friendship based on utility seems to occur chiefly between opposite types: e.g. that of a poor man for a rich one, or of an ignoramus for a scholar; because each, being eager to secure what he happens to lack himself, is prepared to give something else in return. One might introduce here the relation between lover and beloved, or between a handsome person and an ugly one. This is the reason why lovers sometimes make themselves look ridiculous by demanding to be loved as much as they love; if they were equally lovable, this would presumably be a reasonable demand, but when they have no such qualification it is ridiculous. The probability is, however, that one opposite is attracted by the other not essentially but incidentally, and the object of the impulse is the mean (because this is good): e.g. the impulse of the dry is not to become wet but to

1. By the inferior's showing greater affection.   2. Cf. 1157b36.

reach the intermediate state; and similarly with the hot and all the rest. But let us dismiss this topic, since in fact it is somewhat irrelevant.

Friendship and the community

ix. Friendship and justice seem, as we said at the beginning,[1] to be exhibited in the same sphere of conduct and between the same persons; because in every community there is supposed to be some kind of justice and also some friendly feeling. At any rate people address those who are on the same ship or serving in the same force with them as friends; and similarly those with whom they are otherwise associated. But the term of the friendship is that of the association, for so also is the term of their form of justice. And the proverb 'friends have all things in common' is quite right, because friendship is based on community. Brothers and close comrades[2] hold all their possessions in common, and other friends share specified things to a greater or less extent, because friendships too differ in degree. The claims of justice also differ. The duties *of parents to children are not the same as those of brothers to one another, nor are duties the same for comrades as for fellow-citizens; and similarly in the other kinds of friendship. Hence the wrongs committed against these several types of friend differ too; and are aggravated in proportion to the degree of intimacy. For example, it is more serious to defraud a comrade than a fellow-citizen, and to refuse help to a brother than to a stranger, and to strike your father than anybody else. It is natural that the claims of justice should increase with the intensity of friendship, since both involve the same persons and have an equal extension.

All communities are like parts of the political community.

1. 1155a22ff.
2. The Greek word *hetairos* means a comrade in arms or a member of the same guild or religious, political or social 'club' or group.

For when people travel together it is for some advantage,[1] viz. to procure something conducive to better living. Political associations too are believed to have been originally formed and to continue in being for the sake of advantage, for it is this that lawgivers have as their object, and people say that what is to the common advantage is just. Other associations, however, aim at particular advantages; e.g. sailors combine to secure the profits of seafaring with a view to making money or something of the sort, and fellow-soldiers to secure the profits of warfare, whether their object is loot or conquest or the capture of a city; and similarly the members of a tribe[2] or parish [some of the associations seem to be formed for pleasure, e.g. those of religious guilds and social clubs; for these have as their object sacrifices and social activities. All these seem to fall under political association; for this aims not at the advantage of the moment but at that which extends over the whole of life][3] have a common purpose when they offer sacrifices and unite in the celebrations connected with them. In this way they pay due honour to the gods and at the same time provide pleasant relaxations for themselves. For the traditional sacrifices and festivals are, as we can see, held after the gathering in of the harvest, as a sort of harvest-home, because it was at this time of the year that people had most leisure.

It appears, then, that all these associations are parts of the political community; and the secondary friendships that we have described will correspond to these limited associations.

1. Presumably commercial.

2. The tribes (*phūlai*) as reconstructed by Cleisthenes were ten artificial but representative cross-sections of the total citizen population of Athens, and the whole administrative system was based on them.

3. The bracketed words seem to be interpolated from another treatment of the same subject; if they are disregarded the sense runs straight on.

The different kinds of constitution

x. There are three kinds of ⟨political⟩ constitution, and an equal number of perversions or corruptions of them. The constitutions are monarchy, aristocracy, and thirdly the kind that is based on a property qualification (*tīmēma*), which it seems natural to call a timocracy,[1] although most people usually call it a polity. Of these the best is monarchy and the worst timocracy. The perversion of mon*archy is tyranny. Both are forms of one-man rule, but they are vastly different. The tyrant regards his own interest, but the king regards that of his subjects. For a ruler is not a king unless he has independent means and is better off in every way than his subjects are; and such a person needs nothing further, and therefore will study not his own advantage but that of his subjects (for anyone who lacks these qualities will be a sort of titular[2] king). Tyranny is the exact opposite of this sort of rule, because the tyrant pursues his own good. It is more obvious in the case of tyranny that it is the worst of the perversions;[3] and the worst is the opposite of the best.

Change of constitution takes place from monarchy into tyranny, because tyranny is the corruption of monarchy: so a bad king becomes a tyrant. From aristocracy the change is into timocracy, and it is due to the corruptness of ministers, who distribute the resources of the state without regard to merit, and keep all or most of the benefits for themselves, and confine public appointments to the same persons, because they pay most regard to wealth. Thus it is a few bad men,

1. Plato (*Rep.* 545Bff.) had applied the name to a constitution midway between aristocracy (rule by the best-qualified) and oligarchy (which for him meant rule by the rich). A.'s polity was a moderate or middle-class democracy in which the lowest income-group was disfranchised.

2. Literally 'elected', like the King Archon at Athens, an annual magistrate who had certain religious duties but otherwise no powers or privileges.

3. Than it is in that of timocracy that it is the worst of the regular constitutions.

instead of the best, that hold the power. From timocracy the change is into democracy, since they are next-door neighbours; because timocracy too has as its object rule by the people, all who satisfy the property qualification being equal.[1] The least bad[2] is democracy, because it departs little from the form of polity. These are the commonest changes of constitution, because they involve the smallest and easiest transitions.

Analogous relations in the state and in the household

Analogies and (as it were) patterns of these relations can be found in the household. The association of a father with his sons has the form of monarchy, because he is concerned for the welfare of his children. That is why Homer calls Zeus 'father Zeus', because the ideal of kingship is paternal rule. But among the Persians paternal rule resembles tyranny, because they treat their sons as slaves. The relation of master to slaves also resembles tyranny, since in it the object served is the advantage of the master. Now *this* relationship is right, but the Persian one[3] is perverted, because different types of subject require different forms of government.

The association of husband and wife is clearly an aristocracy. The man rules by virtue of merit, and in the sphere that is his by right; but he hands over to his wife such matters as are suitable for her. If the husband asserts control over everything he is turning his rule into an oligarchy, because he is acting without regard for merit, and *not in conformity with his own superiority. In some cases, however, it is the wife that rules, because she is an heiress; such rule, then, is based not on merit but on wealth and power, just as it is in oligarchies.

The association of brothers resembles timocracy, because they are equals except in so far as they differ in age. Hence if the difference is great their friendship ceases to be brotherly.

1. i.e. having equal rights.   2. Of the three perversions.
3. As a father-son relation.

Democracy is most completely expressed in households where there is no master, for in them the members are all on an equality; but it also obtains where the head of the household is weak, and everyone can do as he likes.

Friendship and justice in these various associations

xi.   In each of these types of constitution we find a sort of friendship,[1] to the same extent as there is justice.[2] That of a king for his subjects consists in outstanding beneficence; because he does good to his subjects (assuming that, being good himself, he is concerned to promote their welfare, like a shepherd caring for his flock – which is why Homer called Agamemnon 'shepherd of the people'[3]). A father's affection is also of this nature, but there is a difference in the magnitude of the benefits; for the father is responsible for the child's existence, which is considered to be the greatest good of all, and for its upbringing and education. These benefits are also attributed to ancestors. Also by nature a father is qualified to rule his children, and ancestors their descendants, and a king his subjects. These friendships involve an excess; which is why parents are honoured as well.[4] So in these relations justice too is not the same on both sides, but is in accordance with merit; for this is true of friendship also.

The affection[5] between husband and wife is the same as that[6] in an aristocracy, because it is in accordance with merit, the husband (as superior) receiving the greater good,[7] and each party what is appropriate. The claims of justice are also met in this way.

Friendship between brothers is like that which unites the members of a social club,[8] because the parties are equal in

---

1. Between ruler and ruled.   2. Cf. 1134a26ff.
3. *Iliad* ii.243 and often elsewhere.
4. The excess is one of beneficence on the part of the ruler, which has to be compensated in some way.
5. The word is still *philia*.   6. Between rulers and ruled.
7. i.e. more affection.   8. Cf. note on 1159b32.

standing and age, and such people are usually similar in their feelings and character. This is the kind of friendship that obtains between the members of a timocracy, because ideally the citizens are equal and good; so they hold office in turn, and on a basis of equality; and consequently their friendship has this basis too.

On the other hand in the perverted constitutions friendship, like justice, is little found, and least in the worst; for in a tyranny there is little or no friendship. For where there is nothing in common between ruler and ruled there is no friendship either, just as there is no justice. Their relation is like that of the craftsman to his tool, or of soul to body, or of master to slave; all these instruments *are indeed benefited by those who use them, but there can be no friendship or justice towards inanimate things, and not even towards a horse or an ox, nor yet towards a slave *qua* slave; because there is nothing common to both parties: the slave is a living tool in the same way that a tool is an inanimate slave. Therefore friendship to him as a slave is impossible, although as a human being it is possible. For it is accepted that there is some sort of justice between any human being and any other who can take part in legal action or contract, and therefore there is friendship too in so far as he is a human being. Thus while in tyrannies friendships and justice are little found,[1] they are most commonly found in democracies, because the citizens, being equal, have much in common.

Affection in various degrees of relationship

xii. All friendship involves association, as we have said;[2] but friendship between relations and friendship between the members of a social club[3] might be distinguished ⟨as separate species⟩. Friendships between fellow-citizens or fellow-tribesmen[4] or fellow-voyagers and so on are more evidently friendships of association, because they seem to be based, as

1. Between ruler and subjects.   2. 1159b26ff.
3. Cf. note on 1159b32.   4. Cf. note on 1160a18.

it were, on a sort of compact. With these may be classed also
friendship with foreigners.[1]

   Friendship between relations also appears to be of several
different kinds, but they all seem to be ultimately derived
from paternal affection. For parents love their children as
part of themselves, whereas children love their parents as the
authors of their being. And parents know their children better than the children know their parentage. Also the progenitor has a stronger feeling that the progeny is his own
than the progeny has with regard to the progenitor; because
that which comes from something else belongs to that from
which it comes (as a tooth or hair or whatever it may be
belongs to its owner), whereas the source does not belong to
that which comes from it, or belongs in a lesser degree.
⟨Parental love exceeds the love of their children⟩ in duration too, because parents love their children from the moment of birth, but it is only after the lapse of some time that
children begin to love their parents, when they have acquired understanding or awareness. (These considerations
also make it obvious why mothers love their children more
than fathers do.) Parents, then, love their children as themselves (for one's offspring is a sort of other self in virtue of a
separate existence[2]), and children love their parents as the
origin from which they sprang.

   Brothers love one another as having sprung from the same
origin, because their identity with regard to their parents
identifies them with one another. Hence such phrases as 'the
same blood' and 'the same stock', etc. Thus brothers are in
a sense the same identity in different bodies. Their affection
is much enhanced by a common upbringing and similarity
of age; for 'like age makes like minds' and 'common life
makes comrades'. For this reason the affection of brothers is
like that between members of the *same club.[3] The attach-

   1. Cf. note on 1156a31.
   2. It is 'other' only in virtue of a separate existence, like the offshoot
of a plant; this botanical analogy underlies the thought of the whole
passage.
   3. Cf. 1159b32.

ment of cousins and other relations is an extension of fraternal affection, because it is based on common ancestry; and they exhibit greater or less family feeling according as they are closely or remotely connected with the common ancestor.

The love of children for their parents (and of men towards the gods) implies a relation to an object that is *good* and superior to oneself; for their parents have bestowed on them the greatest blessings: they are responsible for giving them life and sustenance, and subsequently education. Such affection also contains more pleasure and utility than friendship between strangers, inasmuch as their life is lived more in common.

Friendship between brothers has the same characteristics as friendship between comrades (especially if they are good men), and in general between those who are like-minded; inasmuch as brothers are in a closer relation to each other, and have loved each other since birth, and inasmuch as children of the same parents, brought up together and similarly educated, are more closely alike in character. Also in their case the test of time has been longest and most reliable. Friendly feelings between other relations are proportionate to the closeness of the relationship.

The love between husband and wife is considered to be naturally inherent in them. For man is by his nature a pairing rather than a social creature, inasmuch as the family is an older and more necessary thing than the state, and procreation is a characteristic more commonly shared with the animals.[1] In the other animals partnership goes no further than this; but human beings cohabit not merely to produce children but to secure the necessities of life. From the outset the functions are divided, the husband's being different from the wife's; so they supply each other's deficiencies by pooling their personal resources. For this reason it is thought that both utility and pleasure have a place in conjugal love. But it may be based also on goodness, sup-

1. More commonly than association in groups or communities; but cf. 1097b11, 1169b18.

posing the partners to be of good character; for they have each their own special excellence, and this may be a source of pleasure to both. Children too, it is agreed, are a bond between parents, which is why childless marriages break up more quickly. For the children are an asset common to them both, and common possession is cohesive. As for how a husband and wife, or in general a pair of friends, should conduct themselves in their life together, this seems to be nothing other than a question of how it is just for them to do so; because for a given person justice does not seem to be the same towards a friend, a foreigner, a comrade, and a fellow-student.[1]

Friendship and conflicting claims between equals

xiii. As we said at the outset,[2] there are three kinds of friendship, and in each of these three kinds there are both friends who are on an equality and friends who are in a position of superiority (for friendships can be made both between equally good men and *between a better man and a worse, and similarly both between those who are equal and those who are different in the amount of pleasure or benefit that they afford each other). Those who are equal must exhibit this equality by contributing an equal amount of affection and of the other grounds of their friendship, and those who are unequal by making a return proportionate to the other party's superiority.[3]

Complaints and recriminations arise chiefly if not exclusively in utilitarian friendship. This is intelligible, because those whose friendship is based on goodness are eager to benefit each other (since this is an essential feature of goodness and friendliness); and where there is this sort of rivalry there is no occasion for complaints or quarrels. For no one objects to being treated with affection and benefic-

1. Possibly 'put in for a laugh'.   2. 1156a7.
3. i.e. making up in affection their own deficiency in goodness, utility or pleasantness.

ence; on the contrary any decent person requites his benefactor with kindness. And since the one who excels in well-
doing is achieving his object, he cannot complain against
his friend, because every individual aims at what is good.
Nor do complaints arise much between those whose friendship is based on pleasure, because both alike are getting what
they want if they enjoy each other's company. It would
obviously also be ridiculous to complain that one's friend
is not amusing if there is no need to stay in his company. But
utilitarian friendship does give rise to complaints, because
since each associates with the other for his own benefit, they
are always wanting the better of the bargain, and thinking
that they have less than they should, and grumbling because
they do not get as much as they want, although they deserve
it; and the benefactor can never supply as much as the
recipient demands.

In the same way as there are two kinds of justice, one unwritten and the other prescribed by law, so utilitarian
friendship seems to be in some cases a moral, in others a
legal obligation. Thus complaints arise most commonly
when the parties to an association dissolve it in a different
spirit from that in which they contracted it. A legal association is one on fixed terms, either a purely business
transaction from hand to hand, or one more liberally defined in respect of time, but embodying an agreement upon
the terms of repayment. In the latter case while the obligation is clear and indisputable, the provision for deferred
repayment contains a friendly element; which is why in
some states there is no action at law in such cases, the view
being that those who enter into a contract which allows
credit must accept the consequences.

As for the moral type of utilitarian friendship, it is not expressed in set terms, but the gift (or whatever other benefit
it is) is given as to a friend. Still, the giver expects to recover
the equivalent or more, because he feels that he has made
not a gift but a loan; and if he finds himself worse off at the
end of their association than he was at the beginning he will
lodge a complaint. This sort of thing happens because most

people, if not all, although they *wish* to do the fine thing,
choose the course that is profitable. Now it is a fine thing to
confer a benefit without *any thought of a return; but the
profitable thing is to receive benefits. So one ought, if one
can, to repay a kindness at its full value; for one should not
make a man one's friend against his will.[1] Thus one should
repay the benefit as if one had been mistaken at the outset
and had accepted it from the wrong sort of person (because
it was not from a friend, nor from one acting altruistically) –
so[2] the transaction should be terminated as if one had received the benefit on set terms. One would even agree to
make repayment when able to do so[3] (for not even the giver
would have expected it from one who had not the means). If
possible, then, the service should be repaid. But one should
consider carefully at the outset by whom the service is being
done, and upon what terms, so that one may either abide by
the terms or decline it.

How to estimate the value of a service

It is debatable whether in estimating a service and making
repayment for it one should have regard to the benefit of the
recipient or the generosity of the donor. The recipients
assert that what they received cost their benefactors little
and could have been had from other sources – thus trying to
minimize their indebtedness; the donors on the contrary
insist that their services were the greatest that lay in their
power, and could not have been had from elsewhere, and
were rendered in the face of danger or some such emergency.
Probably where the friendship is based on utility the right
standard is the benefit of the recipient; for the request is his,
and the other supplies it in the expectation of getting back an

1. By treating as a gift what was intended as a loan or an exchange of
property.
2. The parenthesis causes a slight anacoluthon.
3. The text and meaning of this sentence, as of one or two others
above it, are rather uncertain.

equal return. So it is the amount of help obtained by the recipient that constitutes the value of the service; and therefore he ought to repay as much benefit as he enjoyed, or even more, because that will be a finer gesture.

In friendships based on goodness there are no complaints, and the measure of the benefit seems to be the intention[1] of the giver; for intention is the decisive factor in virtue and character.

Conflicting claims between unequals

xiv.   Quarrels also occur in friendships that involve superiority; because each party expects to get more, and when this happens the friendship breaks up. The person with the better character thinks that he should have more because more should be assigned to a good man; and so does the one who is more useful, because if a man is of no use, they say, he ought not to have an equal share, since the arrangement becomes more like a compulsory public service[2] than a friendship if the proceeds are not to be worth the effort expended. For they think that just as in a financial partnership those who make the larger contribution receive a larger share of the profit, so it should be in the case of friendship. But the man who is needy, and the inferior character, take the contrary view: that it is the mark of a good friend to help those who are in need. 'For what is the point', they say, 'of being the friend of a good or influential man if there is no prospect of enjoying any advantage from it?'

*Well, it seems likely that both claims are correct and that each should be given a larger share, but not of the same thing: the superior friend should get more honour, and the needy friend more gain; because honour is the reward for virtue and beneficence, whereas the remedy for need is gain. This principle seems to obtain also in public life. The citizen who contributes nothing of value to the community receives no honour; for it is the benefactor of the community

1. *proairesis*.   2. A 'liturgy'; see Appendix I.

that receives what it has to give, namely honour. It is not possible to make money out of public funds and to receive public honour at the same time, because nobody can stand having the worst of every bargain.[1] Accordingly the man who loses financially is accorded honour, and it is only the corrupt official that is given money; for reward in accordance with merit balances and preserves friendly relations, as we have said.[2]

This, then, is also the way in which unequal friends should associate: the one who is benefited financially or morally should give honour in return, making such payment as is in his power. For friendship asks only for what is practicable, not for what is in accordance[3] with merit, for there is actually no such thing in some cases, e.g. in honouring the gods or one's parents; because nobody could ever give them as much as they deserve, but anyone who serves them as best he can is considered to act fairly. Hence it would seem that a son may not disown his father, although a father may disown his son. For a debtor ought to pay his debts, but nothing that a son can do is a due return for what he has received, so that he is permanently in ⟨his father's⟩ debt. On the other hand creditors have the right to remit a debt; therefore so has the father. At the same time it seems improbable that a father would ever break off all relations with a son who was not exceptionally vicious. For apart from natural affection, it is only human not to spurn the assistance ⟨that a son can give⟩, whereas a son (if he is vicious) regards the supporting of his father as something to be evaded or done reluctantly. For most people wish to receive benefits, but avoid conferring them, on the ground that it is unprofitable.

So much for our discussion of this subject.

1. i.e. the state will not reward one to whom it has lost money.
2. Cf. 1158b27f., 1159a33ff. The comment seems to be drily sarcastic.
3. i.e. *strictly* in accordance.

IX

THE GROUNDS OF FRIENDSHIP

Difficulties caused by differences of motive in friendship

i. In all dissimilar friendships it is, as we have said, a proportion[1] that secures equality and preserves the friendship. E.g. in the relations between citizens: the shoemaker receives something of equal value in return for his shoes, and so does the weaver and all the rest. *In these cases a common measure is already provided in the shape of money, and therefore everything is referred to this and is measured by it. But in emotional relations the lover sometimes complains that his devotion is unrequited (it may be because he has no lovable quality); and often the beloved complains that the one who used to promise everything now fulfils none of his promises. Such situations arise when the one loves his beloved on the ground of pleasure and the other his lover on the ground of utility, and they no longer both possess these attributes; because a friendship based on these motives breaks up as soon as the reasons for which the friends loved each other no longer present themselves. For it was not each other that they loved, but each other's attributes, which were not permanent. Hence friendships of this kind are not permanent either. But friendship based on character, being disinterested, is lasting, as we have said.[2]

1. A friendship is dissimilar if the friends differ in quality and make different contributions, e.g. pleasure and profit. The means of equalizing these contributions is not simple proportion (which can only be employed where the contributions are the same in kind), but a sort of diagonal conjunction, as in rectificatory justice; see 1133a5ff.

2. 1156b17.

Any breach of contract causes ill-feeling

Quarrels occur when the outcome of a friendship is different
from what the parties desire, because failure to obtain what
one wants is almost as bad as getting nothing at all. It is like
the story of the man who promised a fee to the harpist, and
the better he played, the higher the fee would be; but when
next morning the harpist asked him for what he had
promised, he replied that he had already paid him pleasure
for pleasure.[1] Now if pleasure had been what both wanted,
this would have been satisfactory. But if one wants pleasure
and the other gain, and one has his wish and the other does
not, the result of the association cannot be fair; for it is what
a man actually needs that he is anxious to get, and it is only
for its sake that he is prepared to give what he has.

*The value of a service, if not fixed in advance, is left to the
discretion of the recipient*

But which has the better right to assess the value of the service,[2] the man who proffers it, or the one who has actually
received it? The latter, because the man who makes the
offer virtually leaves the decision to him. Protagoras,[3] we
are told, acted on this principle: when he had finished
teaching any subject he used to tell his pupil to estimate the
value of the knowledge that he had acquired, and accepted
that as his fee. But in this matter some teachers prefer the
principle

Let the price
Fixed between two friends suffice.[4]

1. The harpist had had the pleasure of anticipating a large fee,
which was payment enough for the pleasure that he had given. The story
was told of Dionysius I of Syracuse (Plutarch, *De Alex. fortuna* ii.1).

2. Where there has been no formal agreement.

3. The famous sophist from Abdera; cf. Plato, *Protagoras* 328B, and
see Appendix B.

4. Hesiod, *Works and Days* 370; i.e. fix a fee and stick to it.

But those who take their fees in advance and then completely fail to carry out their bargain, owing to the extravagance of their pretensions, naturally find themselves exposed to complaints; because they are not fulfilling their agreement. (The sophists are probably compelled to do this,[1] because nobody would pay them money for the knowledge that they possess.) These people, then, are naturally exposed to complaints when they fail to carry out what they have been paid to do.

Pure benevolence cannot be adequately repaid; the beneficiary must make the best return that he can

Where no contract for service is made, those who offer it for their friends' sake are immune from complaint, as we have said,[2] (because friendship based on goodness *does not admit of it) and the return should be made in proportion to the intention of the benefactor (for it is the intention that counts both in friendship and in virtue); and this is probably the right procedure for those who have had a course in philosophy;[3] for the value of this is not measurable in money, nor could such a service be balanced by a gift of honour. Presumably it is enough if (as in the case of the gods or one's parents[4]) the beneficiary makes such a return as lies in his power.

If the parties cannot agree, the beneficiary should decide

But if the gift was not of this kind,[5] but aimed at some object, no doubt the best course is for a return to be made that seems fair to both parties. Failing such an agreement, it would seem not only necessary but also just that the bene-

1. Take their fees in advance. A., like Plato, has a poor opinion of them; see Appendix B.
2. 1162b6ff.   3. Another touch of humour.   4. Cf. 1163b15ff.
5. i.e. not made for the friend's sake.

ficiary should assess the value. For when A has received in return as much benefit as he gave to B, or as much as B would have been content to pay for his pleasure, he will have what is due to him from B. Indeed it is obvious that this is what happens in market transactions. In some states there are laws precluding actions for breach of voluntary covenants, the view being that if you have trusted a person you must conclude the transaction in the same way as you entered into it; because the law considers that it is more just that the assessment should be made by the man to whom it was conceded than by the one who conceded it to him. For in general the owners of a commodity do not set the same price upon it as those who wish to acquire it, since all types of people feel that their own possessions and gifts are of great value. However, what determines the payment is the price fixed by the recipient; but presumably he should value what he receives not at the price that seems fair to him after he received it, but at what he thought it was worth before he got it.

Problems arising from the claims of friendship

ii.   Problems arise also in such cases as these. Ought one invariably to defer to one's father and obey him, or should one when ill entrust oneself to a doctor, or in voting for a general vote for one who has had military experience?[1] Similarly, ought one to help a friend in preference to a man of high character? Ought one to repay a benefactor for his kindness or to spend money on a close friend,[2] if one is not in a position to do both?

Well, it is perhaps no easy matter to lay down exact lines in such cases, because they involve a great many differences

---

1. Instead of a friend of one's father. The example is not quite so cynical as it sounds; an Athenian general's duties were partly ministerial, and in the field he could perhaps rely on the advice of experienced staff officers.

2. Literally 'comrade'; cf. 1159b32.

of every kind in importance and unimportance and in honour and urgency. But it is not difficult to see that no one person is entitled to deference in everything. Then as a general rule it is more important to repay benefits than to make spontaneous presents to one's close friends, just as one should repay a debt rather than give the money to a friend. But presumably there are exceptions even to this. Ought a man who has been ransomed from brigands to ransom his ransomer, whoever he is – or to repay him the ransom-money at his request, *when he has not been kidnapped at all – or to ransom his own father, since it might be thought that he ought to ransom his father even before himself? Well, as we have said, generally speaking the debt should be repaid. But if the gift is the more cogent duty in respect of either honour or urgency, then the balance should incline towards the gift. For there are times when it is not even fair to return the equivalent of the original obligation, as for instance when A has done B a service, knowing him to be a good man, and then B is faced with repaying the service to A, whom he believes to be a vicious one. Indeed there are times when one ought not to make a loan in return to a person from whom one has received one: A lent the money to B, an honest man, expecting to get it back again, but B has no hope of getting his money back from A, who is a villain. Now if this is in fact so, A's demand is not a fair one; and if it is not so, still if B thinks it is, it would not seem extraordinary for B to refuse. So, as we have repeatedly said,[1] discussions about feelings and conduct admit of no more precision than their subject-matter does.

It is not difficult to see, then, that we are not obliged to make the same return in all cases, and that not even a father is entitled to everything, just as Zeus does not get all the sacrifices. And since parents, brothers, comrades and benefactors all have different claims upon us, we must render to each class of benefactor their special and appropriate service. This is what people are actually observed to do. To weddings they invite their relations, because they are

1. 1094b11ff., 1098a26ff., 1103b34ff.

members of the family and presumably have an interest in its affairs; and for the same reason it is thought to be the special duty of relations to attend funerals. It would seem that parents have a special claim upon their children for support, on the ground that it is owed to them, and that it is a finer act for children to furnish this support to the authors of their being than to themselves. It would also seem that, just as honour is due to the gods, so it is to parents – but not every kind of honour; because a father ought not even to receive the same honour as a mother, nor the honour due to a thinker[1] or a general; only the honour due to a father; and similarly with the honour due to a mother. Younger men should always show their elders the respect due to their age by rising at their approach, and giving up their seats to them, and similar courtesies. On the other hand towards brothers and comrades we should exercise frankness and readiness to share anything. As for relations, members of the same tribe,[2] fellow-citizens, etc., we ought always to try to give them all their proper due, comparing their several claims on the basis of their relationship and merit or utility. Between people of the same kind discrimination is comparatively easy: when they stand in different relations to us it is more of a task. However, this is no excuse for shirking; we must draw our distinctions as well as we can.

Grounds for dissolving friendship

iii.   Another problem that arises is whether or not to break off *friendship with those who do not remain the same as they were. Where the bond was one of utility or pleasure there is presumably nothing odd about breaking it when they no longer have these attributes; for it was these that underlay the friendship, and when they fail it is reasonable to feel no affection. But a person might complain if his friend, who liked him only for the profit or pleasure that he got from him, pretended to like him for his character. For (as we said at

1. *Sophos*; cf. 1141a9ff.   2. See note on 1160a18.

the outset[1]) most quarrels between friends arise when the basis of their friendship is not what they suppose it to be. When a person is completely mistaken and has assumed that he is loved for his character although his friend has never done anything to suggest it, he has only himself to blame. But when he has been deceived by the other's pretensions he is justified in protesting at the deception – even more than if it had been a case of uttering false coin, since the offence concerns something more valuable than money.

But if A has accepted B as a friend, in the belief that he is a good man, and he turns out or even appears to be a villain, ought A still to love him? Surely this is impossible, assuming that not everything is lovable but only what is good; and it is not right, either, because one ought not to be a lover of what is bad, or to make oneself like a worthless person; and we have said[2] that 'like is friend to like'. Ought the friendship, then, to be broken off at once? Perhaps not in every case, but only with those whose depravity is incurable. Those who are capable of recovery are entitled to our help for their characters even more than for their fortunes, inasmuch as the character is a higher thing and more closely bound up with friendship. At the same time one who broke off such a friendship would not be felt to be acting oddly, because the man that he made his friend was not like that; so now that he has changed, being unable to restore him to what he was, he gives him up.

But suppose that one friend remains the same, and the other improves and becomes far superior to him in virtue, should he still treat the former as a friend? Surely it is impossible. This appears most clearly in the case of a great disparity, such as occurs in boyhood friendships. Supposing that one person remains a child in intelligence and the other is a man of outstanding ability, how can they go on being friends when they have different interests and different likes and dislikes? They will not even have the same feelings about each other, and without this it is impossible (as we

1. 1162b23.   2. 1155a32ff., 1156b19ff., 1159b2f.

saw[1]) to be friends; because spending their lives together is
out of the question. This has been discussed already.

Is one, then, to behave towards a former friend exactly as
if he had never been a friend at all? Probably one ought to
keep a memory of the former intimacy, and just as we feel
bound to show more favour to friends than to strangers, so
we should for old acquaintance sake show some consideration for former friends – provided that the severance was not
due to excessive wickedness on their part.

Our feelings towards our friends reflect our feelings towards ourselves

*iv. The friendly feelings that we have towards our neigh-
bours, and the characteristics by which the different kinds of
friendship are distinguished, seem to be derived from our
feelings towards ourselves. People define a friend as (a) one
who wishes and effects the good, or apparent good, of
another for the sake of that other; or (b) one who wishes for
the existence and preservation of his friend for the friend's
sake – the same attitude as mothers have towards their
children, or as old friends have towards those with whom
they have fallen out. Others define him as (c) one who spends
all his time with another, and (d) chooses the same things
as he does, or as (e) one who shares his friend's joys and
sorrows (this also is a very special trait of mothers). Friendship, too, is defined by one or another of these characteristics. But each one of them applies to the good man in relation to himself (and applies to others in so far as they suppose themselves to be good; in every case, as we have said,[2]
the standard seems to be ⟨moral⟩ goodness or the good man).
For he is completely integrated[3] and desires the same things
with every part of his soul. Also he wishes and effects the
things that are or seem to be good for him[4] (for it is the

---

1. 1157b17ff., 1158b33ff.   2. Cf. 1113a22–33.
3. He has no inner conflict; see (d) above.   4. See (a) above.

mark of a good man to direct his energies to what is good) and he does it for his own sake (for he does it on account of the intellectual part of him, which is held to be the self of the individual). Also he desires his own life and safety,[1] especially that of his rational part; because for the good man existence is good, and everyone wishes his own good – nobody would choose to have all the good things in the world at the price of becoming somebody else (for as it is God possesses the good[2]), but only while remaining himself, whatever he is. And it would seem that the thinking part is, or most nearly is, the individual self. Such a person likes his own company,[3] because he enjoys being by himself, since he has entertaining memories of the past and good hopes for the future, and these afford him pleasure; also his mind is well furnished with subjects for contemplation. And he has the fullest consciousness of his joys and sorrows,[4] for it is always the same things that vex or please him, and not different things at different times; because he virtually never changes his mind.

Thus it is because the good man has these several feelings towards himself, and extends to his friend the same relation that he has towards himself (for a friend *is* another self), that friendship is regarded as one of the said feelings, and friends as those to whom these feelings apply. The question whether friendship towards oneself is possible or not may be dismissed for the present;[5] but it would seem from what we have said that it *is* possible in so far as the subject is regarded as two or more *persons; there is also the fact that in its extreme form friendship approximates to self-love.

It seems, however, that the qualities that we have been describing belong also to the majority of people, bad as they are. Probably they share in them only in so far as they are

1. See (b) above.
2. And *only* God possesses the supreme good; so to wish for all good, with a change of personality, would mean wishing to be God – which is no more sensible than wishing one's friend to be a god (1159a5ff.).
3. See (c) above.   4. See (e) above.
5. It is taken up explicitly below, 1168a28ff.

self-satisfied and suppose themselves to be respectable; because nobody who is utterly bad and evil has them, or even the semblance of them. It is hardly too much to say that not even ⟨moderately⟩ bad people have them, because they are in conflict with themselves;[1] they desire one thing and will another, like the incontinent, who choose harmful pleasures instead of what they themselves believe to be good. There are others again who through cowardice and indolence shirk doing what they believe is in their own best interests. Others who have committed many fearful crimes and are hated for their villainy actually run away from life[2] and commit suicide. Also bad people seek constant companionship and avoid their own society,[3] because when they are by themselves they recall many disagreeable experiences and expect to have more of the same kind, whereas when they are with others they can forget. Possessing no lovable quality, they feel no affection for themselves;[4] consequently such people have no sympathetic consciousness of their own joys and sorrows,[5] because their soul is in a state of conflict: one part of it through depravity feels pain in abstaining from things, and another feels pleasure; one pulls this way and the other that, as if they would tear it apart. If it is impossible to feel pleasure and pain at the same time, at any rate such a person is very soon sorry that he was glad, and wishes that he had never taken pleasure in such things; for bad men are full of regrets.

It seems, then, that a bad man is not even amicably disposed towards himself, because he has no lovable quality. So if this state is the height of misery, one ought to strain every nerve to avoid wickedness and try to be a man of good character; for in that way one can both be on good terms with oneself and become the friend of somebody else.

1. See (d) above.   2. See (b) above.   3. See (c) above.
4. See (a) above.   5. See (e) above.

Goodwill distinguished from friendship

v. Goodwill resembles friendship but is not identical with it, because goodwill can be felt towards people that one does not know, and without their knowledge, but friendship cannot. This has in fact been said already.[1] Nor is goodwill the same as affection, because it is without intensity or desire, and affection is associated with both. Again, affection implies intimacy, whereas goodwill can spring up quite suddenly, as happens in the case of competitors at *athletic festivals; for the spectators feel goodwill towards them and share their hopes, but they would not do anything to help them, because (as we said) their goodwill is a sudden development, and their kindly feeling is superficial.

Thus goodwill seems to be the beginning of friendship, just as the pleasure at seeing a person is the beginning of love; for nobody falls in love without first feeling pleasure at the person's appearance, although enjoying the sight of a person does not make one in love; it is love when one longs for somebody who is absent and desires that person's presence. Similarly people cannot be friends unless they have come to feel goodwill, although feeling goodwill does not make them friends, because they only wish for the good of those for whom they feel goodwill; they would not actively help them or take any trouble for their sake. One might, then, by a metaphor define goodwill as undeveloped friendship, which in course of time, when it attains to intimacy, becomes friendship – but not friendship based on utility or pleasure, for these never in fact arouse goodwill. A man who has received a benefit does indeed return goodwill for what has been done to him, and this is right and proper. But if a person's motive for doing somebody else a service is the hope of getting, through his help, some substantial advantage, it looks as if the object of his goodwill were not so much the other man as himself – just as a person is not a *friend* if the attentions that he pays have an interested motive.

1. 1155b32ff.

In general, goodwill is aroused by some merit and goodness, when it seems to one that somebody is handsome or brave or something of the kind, as we said in the case of the competitors at an athletic contest.[1]

Friendship and concord

vi. Concord also seems to be a friendly feeling. Consequently it is not the same as agreement of opinion, because that might be present even in people who did not know each other. Nor is the word concord used to describe agreement of views upon any and every subject, e.g. about the heavenly bodies (because agreement about these has nothing to do with friendly feeling). There is said to be concord in a state when the citizens agree about their interests, adopt the same policy, and put their common resolves into effect. Thus concord is concerned with practical ends, and among these only with such as are important, and can be achieved by both parties,[2] or by the whole body of citizens. For example, a state exhibits concord when the citizens unanimously decide that offices shall be elective, or that an alliance shall be made with Sparta, or that Pittacus shall be head of the state (at the time when he himself was willing so to be[3]); but when each of two rivals wishes to rule, as in the *Phoenissae*,[4] there is faction. For the fact that they have the same thought does not mean that the two parties are in concord, no matter what it is; the thought must be in relation to the same object, as when the people *and the upper classes both think that the best men should govern; for in this way they all get what they want. Thus concord is evidently (as the word is actually used) friendship between the citizens of a state, because it is concerned with their interests and living conditions.

1. 1166b35.

2. Where only two (e.g. democrats and oligarchs) are involved.

3. He was 'tyrant' of Mitylene early in the sixth century; the point of the qualification is that he abdicated.

4. See Euripides, *Phoenissae* 588ff.

This sort of concord is found among good men, because they are in accord both with themselves and with one another, having (broadly speaking) the same outlook. For the wishes of such people remain constant and do not ebb and flow like the tides;[1] and they wish for what is just and advantageous, and also pursue these objects in common. But bad men cannot be in concord (just as they cannot be friends) except to a very limited extent, since they are eager to get more than their share of advantages, while they fall short in the performance of difficult tasks and public services; and while each wants the advantages for himself, he keeps a sharp eye upon his neighbour and restrains him; because unless they watch over the public interest it meets with disaster. The consequence is that they are factious, putting pressure on each other, but not wishing to do what is right themselves.

Why are benefactors more loving than beneficiaries?

vii.   Benefactors are thought to love those whom they have benefited more than the beneficiaries love their benefactors, and the apparent paradox calls for explanation. Most people conclude that it is because the latter owe and the former are owed a debt; and so, just as in the case of a loan debtors wish their creditors out of the way, whereas the creditors are actually concerned for the safety of their debtors, in the same way it is thought that benefactors want their protégés to exist, because they expect to receive some expression of gratitude in return; but the beneficiaries are not concerned to repay them. Perhaps Epicharmus[2] would say that people talk like this because they are 'looking on the dark side'; but it is not inconsistent with human nature, because most people have short memories and are more anxious to be

1. In Greek the simile is supplied by changing currents, Mediterranean tides being inconspicuous.
2. See Index of Names. The quotation is otherwise unknown; it seems to mean literally 'watching from a bad seat' (in the theatre).

well-treated than to treat others well. It may be thought, however, that the cause lies deeper in nature, and that the case of the lender is not even analogous. It is not affection that the lender feels, but a wish for the debtor's safety with a view to reimbursement; whereas the author of a kindness feels affection and love for the recipient even if he neither is nor is likely to be any use to him. This is just what happens in the crafts too. Every craftsman loves the work of his own hands more than it would love him if it came to life. *Probably this happens most of all with poets,[1] because they are exceedingly fond of their own poems, loving them as if they were their children. Well, the case of the benefactor is much the same. What he has benefited is his own handiwork; so he loves it more than the work loves its maker. The reason for this is that existence is to everyone an object of choice and love, and we exist through activity (because we exist by living and acting); and the maker of the work exists, in a sense, through his activity.[2] Therefore the maker loves his work, because he loves existence. This is a natural principle; for the work reveals in actuality what *is* only potentially.

There is also the point that for the benefactor there is something fine in the performance of his action, so that he takes pleasure in the person upon whom it is performed; but to the beneficiary there is nothing fine in ⟨his relation to⟩ the agent, but at most some advantage, and this is a weaker ground for pleasure and affection. Thus[3] for the maker his handiwork endures (because what is fine is long-lasting), but for the person affected the utility is transient. It is the activity of a present action, the expectation of a future one, and the memory of a past one, that gives pleasure. But the greatest pleasure is that which accompanies the activity; and it is similarly the strongest ground for love. Besides, the memory of fine deeds is pleasant, but that of useful ones is

1. Cf. note on 1120b14.

2. This is Gauthier's interpretation, which seems to be the best.

3. In the M s this sentence follows the next but one ending in 'ground for love'.

less so or hardly pleasant at all; with anticipation, however, it seems to be the other way round.

Another point is that loving[1] is a sort of active experience, while being loved is a passive one; therefore love and friendly feelings are attributes of those who take the leading part in the action. Again, everyone feels stronger affection for things that have cost him some effort to acquire; e.g. those who have made their money love it more than those who have inherited it. Now it is accepted that no trouble is incurred in receiving a benefit, whereas conferring one takes trouble (this is why mothers are fonder of their children than fathers are, because it cost them more pains to bring them into the world, and they know better that the child is their own). It would seem, then, that this feeling applies also to benefactors.

Is self-love justifiable?

viii. Another problem is whether one ought to love oneself most or somebody else. People are critical of those whose chief concern is for themselves, and call them self-lovers derogatorily. Also a bad man is generally supposed to do everything from a selfish motive, and to be the more selfish the worse he is (e.g. he is accused of doing nothing unless he has to); whereas the good man acts from a fine motive (and the better the man the finer the motive), and for the sake of a friend, and neglects his own interest. But these theories are not borne out by the *facts; nor is this surprising. For they say that a man should love his best friend most. But a man's best friend is the one who not only wishes him well but wishes it for his own sake (even though nobody will ever know it): and this condition is best fulfilled by his attitude towards himself – and similarly with all the other attributes that go to define a friend. For we have said before[2] that all friendly feelings for others are extensions of a man's feelings for himself. Besides, all the proverbial sayings agree on this

1. *philēsis*.   2. 1166a1ff.

point: 'Two friends, one soul',[1] 'Friends share everything',
'Caring is sharing',[2] 'The knee is nearer than the shin'.[3]
All these sayings can be applied most aptly to oneself,
because a man is his own best friend. Therefore he ought to
love himself best. Naturally it is hard to say which of these
opinions we should follow, since both have some plausibility.

Presumably, then, we should take such divergent arguments separately and try to distinguish how far and in what
way each of them is true. Perhaps the difficulty would be
cleared up if we discussed what meaning each side attaches
to the word self-love. Those who give it a pejorative twist
describe as self-loving those who assign themselves the
larger share of money, public honours, and bodily pleasures,
because most people have a craving for these, and set their
hearts on them as the greatest goods, which also makes them
objects of fierce competition. Well, those who try to get more
than their share of these things gratify their desires and their
feelings generally, and the irrational part of their soul; and
such people are in the majority. Hence the word has become a term of reproach, from the fact that the self-love of
most people is a bad thing. Therefore those who are self-
lovers in this sense are rightly reproached. And there is no
doubt that most people regularly describe as self-lovers
those who secure such advantages for themselves. For if
anyone made it his constant endeavour to set an example in
performing just or temperate or any other kind of virtuous
actions, and in general always claimed the prerogative of
acting honourably, certainly nobody would reproach *him*
with being a self-lover.

Yet such a person might be considered to have a better
title to the name. At any rate he assigns to himself what is
most honourable and most truly good; and he gratifies the
most authoritative part of himself, and obeys it in all
respects. And just as in the case of a state or any other
composite body the most authoritative part is considered to

1. Euripides, *Orestes* 1046.   2. Cf. 1157b36.
3. Cf. Theocritus xvi.18: it is an excuse for selfishness, like 'charity
begins at home'.

be most truly the state or body, so too in the case of man.[1] Therefore one who loves this authoritative part and gratifies it is in the truest sense a self-lover. Also a person is called continent or incontinent according as his reason is or is not in control, which implies that this part *is* the individual. Also it is our *reasoned acts that are held to be in the fullest sense voluntary and our own doing. Thus there is no doubt that this part is, or most nearly is, the individual man; and that a good man loves it more than anything else. It follows that he will be in the fullest sense a self-lover – but in a different fashion from the man who incurs reproach, and as far superior to him as life ruled by reason is to life ruled by feeling, and as desire for what is fine is to desire for an apparent advantage. Hence those who are exceptionally devoted to the performance of fine actions receive the approval and commendation of all. And if everyone were striving for what is fine, and trying his hardest to do the finest deeds, then both the public welfare would be truly served, and each individual would enjoy the greatest of goods, since virtue is of this kind.

So it is right for the good man to be self-loving, because then he will both be benefited himself by performing fine actions, and also help others. But it is not right for the bad man, because he will injure both himself and his neighbours by giving way to base feelings. So for the bad man what he ought to do clashes with what he does; but the good man does what he ought to do. For intelligence always chooses what is best for itself, and the good man obeys the guidance of intelligence.

But it is also true to say of the man of good character that he performs many actions for the sake of his friends and his country, and if necessary even dies for them. For he will sacrifice both money and honours and in general the goods that people struggle to obtain, in his pursuit of what is ⟨morally⟩ fine. For he would rather have intense pleasure for a short time than quiet pleasure for a long time; rather

1. The highest part of him, i.e. the rational part, *is* the man; cf. 1166a17, 22, 1178a2, 7.

live finely for one year than indifferently for many; and rather do one great and glorious deed than many petty ones. This result is presumably achieved by those who give their lives for others; so their choice is a glorious prize. Also the good man is ready to lose money on condition that his friends shall get more; for the friend gets money, but he himself gains fineness ⟨of character⟩, so he assigns himself the greater good. He behaves in the same way too with regard to political honours and positions; all these he will freely give up to his friend, because that is a fine and praiseworthy thing for him to do. So it is natural that he is regarded as a man of good character, since he chooses what is fine in preference to anything else. He may even give up to his friend opportunities for doing fine actions, and it may be a finer thing for him to become the cause of his friend's doing them than to have done them himself. Thus we see that in the whole field of praiseworthy conduct the good man assigns himself the larger share of *what is fine. It is right, then (as we said before[1]), to be self-loving in this sense; but not in the sense in which most people are self-loving.

Are friends necessary for happiness?

ix.   There is a disputable point also with regard to the happy man: whether he will need friends or not. For it is maintained that the supremely happy, who are self-sufficient, have no need of friends, because they have their good things; therefore being self-sufficient they need nothing further; but a friend, who is 'another self', supplies what a man cannot provide by his own efforts. Hence the line

When Fortune smiles on us, what need of friends?[2]

Yet it seems paradoxical that, while attributing all good things to the happy man, we should not assign him friends, who are considered to be the greatest of external goods. Besides, if it is more characteristic of a friend to confer than

1. a11ff. above.   2. Euripides, *Orestes* 667.

to receive a benefit, and doing good to others is characteristic of virtue and the good man, and it is better to do a kindness to a friend than to a stranger, the good man will need friends to receive his benefits. Hence arises a further question: Does one need friends more in prosperity or in adversity? because the unfortunate need people to be kind to them, and the fortunate need people to be kind to.

It is also surely paradoxical to represent the man of perfect happiness as a solitary; for nobody would choose to have all the good things in the world by himself, because man is a social creature[1] and naturally constituted to live in company. Therefore the happy man also has this quality, because he possesses everything that is naturally good; and it is clearly better to spend one's time in the company of friends and good men than in that of strangers and people of uncertain character. It follows, therefore, that the happy man needs friends.

What, then, is the meaning of those who uphold the first view,[2] and what truth is there in their arguments? Perhaps the answer is that in the popular view our friends are those who are useful to us; so the truly happy man will have no need of such people, since he already has the things that are good for him. Nor indeed will he require friends on the ground of pleasure, or only to a limited extent, because his life is pleasant and needs no imported pleasure; and since he does not need friends of these kinds he is thought to need none at all. But this is presumably not true. For it was stated at the outset[3] that happiness is a kind of activity; and an activity clearly is developed and is not a piece of property already in one's possession. Now if happiness consists in living and being active, and the activity of a good man is virtuous and pleasurable in itself (as we said at the outset[4]); and if we take pleasure in what is our own; and if we are better able to observe our neighbours than ourselves, and their actions than our own; and if the actions of high-

1. Cf. 1097b11.
2. That the happy man needs no friends (b4ff. above).
3. 1098a7, 16, b31ff.   4. 1099a14, 21.

minded[1] men who are our friends *are pleasant to the good
(because both attributes are naturally pleasant[2]): then it
follows that the truly happy man will need friends of this
sort, because he prefers to contemplate actions that are
honourable and his own, and the actions of a good man who
is his friend are of this nature. Besides, it is assumed that the
happy man ought to enjoy living. Now a solitary man has
a hard life, because it is not easy to keep up a continuous
activity by oneself; but in company with others and in
relation to others it is easier. Consequently the activity,
which is pleasant in itself, will be more nearly continuous,
as the truly happy man's ought to be (for the good man *qua*
good enjoys actions that are in accordance with virtue, but
is disgusted by those that proceed from wickedness, just as a
musician likes beautiful music but is irritated by what is
bad). Also a sort of training in virtue may result from
associating with good people, as Theognis says.[3]

But if we look at the question more scientifically it
appears that a good friend is by nature desirable for a good
man. For (as we have said before)[4] what is by nature good
is in itself good and pleasant to the good man. Now the life
of animals is defined by the capacity for sensation, and that
of man by the capacity for sensation or thinking. But this
capacity is relative to its activity, and its realization depends upon the activity. Hence it appears that to live is
primarily to perceive or to think. But to live is one of the
things that are in themselves good and pleasant, for it is
determinate,[5] and what is determinate is of the nature of
the good.[6] Now what is good by nature is also good for the
good man, and therefore appears pleasant in the eyes of all.
We must not take the case of a vicious and corrupt life, or of
one that is passed in suffering, because such a life is indeter-

1. *spoudaios*.   2. As being both good and virtually one's own.
3. Theognis 25; the words are quoted below, 1172a13f.
4. 1099a7ff., 1113a25ff.
5. i.e. something of which we have a clear conception and which is
capable of full development or actualization.
6. Cf. 1106b30.

minate, just as are the conditions that attach to it. (The question of pain will be made clearer in the sequel.[1]) But assume the following propositions:[2] (a) Life is in itself good and pleasant (as appears from the fact that it is sought after by all, especially by those who are virtuous and truly happy, because their life is in the highest degree desirable, and their existence the truest felicity). (b) A man who sees is aware that he is seeing, a man who hears that he is hearing, and a man who walks that he is walking; and similarly in all our other activities there is something that is aware of them, so that if we percéive, we perceive that we are perceiving, and if we think, that we are thinking. (c) To be conscious that we are perceiving or thinking is to be conscious of our existence (for we saw[3] that existence is sensation or *thought). (d) To be conscious that one is alive is something pleasant in itself (because life is by nature good, and to be conscious that one possesses a good thing is pleasant). (e) Life is a desirable thing, especially for the good, because for them existence is good and pleasant (since they feel pleasure in the consciousness of what is in itself good). (f) The good man feels towards his friend as he feels towards himself, because his friend is a second self to him. If all this is true, it follows that for a given person the existence of his friend is as desirable, or almost as desirable, as his own. But as we saw,[4] what makes existence desirable is the consciousness of one's own goodness, and such consciousness is pleasant in itself. So a person ought to be conscious[5] of his friend's existence, and this can be achieved by living together and conversing and exchanging ideas with him – for this would seem to be what living together means in the case of human beings; not being pastured like cattle in the same field.

If, then, to the truly happy man his own existence is desirable in itself, as being by nature good and pleasant,

1. Book X. i–v.
2. For clarity a long and involved Greek period has been broken up into separate sentences in the translation.
3. a16f.   4. b4f.
5. By sympathetic insight, not outwardly through the senses.

and if the existence of his friend is scarcely less so, then his friend must also be a thing desirable.[1] But what is desirable for him he must have, or else fall short of happiness in that respect. Therefore to be happy a man will need virtuous friends.

How many friends should one have?

x. Should one, then, make as many friends as possible? Or, as the poet has said – aptly, it is thought – on the subject of hospitality,

> Neither let many share thy board, nor none,[2]

will it be the right thing in friendship too to be neither friendless nor, on the other hand, excessively supplied with friends? The principle quoted above would seem to be absolutely the right one in the case of utilitarian friends, for returning the services of a large number of people is a laborious task which life is too short to accomplish. So more friends than are enough to fulfil our own lives are superfluous and a hindrance to living in the right way: therefore there is no need for them. Also a few friends for amusement are quite enough, like a pinch of seasoning in food. But with regard to friends of good character: ought we to have as many as possible numerically, or is there a limit to the number of friends, as there is to the population of a city?[3] – for one cannot have a city with ten people and with 100,000 it would no longer be a city.[4] Presumably there is no one correct number, but anything between certain limits. So also there is *a limit to the number of one's friends; and probably this would be the largest number with whom one can be on intimate terms – because this, as we saw,[5] is the chief factor in friendship – and it is not hard to see that one cannot be intimate, and share oneself, with a large number

1. Strictly 'choosable' (*hairetos*), i.e. rightly desirable.
2. Hesiod, *Works and Days* 660.   3. Cf. *Politics* 1326a35ff.
4. i.e. a properly integrated community.   5. 1157b19.

of people. Besides, they too must be friends with one another, if they are all to live as a group; and it is difficult to have this state of affairs when the numbers are large. It becomes difficult even to sympathize closely with the joys and sorrows of many, because one is likely to be faced with sharing the joy of one and the sorrow of another simultaneously. Probably, then, it is as well to aim at having not as many friends as possible, but only as many as are enough to form an intimate circle. Indeed it would seem to be impossible to be the devoted friend of many, for the same reason that one cannot be in love with more than one; because by love we mean an extreme affection, and this is felt towards *one* person; therefore strong friendship too is felt only towards a few. This seems to be the case in actual life. We do not find that friendships amounting to comradeship are formed by many people: the celebrated cases are reported as occurring between two.[1] Those who have a great many friends and greet everybody familiarly are felt to be friends of nobody (except in the sense that fellow-citizens are friends): the sort of people that are called obsequious.[2] It is possible, indeed, to be friendly with many in the civic sense and not be obsequious – in fact to be a man of really admirable character; but it is not possible to have many friends whom we love for their own sake and for their goodness; we must be content to find even a few of this quality.

Friends in good and bad fortune

xi. Do we need friends more in prosperity or in adversity? because they are sought for in both. Those who are in misfortune need help, and those who are fortunate need companionship and people on whom to exercise generosity, because they want to be beneficent.[3] Thus friendship is more necessary in adversity, and therefore it is useful friends that

1. e.g. Theseus and Pirithous, Achilles and Patroclus, Orestes and Pylades, etc. (Plutarch, *Moralia* 93c).
2. Cf. 1126b11ff.　　3. To pass on their good fortune.

are wanted in that condition; but it is more honourable in prosperity, and therefore the prosperous look for virtuous friends, since they prefer to share their good fortune and spend their time with people like these. For even the very presence of friends is pleasant in prosperity and adversity alike. Grief is lightened by the sympathy of friends; so that one may raise the question whether they share the burden of it, or whether the explanation is simply that the pleasure of their presence and the consciousness of their sympathy lessens the pain. Well, whether it is this or some other reason that makes the sufferer feel better may be dismissed; but at any rate what happens appears to be what we have described.

But the pleasure that their presence gives seems to be a mixed one. The very sight* of one's friends is pleasant, especially in misfortune, and helps one not to give way to grief, because a friend (if he is tactful) tends to comfort one both by his appearance and by his conversation, knowing as he does one's character and one's likes and dislikes. On the other hand it is painful to observe that he is pained at one's own misfortunes, since everyone tries to avoid causing his friends pain. For this reason a man of a resolute nature takes care not to involve his friends in his own troubles, and unless he is exceptionally insensitive cannot stand the thought of causing them pain; and in general does not give them a chance to lament with him, because he himself does not indulge in lamentation either. But womenfolk[1] and men who are like them, enjoy having others to share their moanings, and love them as friends and sympathizers. However, it is clearly right in all circumstances to follow the better example.

In prosperity, on the other hand, the presence of one's friends enables one to pass the time agreeably, and also to enjoy the reflection that they take pleasure in one's good fortune. Hence it may be supposed that we should invite our friends wholeheartedly to share our successes (because generosity is a fine impulse), but hesitate to ask them to

1. The Greek word (a diminutive) has a patronizing tone.

309

visit us in our misfortunes (because one should share one's troubles as little as possible: hence the saying 'Enough that *I* should suffer'[1]). The best time to call friends to one's aid is when they seem likely to do one a great service with little trouble to themselves. Conversely it is probably the proper course to visit friends in misfortune readily, and without waiting to be invited, for it is the part of a friend to do a kindness, particularly to those who are in need, and have not asked for it; because such a kindness is more creditable and more pleasurable to both parties. But as for visiting those who are in good fortune, while one should go eagerly to help in *their* affairs (for friends are needed for this purpose too), if the object is one's *own* well-being the approach should be leisurely (because it does not look well to be eager to receive a benefit). At the same time we should presumably guard against giving an impression of churlishness by repelling their advances; because that does sometimes happen.

The value of friendly intercourse

xii.   Are we to say, then, that just as lovers find the keenest satisfaction in seeing, and prefer this sense to all the others, because they feel that it is the source and stay of love, so to friends there is nothing more desirable than spending their lives together? For friendship is a kind of partnership, and a man stands in the same relation to his friend as to himself, and since the consciousness of his own existence is desirable, the consciousness of his friend's must be the same; and this consciousness becomes actualized in their life together, *so that they naturally desire it. Also everyone wishes to share with his friends the occupation (whatever it is) that constitutes his existence, or makes life worth living. This is why some drink together, others dice together, others go in for athletics and hunting together, or for philosophy, each type spending their time together in the pursuit that gives

1. The source is unknown.

them most satisfaction in their lives; indeed in their desire to spend their lives with their friends they follow these pursuits and share in them as much as possible. Consequently the friendship of worthless people has a bad effect (because they take part, unstable as they are, in worthless pursuits, and actually become bad through each other's influence). But the friendship of the good is good, and increases in goodness because of their association. They seem even to become better men by exercising their friendship and improving each other; for the traits that they admire in each other get transferred to themselves. Hence the saying

> From good men goodness . . .[1]

So much for our account of friendship. Our next subject for discussion will be Pleasure.

1. Theognis 35, alluded to above, 1170a12.

X

PLEASURE AND THE LIFE OF HAPPINESS

The importance of pleasure in ethics, and the conflict of views about its value

i. After this our next task is presumably to discuss pleasure;[1] for it is generally agreed that pleasure is very closely bound up with human nature; which is why those who are educating the young keep them straight by the use of pleasure and pain. It is also thought to be most important for the forming of a virtuous character to like and dislike the right things; because pleasure and pain permeate the whole of life, and have a powerful influence upon virtue and the happy life, since people choose what is pleasant and avoid what is painful. It would seem most improper, then, to neglect such important factors, especially since they admit of a great deal of controversy.

One school[2] maintains that pleasure is the Good; another,[3] on the contrary, that it is wholly bad: some of its members very likely from a conviction that it is really so, and others believing that it is better with a view to the conduct of our lives to represent pleasure as a bad thing, even if it is not; because (they say) most people are inclined towards it and are the slaves of their self-indulgence, so that they need to be urged in the opposite direction; for in this way they may attain to the mean. But probably this view is not correct. For in matters relating to feelings and actions theories are less reliable than facts; so when they clash with the evidence of our senses they provoke contempt and *damage the cause of truth as well as their own. For if a person who

1. Chs. i–v of this book appear to supersede the earlier treatment of pleasure in VII. xi–xv.
2. That of Eudoxus; see 1101b27.
3. Probably that of Speusippus; see note on 1153b5.

denounces pleasure is ever observed to be drawn towards it himself; his backsliding is assumed to imply that he regards all pleasure as desirable; because most people are incapable of drawing distinctions. So it seems that true theories are extremely valuable for the conduct of our lives as well as for the acquisition of knowledge, since because of their agreement with the facts they carry conviction, and so encourage those who understand them to live under their direction.

But enough of these observations; let us examine the views that have been propounded about pleasure.

*Eudoxus' view, that pleasure is the supreme good,
is not above dispute*

ii.   Eudoxus[1] thought that pleasure is the Good, because he observed that all creatures, both rational and irrational, are attracted by it; and that in every case what is desirable[2] is good, and what is most desirable is best; so the fact that all creatures are drawn in the same direction shows that this is what is best for all (since each individual tries to find its own good, just as it does its own food); and that which is good for all, and which all try to obtain, is the Good. His arguments were accepted more for the excellence of his character than on their own account, because he was regarded as exceptionally self-controlled; so it was concluded that he did not state this view because he was a pleasure-lover, but that the facts really were so.

He thought that it[3] was no less evident from consideration of its contrary, because pain, he thought, is in itself something to be shunned by all, and therefore similarly its contrary is to be chosen. He held also that the most desirable thing is that which we choose neither as a means to, nor for the sake of, something else; and that pleasure is, by common consent, a thing of this kind; for no one ever asks a man *why* he is enjoying himself, because it is assumed that

1. Cf. 1101b27.   2. 'Choosable'; cf. below.
3. The goodness of pleasure.

pleasure is desirable in itself. He also said that the addition
of pleasure to any good thing – e.g. just or temperate conduct – makes it more desirable; but what is good is only
increased by itself.[1] Now this particular argument seems
only to show that pleasure is *a* good, no more good than
any other; because any good thing is more desirable when
accompanied by another than it is by itself. In fact Plato[2]
uses this sort of argument to refute the view that pleasure is
the Good; for he says that the life of pleasure is more desirable with the addition of intelligence than without it; and if
the combination is better, pleasure is not the Good; because no addition of anything else to the Good makes it
more desirable. And clearly nothing else can be the Good
either, if it becomes more desirable when accompanied by
something that is good in itself. What, then, is there that
cannot be made better by the addition of some good, and
yet is something in which we share?[3] because it is something
of this sort that is the object of our inquiry.

The view that pleasure is not a good is also open to criticism

On the other hand those[4] who contend that what all
creatures try to obtain is not a good are surely talking
nonsense; for *we hold that what everyone believes is so;
and the man who tries to destroy this belief is not likely to
have a more convincing account of his own. If it were only
irrational creatures that are attracted by pleasure, there
might be something in the theory; but if intelligent beings
are attracted too, how can it be taken seriously? Presumably
there is even in the lower animals some instinct superior to
their own natures which tries to attain their proper good.

1. i.e. is only made more good by the addition of what is good.
2. *Philebus* 60D.
3. The qualification is intended to exclude the Platonic Idea of
Good; see I. vi., especially 1096b32ff.
4. Especially Speusippus and his followers (cf. 1152b12ff.); but some
of the arguments are Plato's; see below, and cf. Appendix H.

It does not seem that their argument about the contrary[1] is valid either. They say that if pain is an evil, it does not follow that pleasure is a good, because an evil can be opposed to an evil, and both opposed to something that is neither good nor evil. There is nothing wrong with the argument, but it does not truly apply to the case under discussion. For if both pleasure and pain are evils, both should be objects of aversion; and if they are neutral, neither should be, or both should be equally, objects of aversion; but as it is we can see that people avoid the one as an evil and choose the other as a good. Therefore it is as good and evil that they are opposed.

Again, even if pleasure is not a quality, it does not follow that it is not a good; because good activities are not qualities either, nor is happiness.

They[2] say that the Good is determinate, whereas pleasure is indeterminate, because it admits of differences of degree. Now if they base this judgement on the fact that people are pleased in different degrees, the same argument will apply to justice and all the other virtues in respect of which people are said explicitly to possess qualities, and act in accordance with the virtues, in a greater or lesser degree; because one person is more just, or more brave, than another, and acts more justly or temperately than another. But if they are judging by the *pleasures*, it looks as if they are not stating the right ground for their conclusion, if pleasures are of two kinds, pure and mixed.[3]

But why should not pleasure be determinate, just as health is, although it admits of degrees? For health does not consist of the same proportion[4] in everyone; it is not even always one and the same in the same person, but when it is in process of breaking up it still persists up to a point, i.e. it

1. Of pleasure, viz. pain; 1172b18f, and cf. Appendix H.

2. The views which follow recall Plato's in *Philebus* 24E, 31Bff., etc.

3. Plato's distinction. It is suggested here that the apparent differences in degree are found only in mixed pleasures and are due to the admixture of pain.

4. Of hot and cold (*Philebus* 25E).

exhibits differences of degree. So this explanation may fit the case of pleasure too.

They assume that the Good is something perfect, whereas movements and processes are incomplete; and they try to show that pleasure is a movement or process. But their argument does not seem to be correct, and pleasure does not seem to be a movement. For it is accepted that every movement has its own quickness and slowness, relative if not to itself – as the movement of the universe[1] is not – then relatively to something else. But neither alternative applies to pleasure. One can *become* pleased quickly, just as one can *get angry, but not *be* pleased, not even in comparison with someone else, as one can walk or grow, etc. Thus it is possible to pass into a state of pleasure quickly or slowly, but not to actualize that state (i.e. be pleased) quickly. Again, how can pleasure be a process of becoming? It is accepted that development is not from *any* one thing into *any* other thing, but that everything is resolved into that from which it came;[2] and where pleasure is the generation of something, pain is the destruction of that something. They[3] also say that pain is a deficiency of our natural condition, and that pleasure is its replenishment. But these are *bodily* experiences. So if pleasure is a replenishment of the natural state, what will feel pleasure is that in which the replenishment takes place; so it will be the body that does so. But this is not generally accepted. So pleasure is not a process of replenishment, although the person in whom the process is going on may feel pleasure, as he would feel pain if he were being cut. This theory[4] seems to have been derived from the pains and pleasures connected with eating: it is assumed that it is because we have experienced a lack, and felt pain, that we subsequently find pleasure in replenish-

1. More accurately, the 'heaven' that carries the fixed stars, which rotates at a constant speed (*De Caelo* I.v, II.iv, vi, viii), fast or slow only in comparison with other movements.

2. See Appendix E.

3. *Philebus* 31E–32D and 42C–D; but no doubt it is still Speusippus that A. is attacking.

4. That pleasure is the replenishment of a deficiency; see Appendix H.

ment. But this does not happen in the case of all pleasures. The pleasures of learning, for instance, have no antecedent pains; neither have some even of the sensuous pleasures, such as those of smell, and many sounds and sights too, and memories and hopes. Of what, then, will these be generative processes? because no deficiency of anything has arisen that can be replenished.

Even the view that some pleasures are bad can be challenged

Against those who cite instances of disreputable pleasures[1] one may argue that these pleasures are not pleasant. They may be pleasant to persons of an unhealthy disposition, but that does not compel us to believe that they are really pleasant (except to these persons), any more than that things are really wholesome or sweet or bitter that seem so to sick people, or that things are white that appear so to people with diseased eyes. Or one might argue that the pleasures are desirable in themselves, but not when they are achieved in a certain way; as, e.g., wealth is desirable, but not as the price of treason, and health is desirable, but not if it involves indiscriminate eating.[2] Or that pleasures differ in kind; for those that come from noble acts are different from those that come from base ones, and it is impossible to enjoy the pleasure of a just man unless one is just, or that of a musical man unless one is musical, and so on. The difference between a flatterer and a friend seems to show that pleasure is not a good, or else that pleasures are different in kind; for the one is considered to associate with others for their good, and the other for their pleasure; and the fact that the latter is blamed whereas the former *is praised implies that the objects of their companionship are different. Nobody would choose to live out his life with the mentality of a child, even if he continued to take the greatest pleasure

1. e.g. Plato, who denounced physical pleasures.
2. A curious qualification. Probably he is thinking of cannibalism in acute food shortage.

in the things that children like; nor would anyone choose to find enjoyment in doing something very disgraceful, even if there were no prospect of painful consequences. Besides, there are many things that we should be eager to have even if they brought no pleasure with them – e.g. sight, memory, knowledge, and the several kinds of excellence.[1] It makes no difference if these are necessarily accompanied by pleasure, because we should choose to have them even if we got no pleasure from them.

It seems clear, then, that pleasure is not the Good, and that not every pleasure is desirable; also that there are some pleasures that are desirable in themselves, being superior either in kind or in respect of the sources from which they come. This may be taken as a sufficient account of the views propounded about pleasure and pain.

Pleasure is not a process

iv.   What pleasure is, or what its differentia is, may become more readily apparent if we make a fresh start to our inquiry.

The act of seeing is regarded as complete at any moment of its duration, because it does not lack anything that, realized later, will perfect its specific quality.[2] Now pleasure also seems to be of this nature, because it is a sort of whole, i.e. at no moment in time can one fasten upon a pleasure the prolongation of which will enable its specific quality to be perfected. For this reason pleasure is not a process; because every process is in time, and has an end (e.g. the process of building), and is complete when it has accomplished its object. Thus it is complete either in the whole of the time that it takes or at the instant of reaching its end. The particular processes that take place in the parts of this time are all incomplete, and different in kind from the

1. Not merely the moral and intellectual virtues; any *aretē* is desirable.
2. Wherein it differs from a process (*kinēsis*), by which the potential becomes actual, the imperfect perfect. See Appendix E.

whole and from one another. For example, the fitting together of the stone blocks is different from the fluting of a column, and both are different from the construction of the temple ⟨as a whole⟩. This last is a complete process (because nothing further is needed to finish the project); but the building of the base, and the carving of the triglyphs,[1] are incomplete, because each is concerned with a part. Therefore they are different in kind,[2] and it is impossible to fasten upon a specifically complete process at any moment: this is found, if at all, in the whole period of time. Similarly also in the case of walking and so on; for if locomotion is a process of moving from one point to another, there are different species of this too – flying, walking, jumping, etc.; and not only so, but also in walking itself (for the starting and finishing points are not the same in the whole running-track as they are in a part of it, or the same in one part as in another; nor is traversing *this* line[3] the same as traversing *that* one; *because the runner does not merely cross *a* line but a line in a certain place; and *this* line is in a different place from *that* one). We have discussed motion in detail elsewhere.[4] It appears, however, that a movement is not complete at any given time; the several movements[5] are incomplete, and differ in kind, since the terminal points constitute specific differences. The form[6] of pleasure, on the other hand, is complete at any given moment.

It is obvious, then, that pleasure and motion are two different things, and that pleasure is something that is whole

---

1. A triglyph is part of the frieze.

2. From the process of building the whole temple.

3. At Epidaurus, Athens, and presumably elsewhere, the stadium was divided into six sections of 100 feet, marked by small pillars on either side of the track. The lines mentioned here are the dividing lines of these sections – in particular the first after the start and the line at the finish.

4. In *Physics* VI–VIII.

5. The general argument is clear enough: that of a movement from one point to another (as of any process, a19–21 above) one can only say that it is complete *either* in respect of the whole time that it takes *or* in the instant of arrival – when its actuality ceases.

6. i.e. specific quality; cf. a14–18 above.

and complete. This might be concluded also from the fact that a movement must occupy time, whereas a feeling of pleasure does not; for that which is instantaneous[1] is a whole.

These considerations also make it clear that it is wrong to speak of pleasure as a movement or process; for this description does not apply to everything; only to things that are not wholes but consist of parts. Seeing,[2] a point, a unit – none of these is the result of a process (nor is any of them a movement or a process); therefore neither is pleasure, because it is a whole.

The relation of pleasure to activity

Each of the senses is active relatively to its object, and its activity is perfect when it is in a good condition and is directed towards the highest object that falls within its range of sensation. (Something like this seems to be the best description of perfect activity; we may assume that it makes no difference whether we speak of the sense itself, or of the organ in which it resides, as being active.) Therefore the activity of any sense is at its best when the organ is in the best condition and directed towards the best of the objects proper to that sense. This activity will be most perfect and most pleasurable; for there is a pleasure corresponding to each of the senses, just as there is to thought and contemplation; and it is most pleasurable when it is most perfect, and most perfect when the organ is in a healthy condition and directed towards the worthiest of its objects; and the pleasure perfects the activity. It does not, however, perfect it in the same way as the object of the

1. 'In the now', i.e. at the *point* of time that separates past and future. What *is not* at one moment and *is* at the next must be a whole without distinguishable parts; it is only a whole of parts that comes into being by a process, 'bit by bit'.

2. The act of seeing is not, of course, instantaneous; nothing *happens* in a point of time; cf. a14ff.

sense and the sense-faculty perfect it when they are good; just as it is not in the same way that health and the doctor are both causes[1] of one's being healthy.

That each of the senses has its corresponding pleasure is obvious, because we say that sights and sounds are pleasant. It is also obvious that the pleasure is keenest when the sensory faculty is at its best, and exercised upon the best object; when both object and organ are at their best, there will always be pleasure so long as there is something to produce it and someone to feel it. The pleasure perfects the activity not as the formed state that issues in that activity[2] perfects it, by being immanent in it, but as a sort of supervening perfection, like the bloom that graces the flower of youth. So long, then, as the object of thought or sensation, and that which judges or contemplates, are in the *right condition, the activity will have its pleasure; for when both subject and object are unchanged and in the same relation to one another, the same result naturally follows.

How is it, then, that nobody feels pleasure continuously? The cause is probably fatigue. No human faculty can be continuously active, so pleasure is not continuous, because it depends upon the activity. Some things please us while they are novelties, but not so much afterwards, for the same reason. At first the mind is stimulated and exercises itself vigorously upon the object, just as people focus their attention in the case of sight; but later the activity declines in vigour and interest is lost; and consequently the pleasure also grows faint.

1. Health being the final and the doctor the efficient cause; cf. 1145a8 (so Gauthier).

2. The *hexis* or fully developed faculty (as distinct from the *dunamis* or mere capability) of vision is an immanent factor in the actualization of it, whereas the pleasure is a sort of extrinsic bonus. See Appendix E.

Pleasure is essential to life

One may suppose that everyone feels drawn towards plea-sure, because everyone is eager to live. Life is a form of activity, and each individual directs his activity to those objects, and by means of those faculties, that he likes best: e.g. the musician occupies himself with the sounds of music by the use of his hearing, and the student with the objects of study by the use of his intellect, and similarly with all the other examples. The pleasure perfects the activities, and so perfects life, to which all are drawn. It is quite reasonable, then, that they should also be eager for pleasure; because it perfects life for each individual, and life is a thing to choose. Whether we choose life on account of pleasure or pleasure on account of life is a question that may be dismissed at the moment; for it appears that they are closely connected and do not admit of separation: as pleasure does not occur with-out activity, so every activity is perfected by its pleasure.

As activities differ in kind, so do their pleasures

v. This affords ground for the view that pleasures also differ in kind. For we assume that things that are different in kind are perfected by things that are different in kind. This is clearly the case with both natural products like animals and trees, and artificial ones like a picture, a statue, a house or a piece of furniture; and we assume that similarly what perfects one kind of activity must differ in kind from what perfects another. But the activities of the intellect differ in kind from those of the senses, and both differ among themselves; therefore so do the pleasures that perfect them.

This can also be seen from the close connection of each pleasure with the activity that it perfects. For the pleasure proper to an activity intensifies it; because those who work with pleasure show better judgement and greater precision in dealing with each class of object: e.g. those who enjoy geometry become good at it and understand its various aspects better, and similarly those who like music or building, and all the other occupations, improve in their proper function if they enjoy it. Thus pleasures intensify their activities; and what intensifies a thing is proper to it; and *things that are proper to things that are different in kind are themselves different in kind.

This may be seen still more clearly from the fact that activities are hindered by pleasures derived from other activities. Thus flute-lovers[1] are incapable of attending to a discussion if they catch the sound of somebody playing the flute, because they enjoy the sound of flute-playing more than their immediate activity; so their pleasure in the flute-playing destroys their active participation in the discussion. A similar result follows in all other cases when a person is engaged in two activities at the same time. The more pleasurable activity interferes with the other, and if it is much more pleasurable, does so increasingly, so that the other activity ceases altogether. Hence if we are greatly enjoying anything we do not effectively do something else; and when we are only mildly interested in one occupation we turn to another: e.g. people who chew sweets in the theatre do it most when the acting is poor. And since our activities are concentrated and prolonged and improved by their proper pleasures, and impaired by the pleasures of other activities, it is clear that the two kinds of pleasure differ widely. Indeed alien pleasures have practically the same effect as proper pains, because the proper pains are destructive of the activity; e.g. if a person finds writing or calculating disagreeable and irksome; one man gives up writing and the other calculating, because the activity is painful to him. So activities are affected in opposite ways by their proper pleasures and pains, 'proper' meaning those that become attached to the activity in virtue of itself.

1. Cf. note on 1097b25 above.

Alien pleasures, as we have said, have an effect very close to that of pain, because they are destructive, only not to the same degree.

Since activities differ in goodness and badness, and some are to be chosen, some to be avoided, and some neutral, their pleasures can be classed similarly, because each activity has a pleasure proper to it. Thus the pleasure proper to a serious activity is virtuous, and that which is proper to a bad one is vicious; for desires too are laudable if their objects are noble, but censurable if they are base. The pleasures involved in activities are more proper to them than the impulses that arouse them, because the latter are differentiated from the activities both by their nature and by the time at which they occur,[1] whereas the pleasures are closely connected with them, and so little distinguishable that it is disputable whether the activity and its pleasure are the same or not. Not that there is any real ground for supposing that the pleasure *is* thinking or sensating (for that would be absurd); but because they are inseparable they appear to some to be identical.

The pleasures, then, are as diverse as their activities. Sight is superior *to touch, and hearing and smell to taste, in purity,[2] so their pleasures differ similarly. Also intellectual pleasures are superior to sensuous ones, and both kinds differ among themselves.

It is thought that every animal has a proper pleasure, just as it has a proper function: viz., the pleasure of exercising that function. This will be clear if one considers individual species; because a horse, a dog and a man each have a different pleasure, as Heraclitus says[3] that a donkey would prefer sweepings to gold, because they are nicer for a donkey to eat. Different species of animals, then, have different kinds of pleasures, but it would be reasonable for the pleasures to be uniform within the same species. However,

1. The *orexis* is the efficient cause of the activity and prior to it in time.
2. Touch and taste (which is a kind of touch) require contact, but the rest do not.
3. Fr. B5 (Diels–Krantz). The 'sweepings' would be chaff.

in the case of human beings at any rate, they show no little
divergence. The same things delight one set of people and
annoy another; what is painful and detestable to some is
pleasurable and likeable to others. This happens in the
case of sweet things too: they do not taste the same to a
feverish patient as they do to a normal person; nor does the
same thing seem hot to an invalid and to a man in perfect
health. The same sort of thing happens in other cases too.

Only the good man's pleasures are real and truly human

But in all such circumstances it is generally accepted that
the good man's view is the true one.[1] If this formula is
correct, as it seems to be; that is, if the standard by which
we measure everything is goodness, or the good man *qua*
good: then the true pleasures too will be those that seem to
him to be pleasures, and those things will be really pleasant
that he enjoys. And if things that displease him seem
pleasant to somebody else, it is not at all surprising; for
humanity is subject to many kinds of corruption and perversion, and the things in question are pleasant only to
these persons in their particular condition. Clearly, then,
we must deny that the admittedly disreputable pleasures
are pleasures at all, except to the depraved; but of those that
are regarded as reputable which, or what sort, should we
pronounce to be the pleasure of man? Probably this will
emerge from a study of human activities, because these are
attended by their proper pleasures. So whether the perfect
and supremely happy man has one activity or more than
one, it is the pleasures that perfect these that can properly
be described as *human*; the remainder, like their activities,
can be so called only in a secondary or far lower degree.

1. Cf. 1099a7ff., 1113a25ff., 1166a12, 1170a14ff.

Recapitulation: the nature of happiness

vi. Now that we have finished our discussion of the virtues, of friendship, and of pleasures, it remains for us to give an outline account of happiness, since we hold it to be the end of human conduct. It may make our treatment of the subject more concise if we recapitulate what has been said already.

We said,[1] then, that happiness is not a *state*, since if it were it might belong even to a man who slept all through his life, passing a vegetable existence; or to a victim of the greatest misfortunes. So if this *is unacceptable, and we ought rather to refer happiness to some activity, as we said earlier;[2] and if activities are either necessary and to be chosen for the sake of something else, or to be chosen for themselves: clearly we must class happiness as one of those to be chosen for themselves, and not as one of the other kind, because it does not need anything else: it is self-sufficient.[3] The activities that are to be chosen for themselves are those from which nothing is required beyond the exercise of the activity; and such a description is thought to fit actions that accord with goodness; because the doing of fine and good actions is one of the things that are to be chosen for themselves.

Happiness must be distinguished from amusement

Pleasant amusements are also thought to belong to this class, because they are not chosen as means to something else: in fact their effects are more harmful than beneficial, since they make people neglect their bodies and their property. However, most of those who are regarded as happy have recourse to such occupations, and that is why those who show some dexterity in them are highly esteemed at the courts of tyrants; they make themselves agreeable by

1. 1098b31ff., and cf. 1095b31ff.   2. 1098a5.
3. Cf. 1097a25–b21.

providing the sort of entertainment that their patrons want,
and such persons are in demand. So these amusements
are thought to be conducive to happiness, because men in
positions of power devote their leisure to them. But what
people of this kind do is probably no evidence, because
virtue and intelligence, which are the sources of serious
activities, do not depend upon positions of power; and if
these persons, never having tasted pure and refined pleasure, have recourse to physical pleasures, that is no reason
why the latter should be regarded as worthier of choice.
Children, too, believe that the things they prize are the
most important; so it is natural that just as different things
seem valuable to children and adults, so they should seem
different also to good and bad men. Thus, as we have often
said,[1] it is the things that seem valuable and pleasant to the
good man that are really such. But to each individual it is
the activity in accordance with his own disposition that is
most desirable, and therefore to the good man virtuous
activity is most desirable. It follows that happiness does not
consist in amusement. Indeed it would be paradoxical if the
end were amusement; if we toiled and suffered all our lives
long to amuse ourselves. For we choose practically everything for the sake of something else, except happiness,
because it is the end. To spend effort and toil for the sake of
amusement seems silly and unduly childish; but on the
other hand the maxim of Anacharsis,[2] 'Play to work
harder', seems to be on the right lines, because amusement
is a form of relaxation, and people need relaxation because
they cannot exert themselves continuously. Therefore
relaxation *is not an end, because it is taken for the sake of
the activity. But the happy life seems to be lived in accordance with goodness, and such a life implies seriousness and
does not consist in amusing oneself. Also we maintain that
serious things are better than those that are merely comical
and amusing, and that the activity of a man, or part of a

1. e.g. 1099a13, 1113a25ff., 1166a12, 1170a14, 1176a15ff.
2. A Scythian sage who visited Greece in the early sixth century, and
to whom a number of maxims were attributed.

man, is always more serious in proportion as it is better. Therefore the activity of the better part is superior, and *eo ipso* more conducive to happiness.

Anybody can enjoy bodily pleasures – a slave no less than the best of men – but nobody attributes a part in happiness to a slave, unless he also attributes to him a life of his own.[1] Therefore happiness does not consist in occupations of this kind, but in activities in accordance with virtue, as we have said before.[2]

Happiness and contemplation

vii.   If happiness is an activity in accordance with virtue, it is reasonable to assume that it is in accordance with the highest virtue, and this will be the virtue of the best part of us. Whether this is the intellect or something else that we regard as naturally ruling and guiding us, and possessing insight into things noble and divine – either as being actually divine itself or as being more divine than any other part of us – it is the activity of this part, in accordance with the virtue proper to it, that will be perfect happiness.

We have already said[3] that it is a contemplative activity. This may be regarded as consonant both with our earlier arguments and with the truth. For contemplation is both the highest form of activity (since the intellect is the highest thing in us, and the objects that it apprehends are the highest things that can be known), and also it is the most continuous, because we are more capable of continuous contemplation than we are of any practical activity. Also we assume that happiness must contain an admixture of pleasure; now activity in accordance with ⟨philosophic⟩ wisdom is admittedly the most pleasant of the virtuous activities; at

1. Which he does not; cf. *Politics* 1280a32.
2. 1098a16, 1176a35ff.
3. Not explicitly, but it has been implied; cf. 1095b14–1096a5, 1141a18ff., 1143b33ff., 1145a6ff.

any rate philosophy is held to entail pleasures that are marvellous in purity and permanence; and it stands to reason that those who possess knowledge pass their time more pleasantly than those who are still in pursuit of it. Again, the quality that we call self-sufficiency will belong in the highest degree to the contemplative activity. The wise man, no less than the just one and all the rest, requires the necessaries of life; but, given an adequate supply of these, the just man also needs people with and towards whom he can perform just actions, and similarly with the temperate man, the brave man, and each of the others; but the wise man can practise contemplation by himself, and the wiser he is, the more he can do it. No doubt he does it better with the help of fellow-workers; but for all that he is the *most self-sufficient of men. Again, contemplation would seem to be the only activity that is appreciated for its own sake; because nothing is gained from it except the act of contemplation, whereas from practical activities we expect to gain something more or less over and above the action.

Since happiness is thought to imply leisure, it must be an intellectual, not a practical activity

Also it is commonly believed that happiness depends on leisure; because we occupy ourselves so that we may have leisure, just as we make war in order that we may live at peace. Now the exercise of the practical virtues takes place in politics or in warfare, and these professions seem to have no place for leisure. This is certainly true of the military profession, for nobody chooses to make war or provokes it for the sake of making war; a man would be regarded as a bloodthirsty monster if he made his friends[1] into enemies in order to bring about battles and slaughter. The politician's profession also makes leisure impossible, since besides the business of politics it aims at securing positions of power

1. i.e. friendly states (cf. 1157a26).

and honour, or the happiness of the politician himself and of his fellow-citizens – a happiness separate from politics, and one which we clearly pursue as separate.

If, then, politics and warfare, although pre-eminent in nobility and grandeur among practical activities in accordance with goodness, are incompatible with leisure and, not being desirable in themselves, are directed towards some other end, whereas the activity of the intellect is considered to excel[1] in seriousness, taking as it does the form of contemplation, and to aim at no other end beyond itself, and to possess a pleasure peculiar to itself, which intensifies its activity; and if it is evident that self-sufficiency and leisuredness and such freedom from fatigue as is humanly possible, together with all the other attributes assigned to the supremely happy man, are those that accord with this activity; then this activity will be the perfect happiness for man – provided that it is allowed a full span of life; for nothing that pertains to happiness is incomplete.

Life on this plane is not too high for the divine element in human nature

But such a life will be too high for human attainment; for any man who lives it will do so not as a human being but in virtue of something divine within him, and in proportion as this divine element is superior to the composite being,[2] so will its activity be superior to that of the other kind of virtue.[3] So if the intellect is divine compared with man, the life of the intellect must be divine compared with the life of a human being. And we ought not to listen to those who warn us that 'man should think the thoughts of man', or 'mortal thoughts fit mortal minds';[4] but we ought, so far

1. To excel other leisured occupations.

2. Probably composite soul, although the word (*suntheton*) is generally used of the composite whole consisting of soul and body.

3. Moral virtue.

4. Cf. *Rhetoric* 1394b24, Pindar, *Isthmians* v.20; similar maxims are common in the dramatists.

as in us lies, to put on immortality, and do all that we can to
live in conformity with the highest that is in us; for even if it
*is small in bulk, in power and preciousness it far excels all
the rest. Indeed it would seem that this is the true self of the
individual,[1] since it is the authoritative and better part of
him; so it would be an odd thing if a man chose to live
someone else's life instead of his own. Moreover, what we
said above will apply here too: that what is best and most
pleasant for any given creature is that which is proper to it.[2]
Therefore for man, too, the best and most pleasant life is
the life of the intellect, since the intellect is in the fullest
sense the man. So this life will also be the happiest.

Moral activity is secondary happiness

viii.   Life in conformity with the other kind of virtue will be
happy in a secondary degree, because activities in accordance with it are human.[3] It is in our dealings with one
another that we act justly and bravely and display the other
virtues, observing what is due to each person in all contracts
and mutual services and actions of every kind, and in our
feelings too; and all these are obviously *human* experiences.
Some of them are even thought to have a physical origin,
and moral goodness is considered to be intimately connected
in various ways with the feelings. Prudence, too, is closely
linked with moral goodness, and moral goodness with
prudence, since the first principles of prudence are given by
the moral virtues, and the right standard for the virtues is set
by prudence.[4] These moral virtues, being bound up with the
feelings too, will also belong to the composite person.[5] But the
virtues of the composite person are human. Therefore the life

1. Cf. 1166a17ff., 1168b35.
2. The reference is perhaps to 1169b33.
3. Whereas intellectual activity is divine; cf. 1177b26–31 above, and
b8–22 below.
4. Cf. 1144a11–1145a6.
5. The concrete man, embodied soul; but cf. 1177b28 above.

331

that conforms with these virtues, and the happiness that belongs to it, are also human. But the happiness of the intellect is separate. Let us leave it at that, because a detailed treatment would exceed the scope of our present inquiry.[1] It would also seem to stand in little need of external accessories, or in less need than moral goodness does. We may assume that both require the necessities of life, and in equal measure (although the politician spends more[2] effort on the provision of bodily needs and the like), because in this respect there may be little difference between them; but there will be a vast difference in what they require for their activities. The liberal man will need money to perform liberal acts, as indeed will the just man to meet his obligations (for intentions do not show, and even the unjust pretend that they wish to act justly); the brave man will need potency[3] if he is to achieve anything valorous, and the temperate man will need opportunity;[4] for how else can he, or any other virtuous person, display his quality?

It is disputed whether the intention or the actions have the greater importance in determining the goodness of conduct, assuming that it depends *on both. Well, its perfection would clearly involve both, and for the performance of virtuous actions many accessories are required, and the grander and nobler the actions the more numerous will these accessories be. On the other hand the contemplative has no need of such things for his activity; on the contrary they are almost a hindrance to his contemplation. However, in so far as he is a human being and a member of society he chooses to act in accordance with virtue; therefore he will need external goods to enable him to live as a human being.

1. The nature of mind or reason is discussed in *De Anima* III.iii–v.
2. More effort than the thinker.
3. He must not be helpless either in himself or through circumstances.
4. For (resisting) self-indulgence.

The view that happiness is contemplation is confirmed by other arguments

That perfect happiness is a kind of contemplative activity may be shown also from the following argument. The gods in our conception of them are supremely happy and blessed, but what kind of actions should we attribute to them? If we say 'Just actions', surely we shall be confronted by the absurdity of their making contracts and returning deposits and all that sort of thing. Well, shall we say 'Brave actions' – facing terrors and risking their persons in the cause of honour? What of liberal actions? They will have nobody to give to; and it is absurd that they should actually have coined money or its equivalent. What form could their temperate actions take? Surely it would be cheap praise,[1] since they have no evil desires! If we went through the whole list we should find that the practical details of these actions are petty and unworthy of gods. On the other hand men have always conceived of them as at least living beings, and therefore active; for we cannot suppose that they spend their time in sleeping, like Endymion.[2] But if a living being is deprived of action, and still further of production, what is left but contemplation? It follows, then, that the activity of God, which is supremely happy, must be a form of contemplation; and therefore among human activities that which is most akin to God's will be the happiest.

This view is further supported by the fact that the lower animals have no share in happiness, being completely incapable of such an activity. The life of the gods is altogether happy, and that of man is happy in so far as it contains something that resembles the divine activity; but none of the lower animals is happy, because they have no way of participating in contemplation. Happiness, then,

1. To impute self-control to them.
2. He was loved by the moon-goddess (in some versions of the story by Artemis or Diana) and granted immortality, but at the price of unconsciousness.

is co-extensive with contemplation, and the more people contemplate, the happier they are; not incidentally, but in virtue of their contemplation, because it is in itself precious. Thus happiness is a form of contemplation.

But its possessor, being only human, will also need external felicity, because human nature is not self-sufficient for the purpose of contemplation; the body too must be healthy, and food and other amenities must be available. *On the other hand it must not be supposed that, because one cannot be happy without external goods, it will be necessary to have many of them on a grand scale in order to be happy at all. For self-sufficiency does not depend upon a superfluity of means, nor does ⟨moral⟩ conduct; and it is possible to perform fine acts even if one is not master of land and sea. Indeed, a man can conduct himself virtuously even from a modest competence (this can be quite plainly seen, for private persons are considered to perform decent actions not less but actually more than those who are in positions of power). It is enough, then, to possess this much; for a man's life will be happy if he acts in accordance with virtue. Solon, too, was presumably right in his description of happy people when he said[1] that they were those who were moderately equipped with external goods, and had achieved what were, as he thought, the finest deeds, and had lived temperate lives; for it is possible for those who have only moderate possessions to do what is right. Anaxagoras, too, seems not to have pictured the happy man as wealthy or powerful when he said[2] that it would not surprise him if such a person were an oddity in most people's eyes, because they judge by outward appearances, which are all that they can perceive. Thus it appears that our arguments are in harmony with the opinions of the wise. Such considerations do indeed carry some conviction; but in the matter of conduct truth is assessed in the light of the facts and of actual life; because it is in these that the decisive factor lies. So we must bring what we have already said to the test of the facts of

1. Cf. Herodotus i.30–32, and see above, 1100a10ff.
2. Cf. *Eudemian Ethics* 1215b6ff.

life; and if it accords with the facts, we can accept it, but if it conflicts with them we must regard it as no more than a theory.

The man who exercises his intellect and cultivates it seems likely to be in the best state of mind and to be most loved by the gods. For if, as is generally supposed, the gods have some concern for human affairs, it would be reasonable to believe also that they take pleasure in that part of us which is best and most closely related to themselves (this being the intellect), and that they reward those who appreciate and honour it most highly; for they care for what is dear to them, and what they do is right and good. Now it is not hard to see that it is the wise man that possesses these qualities in the highest degree; therefore he is dearest to the gods. And it is natural that he should also be the happiest of men. So on this score too the wise man will be happy in the highest degree.

So much for ethical theory. How can it be put into practice?

ix.   Assuming, then, that we have given (in outline) a sufficient account of happiness and the several virtues, and also of friendship and pleasure, may we regard our undertaking as now completed? Or is the correct view that (as we have been saying[1]) in the case of conduct *the end consists not in gaining theoretical knowledge of the several points at issue, but rather in putting our knowledge into practice? In that case it is not enough to know about goodness; we must endeavour to possess and use it, or adopt any other means to become good ourselves. Now if discourses were enough in themselves to make people moral, to quote Theognis[2] 'Many and fat would be the fees they earned', quite rightly; and to provide such discourses[3] would be what is needed.

1. Or 'as they say'; but cf. 1095a5f., 1103b26.
2. Theognis 434.
3. Others translate 'and such rewards should have been provided'; but it is hard to see the point of this.

But as it is we find that although they have the power to stimulate and encourage those of the young who are liberal-minded, and although they can render a generous and truly idealistic[1] character susceptible of virtue, they are incapable of impelling the masses towards human perfection. For it is the nature of the many to be ruled by fear rather than by shame, and to refrain from evil not because of the disgrace but because of the punishments. Living under the sway of their feelings, they pursue their own pleasures and the means of obtaining them, and shun the pains that are their opposites; but of that which is fine and truly pleasurable they have not even a conception, since they have never had a taste of it. What discourse could ever reform people like that? To dislodge by argument habits long embedded in the character is a difficult if not impossible task. We should probably be content if the combination of all the means that are supposed to make us good enables us to attain some portion of goodness.

Goodness can only be induced in a suitably receptive character

Some thinkers hold that it is by nature that people become good, others that it is by habit, and others that it is by instruction. The bounty of nature is clearly beyond our control; it is bestowed by some divine dispensation upon those who are truly fortunate. It is a regrettable fact that discussion and instruction are not effective in all cases; just as a piece of land has to be prepared beforehand if it is to nourish the seed, so the mind of the pupil has to be prepared in its habits if it is to enjoy and dislike the right things; because the man who lives in accordance with his feelings would not listen to an argument to dissuade him, or understand it if he did. And when a man is in that state, how is it possible to persuade him out of it? In general, feeling seems to yield not to argument but only to force. Therefore we

1. 'Beauty-loving' (*philokalos*).

must have a character to work on that has some affinity to virtue: one that appreciates what is noble and objects to what is base.

Education in goodness is best undertaken by the state

But to obtain a right training for goodness from an early age is a hard thing, unless one has been brought up under right laws. For a temperate and hardy way of life is not a pleasant thing to most people, especially when they are young. For this reason upbringing and occupations should be regulated by law, because they will cease to be irksome when they have become *habitual. But presumably it is not enough to have received the right upbringing and supervision in youth; they must keep on observing their regimen and accustoming themselves to it even after they are grown up; so we shall need laws to regulate these activities too, and indeed generally to cover the whole of life; for most people are readier to submit to compulsion and punishment than to argument and fine ideals. This is why some people[1] think that although legislators ought to encourage people to goodness and appeal to their finer feelings, in the hope that those who have had a decent training in their habits will respond, they ought also to inflict chastisement and penalties on any who disobey through deficiency of character, and to deport the incorrigible altogether. For they hold that while the good man, whose life is related to a fine ideal, will listen to reason, the bad one whose object is pleasure must be controlled by pain, like a beast of burden. This is also why they say that the pains inflicted should be those that are most contrary to the favoured pleasures.

To resume, however: if (as we have said[2]) in order to be a good man one must first have been brought up in the right way and trained in the right habits, and must there-

1. Cf. Plato, *Laws* 722Dff.   2. 1179b31ff.

after spend one's life in reputable occupations, doing no
wrong either with or against one's will: then this can be
achieved by living under the guidance of some intelligence
or right system that has effective force. Now the orders
that a father gives have no forceful or compulsive power, nor
indeed have those of any individual in general, unless he is a
king or somebody of that sort; but law, being the pronouncement[1] of a kind of practical wisdom or intelligence, does
have the power of compulsion. And although people resent
it when their impulses are opposed by human agents, even
if the latter are in the right, the law causes no irritation by
enjoining decent behaviour. Yet in Sparta alone, or almost
alone,[2] the lawgiver seems to have concerned himself with
upbringing and daily life. In the great majority of states
matters of this kind have been completely neglected, and
every man lives his life as he likes, 'laying down the law for
wife and children', like the Cyclopes.[3]

*If neglected by the state, it can be supplied by the parent;
but it calls for some knowledge of legislative science*

The best solution would be to introduce a proper system of
public supervision of these matters. But if they continue to
be completely neglected by the state, it would seem to be
right for each individual to help his own children and
friends on the way to goodness, and that he should have the
power or at least the choice of doing this. And it would
seem from what we have said that he will be better able to
do it if he assumes the role of legislator. For obviously
public control is carried out by means of laws, and if the
control is good, by means of sound laws; but whether they
are writ*ten or unwritten, whether they are to regulate the

1. Or perhaps 'rule prescribed by ...'; it is hard to be sure what
logos means in a particular context.
2. Other examples were Crete and Carthage; cf. *Politics* 1272b24.
3. Homer, *Odyssey* ix.114f.

education of one person or of many, would seem to matter
no more than in the case of music or physical education or
any other subject of study. The instruction and habits
prescribed by a father have as much force in the household
as laws and customs have in the state, and even more,
because of the tie of blood and the children's sense of benefits received; for they are influenced from the outset by
natural affection and docility. Moreover, individual tuition,
like individual treatment in medicine, is actually superior
to the public sort. For example, as a general rule rest and
fasting are beneficial in a case of fever, but not, perhaps, for
a particular patient; and presumably a boxing instructor
does not make all his pupils adopt the same manner of
fighting. It would seem, then, that particular cases receive
more accurate treatment when individual attention is
given, because then each person is more likely to get what
suits him. But the best detailed treatment will be given by
the doctor (or trainer or any other instructor) who has a
general knowledge of what is good for all cases, or for a
specific type; because the sciences not only are said to be
but are concerned with common facts. This is not to deny
that in a particular case it is probably quite possible for
the right treatment to be given by one who has no knowledge,[1] but has carefully observed (in the course of his
experience) the effects upon individuals ⟨of different kinds
of treatment⟩; just as some people really seem to be their
own best doctors, although they would be quite unable to
help anybody else. Nevertheless it would presumably be
agreed that anyone who wants to be professionally qualified
with theoretical knowledge must proceed to the study of the
universal and get to know it as well as possible; for it is
with this (as we have said) that the sciences deal. Probably,
then, one who wishes to make other people (whether many
or few) better by supervision ought first to try to acquire the
art of legislation; assuming that we can be made good by
laws. For producing a right disposition in any person that

1. i.e. scientific knowledge.

is set before you is not a task for everybody: if anyone can do it, it is the man with knowledge[1] – just as in the case of medicine and all the other professions that call for application and practical understanding.

Where can such knowledge be obtained? Not from the sophists

Surely, then, the next question to consider is from whom or by what means one can acquire a grasp of legislation. Presumably, as in the case of the other sciences, from the politicians; because legislation is regarded, as we saw,[2] as a branch of political science. But it seems that the case is perhaps not the same with political science as it is with the rest of the sciences and faculties.[3] In all the others we find the same persons both putting their skills into practice and imparting them to others; e.g. doctors and painters. But as for political science, although the sophists profess to teach it, *not one of them practises it; that is done by the politicians, and they would seem to do it from a sort of ability aided by experience rather than by the exercise of reason. For we do not find them writing or lecturing about political subjects (although this would perhaps be more to their credit than composing speeches for the law courts or public meetings); nor again do we find that they have made politicians out of their sons or anyone else that they care for. And yet that would have been their logical course, if they were capable of it. For they could not have left a finer legacy to their countries, nor is there anything that they would rather have had for themselves, and therefore for those dearest to them, than that sort of ability. At the same time experience seems to contribute not a little to success in politics, for otherwise people would never have become statesmen through familiarity with political problems. So it seems that those who aspire to a scienti-

1. i.e. scientific knowledge of the principles involved.
2. 1141b24ff.
3. Cf. Plato's criticisms in *Meno* 91A–100C and *Protagoras* 319D–320B.

fic knowledge of politics need practical experience as well.

On the other hand those sophists who profess to teach politics seem to be very far from actually doing so. They are in fact absolutely ignorant both of the nature of the subject and of the matters with which it deals; otherwise they would not equate it with, or rate it even lower than, rhetoric.[1] Nor would they imagine that it is easy to frame a constitution by making a collection of the laws that have been most highly approved, because then you can select the best of them – as if the actual selection did not call for understanding, and as if a correct judgement were not the crucial factor, just as it is in musical questions. It is only the experts in a given art who can judge its products correctly and understand by what means and methods perfection is achieved, and which elements can be harmoniously combined; amateurs may be content if they do not remain unaware whether the result is good or bad, as in the case of painting. Laws represent the products of the art of politics: *how then can ⟨a collection of⟩ laws teach a man the art of legislation, or help him to pick out the best of them? We do not find people becoming qualified in medicine by reading handbooks, although the authors at least attempt to describe not only general methods of treatment but also possible methods of cure and proper modes of treatment for each type of patient, classifying them by their ⟨bodily⟩ states; and these handbooks are considered to be helpful to the experienced, but useless to the layman. Presumably, then, collections of laws and constitutions may be serviceable to those who are capable of examining them critically and judging what is rightly enacted and what is the opposite, and what sort of legislation is suitable for different circumstances. But those who go through such collections of examples without possessing a formed habit of mind,[2]

1. Cf. Isocrates, *Antidosis* 80, and see Appendix B.

2. It is not clear whether A. is thinking of a moral or an intellectual state, but the latter (fully developed knowledge of the principles involved) seems to suit the context better.

although they cannot assess merit correctly, except by a
kind of instinct, may perhaps improve their understanding
of the subject.

The student of ethics must therefore apply himself to politics

Since, then, the question of legislation has been left un-
examined by previous thinkers,[1] presumably we had better
investigate it more closely for ourselves, together with the
question of constitutions generally, so that our philosophy
of human conduct may be as complete as possible. So let
us first try to review any valid statements (about particular
points) that have been made by our predecessors; and then
to consider, in the light of our collected examples of constitutions,[2] what influences are conservative and what are
destructive of a state; and which have these effects upon
each different kind of constitution; and for what reasons
some states are well governed, while in others the contrary
is the case. For after examining these questions we shall
perhaps see more comprehensively what kind of constitution
is the best, and what is the best organization for each kind,
and the best system of laws and customs for it to use. Let
us, then, begin our account.

1. This concluding passage was obviously written to connect the
Ethics to the *Politics*; but written by whom? Opinions have been sharply
divided. The implication that Plato had nothing of importance to say
about eduction by legislation, or about types of constitution and their
changes, seems perverse and is in fact inconsistent with the actual procedure in the *Politics*, where Plato's views are nearly always traceable as
underlying A.'s thought, and often explicitly criticized or rejected.
At the same time the fact that the outlined programme does not correspond very accurately with the actual treatment may tell for no less
than against authenticity, because an 'editor' might have been expected
to produce a neater and more convincing link. The problem can only
be stated here: it does not yet seem to have been solved.

2. According to tradition A. wrote 158 such *Constitutions*, of which
the *Constitution of Athens* is the only survivor.

APPENDICES

APPENDIX A

PYTHAGOREANISM

PYTHAGORAS of Samos, who founded a religious order at Croton in south Italy in about 530 B.C., was a man of rare genius and had a powerful influence upon the history of Western thought; but it is not easy to explain exactly where his originality lay. He left no writings; much of his teaching was (at least theoretically) secret; he appears to have drawn such mathematical knowledge as he had from Babylonia; and his followers tended to attribute any doctrine of the school at any date to the Master himself. Of the evidence that we have about these doctrines, most is widely scattered, much is late, and not a little is inconsistent or obscure. However, a few statements can be made with some confidence, even about the man himself.

(1) He was primarily a religious teacher.

(2) He believed that the cosmos is rational (since it exhibits order and numerical ratios), living and divine. Other early thinkers, viz. the Milesians, had assumed that the world stuff is alive, and *qua* alive and eternal, divine; but only Pythagoras drew any moral inference from his belief.

(3) He taught that the human soul is immortal and akin to the soul of the cosmos; that since all life is one, souls are subject to transmigration, sin in one life being punished by down-graded reincarnation in the next; and that the object of life is the purification of the soul by the practice of philosophy, which will assimilate it to the divine nature (cf. the accounts put by Plato into the mouth of Socrates towards the end of the *Phaedo* and in the myth of Er in the *Republic*). This emphasis upon the opposition of good and evil led to the development of the first dualistic system of philosophy, as is explained below.

(4) His discovery of the ratios underlying the musical concords, and the mathematical, astronomical and physical theories which he (probably) initiated were secondary and almost incidental to his view of philosophy as a way of life, a contemplative activity for the emancipation of the soul. This view, transmitted by Plato, undoubtedly influenced Aristotle's doctrine of *eudaimonia* in Book X.

Of the views attributed to the Pythagoreans in the *Ethics* one, the equation of justice with reciprocity, needs no explanation, although it may be noted that Alexander,[1] commenting on *Metaphysics* 985b29, states that they also identified justice with squareness and the number 4 (or 9). The allusions at 1096b5 and 1132b21 refer to a doctrine described by Aristotle at *Metaphysics* 986a22 as held by 'others of this same school' – not, apparently, by all – that there are ten principles, each consisting in a pair of contraries, set out in two columns thus:

Limit	Unlimited
Odd	Even
Unity	Plurality
Right	Left
Male	Female
Rest	Motion
Straight	Crooked
Light	Darkness
Good	Bad
Square	Oblong

The selection of these pairs seems rather capricious, and some look rather like stop-gaps brought in to make up the venerable number Ten; but evidently there is system of a sort: the first column is meant to exhibit order, unity and goodness, and the second the corresponding defects. Aristotle makes this point when (1096b6) he speaks of the 'column of goods'. Moreover Limit is clearly a formal and Unlimited a material principle. There is not space here to debate the implications of this doctrine, although it will be touched upon again in Appendix C; the reader who wishes to pursue the fascinating study of Pythagoreanism should consult Guthrie's excellent account in Vol. I of his *History of Greek Philosophy*, and (if possible) W. Burkert's *Lore and Science in Early Pythagoreanism*.

1. See Appendix J, p. 363.

APPENDIX B

THE SOPHISTS AND SOCRATES

To describe briefly what the Sophists were and what they stood for is difficult, and to do so fairly is probably impossible; we know too little, and the evidence comes mainly from hostile or at least critical sources. Besides, they differed widely in character, personality, aims and methods, and even in the period of their activity; for the 'movement' had started well over a century before Aristotle wrote the *Ethics*. Finally, there is still sharp disagreement on the question whether their influence was generally beneficial or pernicious.

A few facts are undisputed. Sophists were professional teachers who travelled about lecturing, leading discussions, and generally giving instruction; usually in rhetoric (as the key to success in public life), but also in many other subjects, theoretical and practical; thus supplying a kind of higher or further education. They converged upon Athens as the cultural centre of Greece (only one or two of them were Athenian born). They charged fees for their services. Some of them challenged (or appeared to challenge) accepted views about religion and morality.

That the effect of their teaching was stimulating can hardly be doubted; how far it was salutary, and how far confusing or subversive, is much less certain: there is probably no simple answer. But the philosophers – at any rate Plato and Aristotle and their followers – considered them to be (upon the whole) superficial; more concerned with plausibility and expedience than with truth and goodness; and actuated largely by mercenary motives. Certainly the sophistic movement was closely associated with scepticism, but both might be attributed to the deadlock caused by conflicting philosophical theories.

Socrates may be called a contemporary of the sophists, although the two earliest, Protagoras and Gorgias, were his seniors by ten or twenty years. Even if the encounters described by Plato in his dialogues are imaginary, Socrates must have met and talked to most if not all of them; he would certainly have known their views, and generally disagreed with them. Against scepticism he set a confident belief that knowledge is possible, although he did not

347

claim to possess it; against atheism or agnosticism, a resolute faith in divine providence; against materialism, an insistence upon the superiority of soul to body; and against extreme relativism, a conviction that goodness is something positive and absolute, however differently it may be manifested in particular circumstances.

How, then, could Socrates be described as a sophist, as he was by Aristophanes in the *Clouds*? The short and obvious answer is that the poet wanted a well-known citizen (not a foreigner) to represent the new trend of education that he wanted to attack, and Socrates was an ideal subject for caricature.[1] But there was another reason, more logical, although resting on an equivocation. The sophists claimed to teach *aretē* in the sense of efficiency: to make people good speakers, good citizens, successful in public life. Socrates too was interested in efficiency, as any logically-minded person must be; but for him *aretē* was not particular but total: the object of knowledge was not merely to become good at this or that, but to become a good man. Hence although (according to Plato, at any rate) he did not even claim to possess knowledge, much less to impart it,[2] he urged and helped his friends and anyone else who would listen to him to seek knowledge as the necessary and sufficient condition of all the virtues[3] and of *aretē* itself in the sense of moral goodness; because he believed that all wrongdoing was due to ignorance.[4] This was why he set himself to question people about their beliefs, to see whether they were rationally defensible; his object being to rid their minds of false or muddled notions as a first step towards the acquisition of real knowledge. Many found the experience humiliating; and this was a major cause of his unpopularity (*Apology* 21C–23D). But his questionings also had a positive and fruitful result. Aristotle himself tells us (*Metaphysics* 1078b27) that Socrates could fairly be credited with two innovations: inductive arguments and general definition. Since both

1. See Guthrie, op. cit. iii.361–77, and the introduction of K. J. Dover's edition of the *Clouds* (Oxford, 1968).

2. Cf. 1127b25.

3. 1116b4, 1144b18ff.

4. 1145b23, 1147b15. For him, apparently, to see what was right was to do it. Plato discerned that inner conflict is not uncommon – reason pulling one way and appetite the other; and that reason may lose unless supported by the 'spirited element' in the soul (*Rep.* 439C–441A.). A.'s doctrine of *proairesis* (1139a3ff.) stems from this.

Xenophon (in the *Memorabilia*) and Plato (in the earlier 'Socratic' dialogues) show Socrates seeking definitions and employing arguments that are based on analogy if not formally inductive, the attribution can be accepted with confidence. The innovations had an important bearing upon Plato's thought.

APPENDIX C

PLATO'S THEORY OF FORMS

THIS remarkable and influential theory has been much debated, often misunderstood, and sometimes misrepresented. All that will be attempted here is to indicate some of the sources from which Plato drew inspiration, and to give an (admittedly over-simplified) account of the theory as a whole. For a classic exposition see W. D. Ross, *Plato's Theory of Ideas*, Oxford, 1951.

Several earlier thinkers had recognized that the evidence of the senses is unreliable, but held nevertheless that critical use of it by the mind could lead to knowledge. Parmenides was the first to insist that truth and see ing a e entirely different: that *what is* is one, changeless and eternal, whereas the world of which the senses tell us is manifold, mutable and transient; either not real at all or (more probably) corresponding only remotely to reality; in either case only *what is* can be known. Others, especially Heraclitus, the Pythagoreans, and Empedocles, had felt the need for a formal cause to account for the differentiation of the world-stuff. Heraclitus had found this in the concept of *measure* (fr. 30), and his *Logos* was itself a directive principle. He also stressed the instability of the sensible world, which never *is*, being always in process of *becoming*. For the Pythagoreans Limit was an *archē*, and it was expressed in terms of numbers or numerical ratios. Empedocles enunciated, in the case of certain natural substances, the constitutive formula or proportion of the elements that composed them; and presumably he intended every substance to have its formula.

Thus from several sources Plato inherited a belief that nothing in the sensible world is knowable *per se*, but only in so far as it corresponds to some intelligible reality. What, then, was the relation between the sensible and the intelligible?

Socrates, in his quest for knowledge, had developed an inductive technique through which, by considering a number of particular instances of some attribute or notion, he had succeeded in isolating their common character in the form of a general definition. Also the study of geometry, in which Plato was especially interested, must have suggested to him that the particular figures that were drawn (scratched on a waxed tablet, or even more roughly in dust or sand) were only poor and short-lived copies of the perfect and eternal circles, triangles, etc., with which our knowledge is concerned. It was natural to extend this analogy to the objects that we perceive around us. Apples, turnips, peas and play-balls are (broadly speaking) round; some more so than others, but they are all instances of roundness. Plato would have said that they all participate or share in the Form of roundness (or rather sphericity). Where the common characteristic was visible he often used the metaphor of copy and pattern to illustrate the relation; this was apt, inasmuch as the copy is generally inferior to the pattern, and less real. (Hence also the name Form and its alternative Idea, from the Greek words *eidos* and *idea*, both meaning 'shape' or 'appearance'.) But the common feature need not, of course, be visible or even perceptible – only intelligible.

But how do we acquire knowledge of the Forms? Here the Pythagorean belief in metempsychosis or transmigration suggested a solution: the soul in its disembodied state between one life and the next apprehends the Forms directly; and although this knowledge is lost at birth, it can be recovered by intelligent reflection on the data of sense-perception (the doctrine of Recollection: *Phaedo* 72D–76E, *Phaedrus* 249E–250A, *Meno* 81B–D).

Plato never wrote a straightforward exposition of his theory, and it is likely that he developed and modified it from time to time – though perhaps not so much as some of his interpreters have supposed, because apart from other special considerations apparent development may be no more than a fresh stage of gradual presentation. Such stages may perhaps be seen at *Euthyphro* 5D, 6D; *Meno* 72C–E; *Cratylus* 389A–B, 438D–440B; *Phaedo* 65B–66A, 72E–75E, 78B–79D, 140B–D; *Symposium* 210A–212A, *Republic* 504D–517C. In this last passage we meet the Form of Good, or universal good, to which Aristotle takes exception. The analogies of the Line and the Cave are illustrations, not methodical descriptions; and the precise nature of the Good, and its relation to the other Forms, must remain largely conjectural; this arcane doctrine Plato imparted, it seems, only by word of mouth. But the following account is submitted for the reader's consideration.

When Plato began to introduce the Forms into his dialogues he was compelled to use figurative language. The metaphors of imitation and participation were probably the best available; but to the literal-minded both suggest something too concrete and physical, and this led to some of the misunderstandings that are exposed in the *Parmenides*. Here and later (especially in the *Sophist* and *Timaeus*) Plato made it clear that the Forms are much more like formulae expressing the laws or principles that govern the physical world. They are also the forerunners of Aristotle's essence and substance, genus and species; indeed Plato begins to use the word *genos* in the *Sophist*; and it seems that he already envisaged a hierarchical system of Forms, logically and ontologically inter-related, with Being as *summum genus* at the top, and the multiplicity of Forms that characterize *infimae species* at its base; the whole con-stituting a sort of blueprint of reality, the 'pattern' which the Artificer follows (*Timaeus* 27D–29A) – and the parent of Aristotle's system of classification to which the Latin name *Scala Universi* be-came attached.

How the Good, like the sun, illuminates the whole system and renders it intelligible is not really relevant to Aristotle's criticism in Book I ch. vi; what he objects to is the concept of any universal good. In this he seems to be at fault. It is true that the precise ap-plication of the word 'good' varies not only between different categories but even within the same one: the goodness of a saint is not exactly the goodness of a detergent or an insecticide. But this is not really a valid objection. Aristotle seems to have regarded the Form of Good as something like one of his own species, of which all the members are coordinate; but Plato cannot have conceived of the Good in this way. He must surely have meant by it goodness in the most comprehensive sense: that excellence or perfection to which anything can approximate *in its own kind*; and which in a teleological system is the Final Cause. Indeed Aristotle's First Mover owes much to Plato's Form of Good.

APPENDIX D

THE CATEGORIES

A CATEGORY, as Aristotle used the word in Book I ch. vi, is simply a predicate or kind of predicate. The doctrine of categories, which must have had its origin in the Academy, whether or not it was developed by Aristotle, amounts to this (the account is neither complete nor strictly accurate, but may serve to show what Aristotle is talking about; for a full discussion see J. L. Ackrill, *Aristotle's Categories and De Interpretatione*, Oxford, 1963). In a judgement of the type S is P, the predicate P may be any one of ten kinds:

(1) a Substance, i.e. a member of a species, e.g. a horse or a man.
(2) a Quality, e.g. white or cold.
(3) a Quantity, e.g. three-foot or ten-litre.
(4) a Relation, e.g. dear (to) or bigger (than).
(5) a Time, e.g. in spring, at noon.
(6) a Place, e.g. at home, in Athens.
(7) a (temporary) Position or disposition, e.g. sitting or pleased.
(8) a (permanent) State, e.g. crippled or educated.
(9) an Activity, e.g. cutting.
(10) a Passivity, e.g. being cut.

The last six are often passed over, since they are all reducible to (2), (3) or (4).

In the above-mentioned passage Aristotle is using the doctrine to argue that there cannot be a universal good such as Plato, in his Theory of Forms, held to be the supreme reality. This was, in a sense, an anticipation of the controversy that exercised the medieval schoolmen: whether general or universal terms express something that actually exists (Realism), or whether they are merely names used for analytical convenience (Nominalism). Plato's view is probably right; see Appendix C *ad fin.*

APPENDIX E

SUBSTANCE AND CHANGE

Matter and Form

FOR Aristotle substance (*ousia*), i.e. what *is* in the fullest sense, is an individual person or thing. Or rather, he normally describes the individual as substance in the primary sense. But logically and epistemologically the individual is less knowable than the species to which it belongs; this is because the individual is a concrete whole (what Aristotle calls a *sunolon* or *suneilēmmenon*), a combination of form and matter; and only the formal element is constant and definable, and therefore knowable. Hence he often identifies substance with the form or essence of a thing; and this seems to be the outcome of his long and careful discussion in *Metaphysics* Z. He has been accused of not being quite consistent on this point.

But the matter – form relation is not in fact as simple as it sounds. Prime matter – matter devoid altogether of form – does not occur, and could not be perceived if it did; it is barely conceivable. Matter is, however, progressively informed: first as one of the simple bodies or elements,[1] say earth, then as a species of earth, e.g. clay; then as clay treated, shaped and baked into bricks; and bricks in their turn can be so arranged as to constitute a wall or a house. At each stage the proximate matter, already informed at the preceding stage, is combined (just as if it were bare matter) with a fresh form to produce a more highly organized entity. Thus all the constituents – both physical and non-physical – of the individual have a formal element, which is knowable; not only his physical characteristics, but all his idiosyncrasies fall under recognizable types; in fact his is a composite form, and knowable in much greater detail than the species. To put it in another way, the species is more knowable in theory, the individual in practice. Moreover, matter and form are really correlative, though logically distinct; informed matter and inmattered form are two different ways of looking at the same thing.

1. The elements themselves are combinations of the four primary contraries hot, dry, wet and cold; but this is more a matter of logical analysis than of physical constitution.

354

Causation

Matter and form are factors in Aristotle's theory of causation.[1] In artificial processes he distinguishes four causes or conditions necessary for producing the required result: (1) the Material, e.g. bricks, stone, wood, etc.; (2) the Formal, i.e. the shape or design which is imposed upon the materials, e.g. the form of a house; (3) the Efficient, i.e. that which originates the process: in the case of the house, the builder or his (or the architect's) idea of the completed structure; and (4) the Final cause; the end or purpose of the operation, viz. the house considered as a place of shelter for occupation. The last three are obviously closely related, and in many cases (especially in natural processes) they are barely distinguishable aspects of the one formal cause.

Change and Process

But how does matter pass from one state to another? How does change take place?[2]

Change (*metabolē*) is either (1) of substance, viz. coming to be (*genesis*) and ceasing to be (*phthora*); or (2) of quality, viz. alteration (*alloiōsis*); or (3) of quantity, viz. increase (*auxēsis*) and decrease (*phthisis*); or (4) of place, viz. locomotion (*phora*). The last two present no special problem. All the last three are usually described by Aristotle as kinds of movement, *kinēsis*; but both *genesis* and *kinēsis* are sometimes used in the more general sense of process.

All change involves three factors: (1) something that persists, and (2) and (3) two states or qualities or other determinants, one of which is exchanged for the other. What persists is the substrate or subject, *hupokeimenon*. In change of quality this is the substance: a round bowl is battered out of shape and is no longer round, but it is still a bowl; an unripe apple becomes ripe, and is still an apple, because transformation has not affected their *essential* qualities. But in change of substance the essential form is lost, and what persists is only matter. Melt down the bowl, and all that is left is metal; keep the apple long enough, and it will disintegrate.

Change is between either contraries or contradictories. Substantive change is only between contradictories, because substance has no contrary; what is not a bowl or an apple becomes a bowl or

1. See *Metaphysics* 983a24–b3 and *Physics* 189b30–192b4, 194b16–200b8.

2. See *Metaphysics* 1069a3–34 and *Physics* V, especially 224a21–226b17.

an apple, and vice versa. Qualitative change is usually between contraries: either between the extremes of a qualitative continuum (e.g. white and black) or between two points in the continuum (e.g. white and grey, or light grey and dark grey, or grey and black). Such change may also be viewed as change between contradictories, between white and not-white – that is, between any positive quality or state, *hexis*, and the negation or absence of that quality or state, which Aristotle calls privation, *sterēsis*. Of course the reverse process from *sterēsis* to *hexis* is equally possible, and is indeed normal in natural development; but it is generally expressed in a different way.

Potentiality and Actuality

This brings us to one of Aristotle's most valuable contributions to the analysis of change. Earlier thinkers had been unable to explain how not–A can become A. Plato in the *Sophist* had gone some way towards solving the problem; but it was Aristotle who provided the neat solution that what is not–A actually can be A potentially. In the case of qualities this is self-evident: to say that a thing is not hot is pointless unless it *can* be hot. So each contrary quality or state is potentially the other, and the substrate is potentially both, because it can become either, given the requisite conditions. In fact the antithesis of potentiality and actuality is that of matter and form viewed dynamically. Bricks are not actually, but are potentially, a house; a lump of bronze is potentially a statue. So too in the organic sphere: the seed is potentially a tree, and the fertilized ovum is potentially an animal or a human being.

The antithesis appears also in a slightly different form as part of Aristotle's theory of education and character-training. The word *dunamis* (see the Glossary) also means a faculty or capacity which can, through practice, become a settled state or 'habit', *hexis*: an aptitude for music can be developed into musicianship. But the *hexis* when acquired may remain dormant; only when in full use does it become *energeia*, actuality or activity.

Two other points about change and process have special relevance for Aristotle's doctrine of Pleasure. (1) They involve lapse of time (indeed time is only measurable in terms of change). (2) When complete, they cease, because they are relative to an end distinct from themselves; in this they differ from an activity, which is an end in itself, since its very being is activity.

APPENDIX F

NATURE AND THEOLOGY

PHUSIS, the Greek word which we translate by 'nature', had the basic meaning of growth, with the emphasis sometimes on origin, sometimes on development, sometimes on the developed state. Several of the Presocratic philosophers had used the word of the primary world-stuff and its modifications, and Aristotle continues this use; for him nature includes everything that – as he puts it – contains in itself a principle of movement. The natural world, then, exhibits process.

It also exhibits an orderly system. Aristotle's special interest was in biology, and his careful study of plants and animals led him to group and classify the latter[1] by genera and species, on a principle suggested by Plato's 'division' and the hierarchy of Forms, but more methodically applied. His *Scala Naturae* or theory of the organization of nature begins with the elements, which make up simple bodies, i.e. inorganic matter as we encounter it in nature. The grades of soul – nutritive, sentient, intellective – and the forms of life that accompany them range upwards from plants through zoophytes, molluscs, insects, fishes, etc., to the higher animals and man.

The 'principle of movement' by which Aristotle characterizes natural bodies is not a spontaneous movement but a response to external attraction.[2] The element or inanimate body is attracted (downwards or upwards) to its proper region; the living creature grows or moves towards what is good for it or what it desires (in intelligent creatures there is a complication: see Appendix G). This principle extends beyond the sublunary world. The astronomer Eudoxus had calculated that the apparent movements of the sun, moon and five planets (all that were then known) could be accounted for by a system of concentric spheres rotating on different axes (and in some cases in contrary directions). Aristotle took over these calculations (as revised by his friend Callippus) and converted them (with some additions of his own) into a mechanical explanation of the said movements. Each of these heavenly bodies

1. His work 'On Plants' is unfortunately lost.
2. *Physics* 255b29–256a3.

357

is attached to the periphery of one of the spheres, which being perfectly transparent are invisible. The outermost sphere of all (called 'the first heaven') carries round the fixed stars. The spheres are eternal, and each is kept eternally rotating by its own mover.[1] All these movers, and the outermost sphere or 'first heaven', are themselves moved by the unmoved First Mover, the ultimate reality and pure form, Mind or God, whose ceaseless activity is self-thinking thought, since no other activity or object is worthy of him. He is the final Good, and it is as an object of love and desire that he ultimately causes and sustains all movement and life in the cosmos. Nature, which Aristotle occasionally seems to personify, is (as it were) the collective response of the sublunary world to the divine mind: all creatures are drawn towards the perfection of their own 'nature' or natural state; that is how all development and all actualization comes about. There is, however, inherent in matter a certain element of imperfection and intransigence, and that is why even in nature things sometimes go wrong.

This very brief sketch may raise a smile. The sketch itself is absurdly inadequate, and the views upon which it touches are often obscure or apparently inconsistent in detail; some may seem naïve in themselves, especially the concept of teleology, which is not now fashionable. Certainly the reader should seek more information.[2] But enough may have been said to rouse his curiosity, and perhaps even his admiration for Aristotle's ingenuity in working out such a comprehensive system; enough at any rate to supply some background for his ethical theory, and to show some of the reasons why he identified *eudaimonia* with contemplation.

1. Sometimes called an Intelligence: a rational being intermediate between man and God; but A.'s account is rather vague.
2. See the Bibliography, especially items 15–17.

APPENDIX G

THE PRACTICAL SYLLOGISM

ACCORDING to Aristotle desire directly attracts inanimate objects (perhaps by a kind of magnetism; the properties of the lodestone were common knowledge, as is shown by Plato's simile at *Ion* 533), and operates mechanically upon animals (the presentation, by means of the senses, of a good to the appetitive part of the soul acts upon the heart, which sets up movements in the joints, so that the animal approaches the good and enjoys it in the appropriate way). In man the process is complicated by his possession of the rational faculty of deliberation. Deliberation implies the exercise of judgement; and this is where the practical syllogism comes in. It differs from the familiar demonstrative syllogism in that (1) the major premiss is a judgement of value, 'all dry food is wholesome', or an imperative, 'all dry food ought to be eaten'; and (2) the conclusion following from the combination of such a major premiss with a minor such as 'this is dry food' is not merely a statement but an action: the subject eats the food.

In ch. iii of Book VII Aristotle uses the practical syllogism to account for incontinence, or rather to show how it is, in a sense, due to ignorance. In the example there given the subject is confronted with two major premisses, not actually incompatible, but leading naturally to contradictory conclusions: (a) All sweet food is unwholesome,[1] and (b) All sweet food is pleasant. He also has the minor premiss: This is sweet food. His appetite leads him to attend to (b) and ignore (a); consequently he eats the sweet food. Thus there is a sense in which he acts from ignorance.[2]

1. As promoting acidity.
2. For detailed discussions of the Practical Syllogism see the Bibliography, items 79–85.

APPENDIX H

PLEASURE AND PROCESS

SPEUSIPPUS had argued that pleasure consists in the supplying of a deficiency and the remedying of any debility or malady resulting therefrom: i.e. that it is a remedial process, perceptible by the subject. Its object is the restoration of health or normality, which is good. But no process is the same as the end to which it leads: therefore pleasure is not a good.

To this argument Aristotle brings two objections.

(1) What we call good or bad generally may not be such for a particular subject in particular circumstances; and therefore a process which is good or pleasant in one sense may be bad or unpleasant in another. This line of reasoning, which of course can be used against any generalization, seems to have special force in this context owing to the fact that physical pleasures are in any case mixed, i.e. contain an element of pain.

(2) When a person suffers from a deficiency, only a part of his normal state is impaired, the rest remaining healthy. The process by which the affected part is restored to health is not really pleasant (medical treatment is often painful); or if pleasant at all, is so only indirectly, because the activity of the healthy part is now unimpeded. It is upon activity that pleasure supervenes.

Aristotle's other criticisms of Speusippus are for the most part easy to follow, but there is an exception at 1153b4–7, echoed at 1173a6–13. There we find that Speusippus argued (against the view that pleasure, being the contrary of pain, which is an evil, must be a good) that good is contrary to both pleasure and pain, just as 'greater' is to both 'less' and 'equal' and that this objection fails 'because he would not say that pleasure is a species of evil'. Since this appears to be just what Speusippus *would* say, attempts have been made to get round the difficulty – without any great success. Hence Gauthier has suggested that the orthodox representation of Speusippus's scheme

Pain	Absence of pain	Pleasure
(evil)	(good)	(evil)

should be replaced by another, based on Plato's account at
Philebus 44A–C, which is generally held to refer to Speusippus:

Pain——————————————————————→Absence of pain		
(Evil	Pleasure	(Good
reality)	(Process)	reality)

in which pleasure is a process from pain to its absence, and is contrasted with both, just as 'equal' is opposed to both 'greater' and
'less'. To this Aristotle rightly objects that (contrariety being
maximum opposition) nothing can have more than one contrary.

Gauthier's suggestion gives a good sense, and seems to fit the
evidence better than any version of the traditional interpretation.

APPENDIX I

LITURGIES

WEALTHY Athenian citizens were required to perform certain public services, called *liturgies*, at their own expense – thus benefiting the state and acquiring popularity. Among the most notable of these liturgies were the following, all mentioned or alluded to by Aristotle in the *Ethics*: *chorēgia*, the training and equipment of a chorus for a dramatic or musical performance (the word came to be used metaphorically of equipment or 'properties' in general; cf. 1101a15, 1122b22, 1123a23, 1177a30, 1178a24, 1179a11); *triērarchia*, the command, maintenance and repair of a warship (1122a24, b23); *architheōria*, the leadership of a delegation to a foreign festival (1122a25); and *hestiāsis*, the provision of a banquet for one's *phulē* (cf. 1122b23 and note on 1160a18).

APPENDIX J

ARISTOTLE IN THE MIDDLE AGES

AFTER the death of Aristotle's pupil Theophrastus, who presumably supervised Nichomachus's editing of his father's notes, Peripatetic interest in ethics seems to have declined. The list of Aristotle's works drawn up perhaps by Ariston of Ceos (who became head of the Lyceum *c.* 225) mentions only one ethical treatise which – as it consisted of five books – must surely have been the *Eudemian Ethics*, and this implies that our *Ethics* was not available in the library. However that may be, it survived somewhere. It was known to the author of the *Magna Moralia* (written about 100 B.C.), although he based his work mainly on the Eudemian treatise; and it was known also to Cicero, although he seems to have believed it to be an original work by Nicomachus (*De Finibus* V.5). It was edited (i.e. copied and published) between 40 and 20 B.C. by Andronicus of Rhodes, who became head of the Lyceum at about the same time. But the living issues of ethics had been taken over for the most part by the post-Aristotelian schools; and the refoundation of Byzantium as Constantinople to be the eastern and Christian capital of the empire, and the inauguration of its university (A.D. 330 or soon after) led to a recession of Greek studies at Rome. The last important Roman writer on Greek philosophy was Boethius (480–524), who translated and wrote commentaries on Aristotle's logical works and intended to deal similarly with the rest of his and all Plato's writings; but he incurred the suspicion of Theodoric and was imprisoned and put to death. In prison he wrote his celebrated *Consolatio Philosophiae*, containing many echoes and aphorisms of Greek philosophers. He is perhaps best known for having provoked the age-long scholastic controversy of Nominalism v. Realism (see Appendix D).

In the Eastern part of the empire a succession of Greek scholars wrote commentaries on Aristotle's works. The earliest and therefore the most important as a witness was Aspasius (*c.* A.D. 100); more than half of his commentary on the *Ethics* (I–IV, part of VII, and VIII) is preserved, and is valuable for its familiarity with Peripatetic tradition. Unfortunately Alexander of Aphrodisias (*c.* A.D. 200), the ablest member of the series, left no commentary on the

Ethics, but two of his own ethical treatises throw some light on Aristotle's doctrines. In the latter part of the third century Porphyry, the pupil and assistant of Plotinus, wrote a commentary on the *Ethics* which has not come down to us, but became known to Arab scholars (see below). Others carried on the tradition for nearly four centuries. Meanwhile at Constantinople itself Aristotle's teaching had been expounded by Themistius (*c.* 317–88). From one or more of these centres interest was aroused at seats of learning in Syria, and Syriac commentaries on some of the logical works – in some cases Syriac translations too – were made in the fifth and sixth centuries. These in turn stimulated the curiosity of the Arabs; and in the ninth century there began a flow of Arabic translations from the Syriac versions of the works of Aristotelian scholars and of Aristotle himself. So in a dark educational age Peripatetic logic followed the conquering Arabs across North Africa and re-entered Europe by the back door, by way of Spain.

But both in Spain and in the schools set up by Charlemagne in France Aristotle was studied only in Latin translations and for the sake of his logic and rhetoric. It was again from the East that a new impetus came. Arab philosophers, especially Avicenna (980–1037) at Isfahan, began writing on the non-logical works, including the *De Anima* and *De Caelo*, the *Physics* and the *Metaphysics*. Avicenna was familiar, as Gauthier shows (note on 1124b24–26), even with Aristotle's Magnificent man. These and other commentaries reached Toledo in the twelfth century and were there translated into Latin. At nearly the same time in France the brilliant Abelard, who, having no Greek, knew Aristotle only through Latin translations, set him above Plato, but succeeded in reconciling their teachings, and adopted the central position called Conceptualism in the great scholastic controversy between Realism and Nominalism. He mentions Aristotle three times in his ethical treatise *Scito te ipsum*, but the references are all to the *Categories*. He died in 1142. Thirty-five years later the Arabian scholar Averroes (1126–98) completed his translation (with periphrastic commentary) of the *Ethics*. He was well acquainted with neo-Platonism, but gave his primary allegiance to Aristotle, writing abstracts or expositions of most of the major works. Towards the end of the century appeared an anonymous Latin translation of *Ethics* II and III (down to 1119a34), based apparently on at least two Greek MSS. Roughly a century later, in about 1300, a further anonymous Latin translation supplied the missing Book I, the rest of III, and IV–X.

Meanwhile the Oxford scholar Robert Grosseteste applied himself to the study of Greek, and after his consecration as Bishop of Lincoln gathered together a group of Hellenists for the purpose of translating Greek authors both sacred and secular. These produced in 1246–7 a Latin translation (based partly on the earlier anonymous version mentioned above) of the *Ethics* and of selected Greek commentaries thereon, together with notes by Grosseteste himself – most of which have unfortunately been lost. Grosseteste's translations were used by the great Dominicans Albertus Magnus (1193–1280) and his pupil Thomas Aquinas (1225?–74). Both were fine scholars and had considerable influence, but Thomas far outshone his teacher. Apart from his original doctrines, his main achievement was the harmonization of Aristotelian logic and metaphysics with Platonic idealism and Christian theology – a feat which, though evoking some cheap gibes, has had a profound and generally enlightening influence upon Western thought. Unlike Albertus, he did not merely paraphrase Aristotle but commented at length upon most of the important non-biological works. His knowledge of Greek was perhaps only moderate. Better, though still imperfect, was that of William of Moerbecke near Ghent, who carried out or supervised the translation of all the available works of Aristotle into Latin in or about 1273. The translation is so literal that (being based upon good and early MSS now lost) it often helps to decide points of textual criticism.

By 1300, then, all the surviving works of Aristotle[1] were available in Latin versions, some of which were taken directly from Greek MSS. But there was some discrimination against him. At a Council held at Paris in 1210 it had been ordered that 'neither the books of Aristotle on natural philosophy nor comments on the same should be read either privately or publicly': and in 1215 the statutes for the University of Paris ordered the study of the books on Dialectic (i.e. logic), but forbade that of the *Physics* and *Metaphysics*. Yet in 1255 these last were included among the subjects prescribed in the Faculty of Arts at Paris; and although Roger Bacon, deploring the slow progress of Aristotelian studies, wrote 'There have been few . . . who have been of any account in the philosophy of Aristotle up to this year of grace 1292 . . . The *Ethics* has but slowly become known, having been only lately, and that

---

1. Except the *Constitution of Athens*, which was lost quite early and not rediscovered until 1890.

seldom, expounded by our masters', by 1366 candidates for the Paris M.A. were required to read the greater part of it, together with at least three books of the *Meteorologica*.

It was perhaps just before the Renaissance that Aristotle's reputation reached its peak. To Bacon, who scorned scholasticism, he was a fount of wisdom who must be studied at first-hand; to Dante he was *il maestro*, the ultimate secular authority – quoted (not, of course, in Greek) far more often even than Virgil. It was the spread of Greek learning generally, and the rediscovery of Plato in particular, that set him back in a truer perspective. Then followed the rising tide of fresh knowledge that swept away most of his astronomical and physical theories and eroded much of his philosophical authority. In spite of estimates like Darwin's well-known 'Linnaeus and Cuvier have been my two gods, but they were mere schoolboys to old Aristotle', people still talk as if this one man had blocked the advance of science, and left no place for experiment and research, by claiming omniscience. But he made no such claim, and it is doubtful whether the blindest of his admirers made it for him. It would be better to reflect that, but for him, Western science might well have died in infancy, or survived only at a primitive level. As for his ethical teaching, the closing words of Professor D. J. Allan in his *Philosophy of Aristotle* (1952) could hardly be bettered as a fair and sober judgement: 'One lesson of our age is that barbarism persists under the surface, and that the virtues of civilized life are less deeply rooted than used to be supposed. The world is not too richly endowed with examples of perseverance and subtlety in analysis, of moderation and sanity in the study of human affairs. It will be a great loss if the thinker who, above all others, displays these qualities, is ever totally forgotten.'

GLOSSARY OF GREEK WORDS

ARISTOTLE's terminology is not absolutely consistent; besides, even technical terms are subject to the normal hazards of translation: there are few, if any, exact equivalents, and implications are affected by context. Hence although capricious variations of rendering have been avoided, strict uniformity has not been attempted.

This glossary – which is only selective – has two principal aims: to give the Greekless reader a clue to the connotations of some of the words that Aristotle uses to express his ideas, and to help the reader who has some Greek to identify the Aristotelian concept that underlies the English rendering in a given passage. It also represents a certain saving in respect of footnotes. Adjectives are not listed separately unless they differ substantially in appearance from the corresponding nouns.

adikia   injustice, wrongdoing (opp. *dikaiosunē*).
agroikia   boorishness, dullness, rusticity.
agathos   (see *aretē*).
aidōs, aidēmōn   modesty, respect, sense of shame.
aischros   ugly, disgraceful (opp. *kalos*).
aisthēsis   sensation, perception.
akolasia (akolastos)   licentiousness, intemperance, lack of restraint (opp. *sōphrosunē*).
akrasia (akratēs)   incontinence, lack of self-control (opp. *enkrateia*).
anaisthesia   insensibility, insensitivity, indifference.
aneleutheria   illiberality, meanness (opp. *eleutheriotēs*).
apeirokalia   tastelessness, indifference to beauty.
archē   starting-point, source, origin, originative cause, first principle, rule, authority.
aretē (agathos)   goodness, excellence, virtue, efficiency.
asōtia   prodigality, ruinous extravagance.
autarkēs   self-sufficient, independent.

boulēsis   wish.
bouleusis   deliberation.

deilia   cowardice (opp. *andreia*).

deinotēs (deinos)   cleverness.

dianoia   thought, discursive thinking, intelligence.

diathesis   disposition.

dikaisosunē (dikaios)   justice, integrity.

doxa   belief, opinion, reputation.

dunamis   power, capacity, faculty, potency, potentiality (opp. *energeia*).

eidos   form, kind, species.

eirōneia   irony, self-depreciation, understatement.

eleutheriotēs (eleutheros)   liberality, generosity, good breeding.

energeia   activity, actuality, actualization, exercise.

enkrateia (enkratēs)   continence, strength of will or character.

epieikeia (epieikēs)   equity, fairness, decency.

epistēmē   (scientific) knowledge, science.

epithūmia   desire, appetite.

ergon   deed, function, product, result.

ethos   habit.

ēthos   character.

euboulia   deliberative ability, judiciousness.

eudaimonia   happiness, felicity, prosperity.

euprāxia   good action, prosperity.

genesis   becoming, development, process.

gnōmē   judgement.

hairetos   choosable, to be chosen, (rightly) desirable.

harmonia   joining, combination, adjustment.

hexis   settled or fully developed state or habit.

hūbris   insolence, wanton misbehaviour.

hupothesis   assumption.

kakia   vice, evil, wickedness (opp. *aretē*).

kalos   beautiful, fine, admirable, noble (opp. *aischros*).

karteria   endurance.

kinēsis   movement, change, process.

logos   A very common word with a very wide connotation. Its early meaning of *picking up* became generalized through the notion of *counting* or *reckoning* to convey a wide range of concepts more or less closely related to the English word *account*: e.g. estimation, measure, relation, proportion; explanation, coherent discourse, discussion, argument, rule or principle, law; thought, reasoning, reason; speech and its subject-matter. The list is far from exhaustive. Naturally it is often hard to say which sense predominates in a given context; Aristotle himself sometimes offers guidance, as at 1102b31ff.

makarios   blessed, truly happy, but sometimes a mere variant for *eudaimōn*.
megaloprepeia   magnificence, the grand manner.
megalopsūchia   greatness of soul, magnanimity, dignity, proper pride.
mikroprepeia   pettiness, meanness.
mikropsūchia   pusillanimity.

nemesis   just indignation.
noēsis   intellect, thought.
nous   intelligence, intuition.

orexis   appetite, appetition, impulse, desire.
orgē   anger.

pathos   susceptibility, feeling, emotion, experience, effect, affection, passion.
phantasia   appearance, presentation, imagination.
philia   love, affection, friendship, friendliness.
philotīmia   love of honour, ambition.
phronēsis   prudence, practical wisdom or common-sense.
phusis   nature, natural faculty, tendency or state.
poiēsis   making, production.
polis   state, city-state, civilized community.
prācton   act, thing done.
prāotēs   gentleness, good nature, patience.
prāxis   action, conduct (always purposive).
proairesis   choice, preference, purpose, intention; cf. *hairetos*.

sophia   skill, wisdom, often implying genius (cf. 1141a9).
sōphrosunē (sōphrōn)   temperance, self-control (literally soundness of thought or mind; cf. 1140b11).
spoudaios   earnest, serious-minded; sometimes a mere variant for *agathos*.
sumbebēkos   accident.

sunesis   understanding.
sungnōmē   sympathy, pardon.
sunolon
suntheton }composite thing, concrete whole.

technē   art, craft, skill.
teleios   complete, final, perfect.
thēriotēs   brutishness, stupid (and often savage) self-indulgence.
thūmos   eagerness, mettle, spirit; sometimes anger.

INDEX OF NAMES

371

SUBJECT INDEX